Taking a Detailed Eating Disorder History

Taking a Detailed Eating Disorder History educates health care clinicians of all backgrounds on how to best acquire a detailed eating disorder history and expands the clinical standard and effectiveness of history taking for a more thorough treatment of eating disorders. It describes the vast permutations and possible combinations of over 100 eating disorder behaviors as well as their connections to emotional and social triggers. Readers will also gain a stronger understanding of complicating factors related to eating disorders, such as diabetes, pregnancy, inflammatory bowel disease, and metabolic disorders, as well as drug and alcohol use, difficult relationships, and emotional strife. This informative new resource will be essential for any care provider of those with eating disorders.

James R. Kirkpatrick, MD, has managed the care of adolescents and adults with eating disorders in private practice, community-based eating disorder programs, and hospitals for over 30 years. He is a clinical assistant professor at the University of British Columbia, a member of the Academy for Eating Disorders, and a member of the World Health Organization's Global Clinical Practice Network.

Taking a Detailed Eating Disorder History

A Comprehensive Guide for Clinicians

James R. Kirkpatrick

Routledge
Taylor & Francis Group
NEW YORK AND LONDON

First published 2019
by Routledge
711 Third Avenue, New York, NY 10017

and by Routledge
2 Park Square, Milton Park, Abingdon, Oxon, OX14 4RN

Routledge is an imprint of the Taylor & Francis Group, an informa business

© 2019 Taylor & Francis

The right of James R. Kirkpatrick to be identified as author of this work has been asserted by him in accordance with sections 77 and 78 of the Copyright, Designs and Patents Act 1988.

All rights reserved. No part of this book may be reprinted or reproduced or utilised in any form or by any electronic, mechanical, or other means, now known or hereafter invented, including photocopying and recording, or in any information storage or retrieval system, without permission in writing from the publishers.

Trademark notice: Product or corporate names may be trademarks or registered trademarks, and are used only for identification and explanation without intent to infringe.

Library of Congress Cataloging-in-Publication Data
Names: Kirkpatrick, Jim, Dr., author.
Title: Taking a detailed eating disorder history : a
    comprehensive guide for clinicians/James R. Kirkpatrick.
Description: New York, NY : Routledge, 2019. | Includes
    bibliographical references and index.
Identifiers: LCCN 2018011649 | ISBN 9780415793575
    (hardcover : alk. paper) | ISBN 9780415793582 (pbk. : alk.
    paper) | ISBN 9781315210957 (e-book)
Subjects: | MESH: Feeding and Eating Disorders—diagnosis |
    Medical History Taking—methods
Classification: LCC RC552.E18 | NLM WM 175 | DDC
    616.85/26075—dc23
LC record available at https://lccn.loc.gov/2018011649

ISBN: 978-0-415-79357-5 (hbk)
ISBN: 978-0-415-79358-2 (pbk)
ISBN: 978-1-315-21095-7 (ebk)

Typeset in Garamond
by Apex CoVantage, LLC

For my mother, Helen

In loving memory of Elise
A warrior

Contents

	Acknowledgments	viii
	About the Author	ix
	Preface	x
1	Introduction	1
2	Fundamentals of Taking a Detailed Eating Disorder History	42
3	General Eating Disorder History	62
4	Eating Disorder Behaviors	116
5	Eating Disorder Behavior Parameters	205
6	Medical Symptoms and Complicating Health Concerns	224
	Index	278

Acknowledgments

I would like to thank all of those I have served with eating disorders, as well as their families, for providing me with a wealth of knowledge. This book has been written out of a crucible of clinical and emotional experiences.

Many thanks to Jerry Davidson, Don Wilkes, and Leigh Cohn as well as to Stephanie Ustina and Lori Vogt. I am most grateful to my wife, Gail, and kids, Amy and Paul, for their encouragement over the years.

About the Author

James R. Kirkpatrick is a founding member of the B. C. Eating Disorders Association. He has been medical consultant for the Ministry of Health as well as the South Vancouver Island Eating Disorders Program of the Ministry of Children and Family Development in Victoria, British Columbia, for almost three decades. He completed his undergraduate education as well as medical training from the Department of Family Medicine, Faculty of Medicine at the University of Saskatchewan. He is editor emeritus for the journal *Eating Disorders: The Journal of Treatment and Prevention*. Dr. Kirkpatrick is currently Clinical Assistant Professor for the Department of Psychiatry, Faculty of Medicine, University of British Columbia and the Island Medical Program at the University of Victoria. He has been a member of the World Health Organization's Global Clinical Practice Network as well as the Academy for Eating Disorders. As well as his work in the field of eating disorders, he has been a clinician at the Island Sexual Health Society for 27 years. The Canadian Medical Association commissioned his first book, *Eating Disorders* (Kirkpatrick & Caldwell). He was honored with the B.C. Community Achievement Award by the lieutenant governor of British Columbia in 2015 for advocacy and leadership in developing treatment for those with eating disorders, university teaching and clinical dedication. He has also published a music instruction book, *Electric Bass Beginnings*. He coauthored several neuroscience research papers. He currently resides in Victoria, British Columbia, with his wife, Gail, and has two children, Paul and Amy.

Preface

"An eating disorder is like a tornado that tears through your life, and hope never returns."

These are the heartfelt words of a parent whose daughter had an eating disorder. No truer words.

Taking a Detailed Eating Disorder History: A Comprehensive Guide for Clinicians is primarily a book of understanding. The currency of meaningful exchange in treatment is respect, a product of understanding. While this book is not especially designed to be a source of treatment options, it does provide an important therapeutic tool, the act of creating a detailed eating disorder assessment. Building an assessment, though technically an impartial task, is a remarkably intimate process. The somewhat detached professional veneer we present to those we are supporting is embedded in an emotional connection running in the background whether we are aware of it or not. This is much like the operating system of a computer that silently runs computer functions of which we are unaware. It is a combination of factual knowledge we acquire plus the emotional and humanitarian bedrock possessed by the professional clinician who delivers a therapeutic agent for positive change.

Taking a history is a shared experience that helps establish a bond. It is an opportunity to show our stripes as to the kind of person we are as well as a professional. Over the time period it takes to gather an assessment, we are able to display how we listen without judgment or criticism and with patience. We demonstrate our capacity to go with the flow of conversation without necessarily needing to direct it. We begin to determine an individual's communication style and what he or she will tolerate with regard to answering very personal questions. When in conversation with Professor Arthur Crisp, an eating disorder specialist from the UK, I mentioned that I did not like the term psychotherapy much. I felt it had a rather impersonal or clinical tone. He then defined psychotherapy as "Change through communication." In short, we bring change through our communication styles that are in sync or resonate with those we support.

A history does not necessarily need to be linear, that is, be acquired in any particular order of questioning. It is a real-time task. Aside from risk assessment, which needs to be clearly defined up front, the remaining history may be directed by a particular line of questioning that seems appropriate at the time. So, if the presenting reason for contact between a clinician and someone with an eating disorder happens to be regarding substance abuse, a family matter, or the need to drop out of university, then this will be the point of entry that leads to the individual's eating disorder world.

A history isn't just about data collecting. It creates a nexus into a person's life and exposes communication corridors. These corridors lead to potential therapeutically accessible vistas. We realize that these vistas of varied life experiences are connected and, to some degree, may feel one and the same. A history can begin at different portals of entry that allow us to view an individual's life from different perspectives. It doesn't matter at what point one enters a maze; the end point is the same. Each focus of the history, including the eating disorder, family, medical, psychological, or social assessments, is at some level a microcosm of the whole person's life experience. Similar to holograms, where any given smaller piece of the hologram retains the entire image of the original, each parcel of history contains an imprint of the individual's larger being. As an example, if the clinician begins a person's history focused on eating disorder behaviors, the conversation will very likely turn to family, moods, school, substance abuse, or any other concerns in life. As likely, if the history begins discussing the family, other areas of the person's life including the eating disorder will soon come to light. I remember attending a concert at the Royal Albert Hall. There were dozens of doors through which one could enter the concert hall. Regardless of the entry point or seating assignment, we all saw the same concert, just from different viewing points. Taking a detailed history is similar in kind.

At many points in history taking, we are given opportunities to interject comments along the way. Comments may be in the form of advice or opinions. As clinicians, we have the opportunity to teach and mentor. Our own personal experiences become a wellspring of knowledge that can be imparted to those we provide care for. It provides a valuable therapeutic resource not found in books or other clinicians.

Therapy need not begin only after a completed assessment but during the process of obtaining in. It provides the opportunity to plant seeds of change during the assessment process. This is akin to a farmer tilling the soil and simultaneously planting grain along the way, as opposed to tilling a whole field first then going back and planting later. The interjected

xii Preface

therapeutic tidbits are then given time to percolate, creating a therapeutic brewing process. Because new ideas take time to process, getting going on effecting change can't start too soon.

About the Book

This book presents four main themes. The first is we need to ask *one more question* and the second is to *never assume, always ask, always know*. Much time and resources can be wasted by not knowing enough history or by making inaccurate assumptions. Thoroughness and accuracy are at the heart of a meaningful assessment. The third theme is that *triggers-trigger-triggers*. This means that single life events trigger further consequences much like a billiard ball colliding with others, resulting in a kind of chain reaction. Knowing details in a history helps to identify this lineage of reactions, thus helping us to anticipate potential emotional and behavioral responses. The fourth theme is that *we cannot rely on other clinicians' assessments*. It is up to us and us alone to determine accurate diagnoses and all historical content. Sometimes piecemealing a history from other sources introduces inaccuracies that can misdirect our clinical judgment. Collateral information needs to be filtered for authenticity.

Obtaining details from a history requires a multidimensional approach. In Chapter 1: *Introduction*, we learn what motivates those with eating disorders to be driven toward eating disorder pursuits. We learn about body image awareness as well. Chapter 2: *Fundamentals of Taking a Detailed Eating Disorder History*, outlines the basics of acquiring a thorough history. If there is no meaningful connection with those we support, our ability to provide useful treatment options may be challenged. We then need to know about the person's general psychosocial and medical experiences and how they may be integrally intertwined with the eating disorder. This is described in Chapter 3: *General Eating Disorder History*. We also need to know, from the dozens of eating disorder behaviors, which ones are currently being engaged in. As well, we need to be aware of any eating disorder behaviors the person has ever been involved with previously or might be in the future. This is described in Chapter 4: *Eating Disorder Behaviors*. Each eating disorder behavior may have multiple variables or parameters attributed to it, as described in Chapter 5: *Eating Disorder Behavior Parameters*. Chapter 6: *Medical Symptoms and Complicating Health Concerns* focuses attention on medical symptoms and complicating health concerns that compound resistance to recovery efforts.

Following topic sections there are sets of *Questions* that can be asked relating to the subject previously addressed. These sets of questions are not intended to be complete but introductory or starter questions that may help with broaching a topic. They are meant to be a primer for more detailed history taking, as described in the Chapter 5: *Eating Disorder*

Behavior Parameters. They are intended to be selected depending on their relevance. Others focus on lesser-known fine points of a subject. The order of their use is strictly up to the clinician to determine. Questions have been added to some sections but not others, as questioning may be more self-evident depending on the topic. Questions may reflect what has already been stated in the text or provide new information. Some questions are general while others are specific and directed. The questions help demonstrate to the clinician questioning techniques and what subject matter to hone in on.

Excerpts of *personal stories* written by those with eating disorders have been distributed throughout the book. They provide a sense of reality or authenticity to given topics.

About Myself

My medical training is in family medicine or general practice. Because there were no dedicated resources for those with eating disorders locally and little province wide, I was put in a position to deal with multiple aspects of the care for those with eating disorders. I saw those with eating disorders in my private office initially to do medical monitoring but very quickly was required to manage eating disorder attitudes and behaviors. I dealt with urgent mental health concerns such as depression, anxiety, and suicidal ideation. I managed both eating disorder related health issues and typical family doc medical situations. For a number of years, I also provided the maternity care of those with eating disorders. I spent many hours in delivery rooms. It was necessary to also provide nutritional support as well as any and all counseling required for eating disorder and mental health concerns. I used to ask those I saw for the first time how they knew about me. One young woman said she saw my name and office phone number written on the wall of a woman's restroom stall at the university—a lofty recommendation to be sure.

Aside from my office practice I admitted adolescents to pediatric wards and adults to any adult ward that had an empty bed, such as surgery, internal medicine, gastroenterology, and gynecology services. I also admitted to the emergency rooms in two hospitals as well as to the pediatric and adult psychiatric wards. I invested over 80,000 hours of call for emergency rooms and hospital wards during a 12-year period. I was very busy. Fortunately, I had a small cadre of specialists and nutritionists with whom I shared care. From these experiences, I gained an exceptionally broad knowledge and experiential base, from which this book has largely been derived.

As well as my eating disorder clinical work, I continued in general practice for some time. I have also worked in a sexual health clinic for almost three decades. For a time, I worked with those with drug addiction at a methadone clinic and as the medical officer on a military base. These various clinical engagements have helped to round out my service base for those with eating disorders.

Prior to becoming a physician, I was a musician. I toured and I was a studio musician. My first published book was a music instruction book. I play electric bass guitar, flute, and classical guitar. My experiences of being tutored in music and having collaborations with other musicians has provided a reservoir of artistic creative energy, precision, and competitive spirit that, in turn, helps me engage with those who have artistic muses. These experiences also roll over to assist in connecting with others who demonstrate competitive aspirations, as with elite athletes. Being a music teacher may have helped me to communicate the abstract concepts that music and, indeed, eating disorders possess.

In all, this book is about optimism. It provides therapeutic tendrils that are capable of entering any and all aspects of the lives for those we serve. The chance for productive recovery options increase from the deep knowledge base we obtain of an individual's eating disorder world and her life as a whole.

All the best and enjoy!

James R. Kirkpatrick

Chapter 1

Introduction

> "*Most people don't really know the challenges and struggles I and millions have endured in the face of an eating disorder.*"

This book has been written to aid clinicians in taking a detailed eating disorder history. It does this through providing a structure to history taking, a method of approaching detailed questioning, and in-depth descriptions of eating disorder behaviors as well as other subjects and patients' personal writings.

In order to take a thorough history, clinicians need to have an extensive understanding of the nature of eating disorders. This includes learning about as many eating disorder behaviors as possible with an extensive knowledge about each behavior. Taking open-ended questions and questioning regarding the few behaviors that are commonly known will only get us so far.

What complicates assessing those with eating disorders further is not just the sheer number of possible eating disorder behaviors and the complexities of each, but that these behaviors are often intimately linked to several aspects of one's life. The eating disorder can profoundly affect family dynamics, drug and alcohol use, mental health status, and self-worth as well as relationships with friends, peers, and coworkers and tarnish academic and career possibilities. The reverse is true in that any aspect of one's life can ramp up eating disorder attitudes and behaviors. It's a two-way street.

Further difficulties come with assessing those with eating disorders in that there are potentially far too many scenarios in an individual's life to assess and deal with in a short period of time. We have to be selective in our questioning and learn to focus on what is important in the here and now and put aside temporarily what can be dealt with later. We need to determine when we need to share the care with other clinicians or family. We can't deal with it all due to time restraints, our limitations on clinical knowledge and skills, and financial limits available for treatment options.

2 Introduction

Diagnostic Criteria for Eating Disorders

Over the years there have been several attempts to set clinical or diagnostic criteria to define anorexia nervosa, bulimia nervosa, binge eating disorder and other eating disorders that cannot be defined by these fundamental ones. Classifications have been established by the World Health Organization and the American Psychiatric Association. Every so many years the classifications are redefined. The diagnostic criteria, however, change quite drastically with each revision, moving the line in the sand significantly as to what we can call an eating disorder. What does not change are the staggering number of eating disorder behaviors and emotional driving forces those with eating disorders engage in. Regardless of current diagnostic criteria, one's eating disorder is what it is. A rose by any other name. . . ! Treatment options depend on the nature of one's eating disorder and connected life stressors and not on the diagnosis.

For example, an individual who binge eats or binges and vomits once a week, is medically stable, is normal weight, and does not utilize any other eating disorder behaviors, as well as is able to carry on with normal life functioning, has a diagnosis of bulimia nervosa or bulimia. Another who engages in six sessions of bingeing and vomiting daily, where they vomit 10 times each session, takes 30 laxative tablets daily, and has life-threatening electrolyte levels associated with near-lethal cardiac rhythms as well as can't survive outside of a hospital setting also has a diagnosis of bulimia. Both individuals have the same diagnosis but a very different eating disorder and risk factors. Treatment choices will need to be different regardless of the diagnosis.

So, what value do classifications have and why should we pay attention to them? They will be necessary in order to receive insurance funding. Insurance companies require clearly defined clinical criteria, otherwise claims may be rejected. Accurate diagnoses may be necessary in order to obtain permission to drop or defer university classes or to defer student loan payments. Once a diagnosis is documented in a medical report, it is there forever. Organizations that employ people, such as government agencies, including the military, hospitals, school boards and any number of corporations, often request copies of medical reports before hiring. Institutes may reject anyone on medical grounds based on legitimate reasons or due to negative biases, including those with a history of mental health diagnosis. Don't make a diagnosis unless it is likely accurate. Also, state clearly if the diagnosis is uncertain.

Another reason to state clear diagnoses is when records are requested by a lawyer. Records could be used in litigation against yourself or others. A sloppy diagnosis could bring into question treatment choices and outcomes. For individuals or families who go into major debt because of expenses required to pay for eating disorder treatments, they may feel failed treatment is due to negligence or incompetence. For the person with the eating disorder, a precise diagnosis may help him or her to come to terms with their eating disorder. An incorrect diagnosis is crazy making, to say the least.

Motivations for Engaging in an Eating Disorder

In efforts to stick to weight control goals, some will establish motivational objectives. These objectives help to encourage serious attention to weight control goals. Any reason to engage in eating disorder behaviors are themselves motivations. Aside from these reasons there are other motivating devices.

Being motivated usually implies a desire to do something. There is a positive incentive to engage in a behavior or a reward for doing so. There can be *negative motivating forces* that compel people to do something they do not want to do. For those who are engaged in vomiting, it may be because they are not in control to prevent it even when loathing having to do it.

Motivations to control weight may be self-imposed, either deliberately or out of one's control. There indeed could be subconscious motivating forces at work as well. All may be in play at the same time or may vary depending on triggers. Motivations may be *external, internal,* or a *mixture* of both.

Apps

The term *apps* refer to software applications that are designed to run on mobile devices as well as desktop computers. Mobile devices are typically smart phones and computer tablets (Tan, Kuek, Goh, Lee & Kwok, 2016).

In the area of eating disorders there are many apps that are designed to aid in recovery and provide general information about eating disorders for anyone interested in learning about eating disorders, as well as those that support engaging in eating disorder attitudes and behaviors. The latter apps are referred to as *ana apps* (Pro-Ana apps) or thinspiration apps. There are many apps for mental health diagnoses that are educational and support recovery. This includes drug and alcohol apps.

Internet

> *"It seems so simple, so innate, yet I couldn't do it. I pored over food blogs, trying to get a sense of what a normal person eats; unfortunately, many of the food bloggers out there have their own issues, and thus my attempts to eat like them did not help me."*

The internet provides an ocean of information about nutrition and eating disorders (Llado, Gonzalez-Soltero & Blanco Fernandez de Valderrama, 2017). Individuals search the net for nutrition information regarding calories, protein, and fat as well as carbohydrate content, including sugar quantities. When attempting to restrict, all of these factors matter. They also may search looking for healthy food.

There are sites specifically targeted for those with eating disorders. Some offer support around recovery while others provide harmful suggestions to help escalate eating disorder attitudes and behaviors. These latter websites are referred to as *pro-ana* and *pro-mia* websites (Rodgers, Lowy, Halperin & Franko, 2016).

Pro-ana and pro-mia websites offer a large assortment of options assisting in supporting eating disorder ways. Typically, they offer information regarding *thinspirational pictures*, calorie-burning foods, "tips" on how to lose weight better, advertisements for purchasing laxatives and diet pills, connections to other harmful eating disorder websites, and punitive articles to make people feel bad about themselves if they do not give in to the eating disorder.

There may be web portals from these sites linked to destructive web pages. Some encourage self-harm and even provide helpful hints how to commit suicide. These sites also display bloody images of some having cut themselves. Photos of dead anorexics and bulimics are displayed here. They provide a kind of "Suicide for Dummies" scenario.

Questions

- Do you use the internet for any eating disorder purposes?
- What sites do you view?
- Do you look for nutrition information?
- Do you look for information regarding how to lose weight?
- Do you connect with pro-ana or pro-mia web pages?
- Are you involved with eating disorder chat rooms either focused on encouraging eating disorder attitudes and behaviors or recovery?
- Which pro-ana sites do you visit?
- Do you look up thinspirational sites and download this information?
- What do you do with the downloaded information?
- Do you view pro-ana "tips"?
- Do you look at self-harm sites, including those with suicide suggestions, and why?
- Do you look up photos of dead anorexics or bulimics, and why?
- Do you look up sites dedicated to recovery from eating disorders?
- What computer apps do you use for eating disorder purposes?
- What computer apps do you use that are recovery oriented?

Social Media

Social media has become the mainstay of communication for many around the world. There are multiple venues for individuals and social groups to connect. The ever-evolving creation of new venues allows a plethora of social interaction. Not that many years ago, communication with others would involve an expensive phone call or paper letter requiring weeks between responses. Modern electronic social media allows for near-instant contact as well as expected immediate responses. The sharing of information verbally, visually, and in text form can be performed by single electronic devices. Multiple individuals utilizing various simultaneously connected electronic devices has become the norm.

The negative influences of social media include (Mingoia, Hutchinson, Wilson & Gleaves, 2017):

- Bullying
- Instant access to pro-ana and pro-mia websites
- Continuous contact with those with eating disorders
- Connections with stalkers
- Unwanted personal information going viral

Questions

- Do you use social media, and which venues?
- Do you use social media as part of your eating disorder directive, and why?
- Do you take thinspiration photographic images from social media sources and store them on your cell phone or computer?
- What is the purpose of these photos?
- Are the photographic images of yourself, friends, celebrities, or unknown individuals?
- Have you experienced cyberbullying, and by whom?
- Does it upset you if others do not respond to your texts or other social media transmitted messages?
- Do you think the use of social media is a toxic influence on the eating disorder or to your self-worth?
- How does it affect your body image?
- Do you know that your comments could prevent you from getting a job or crossing international borders or ruin a chance to connect with a partner?
- Have you ever been hurt by what others post about you or say to you?

Cyberbullying

An increasingly escalating source of destructive body image triggering is electronic bullying or cyberbullying (Fairweather-Schmidt & Wade, 2017). Emails were the first source of this, followed by the ability to post electronic messages and photographic images on the internet. As more and

6 Introduction

more electronic social media devices and apps develop, the more derogatory comments and images can be disseminated.

Today these comments and images become permanently available for all to view. As a result of this, employers, governments, educational institutes, and others seeking knowledge of individuals may access salacious and embarrassing data. Those dating, as well as their parents, can look up details of potential dating partners on the internet. Postings of lies or false information can ruin the reputation of others. What are the chances of someone getting a job in a health care or teaching capacity who has had falsely reported accusations of pedophilia posted on social media? Whether accusations are true or false, the damage is done and likely permanent. Accurate information of previous drug use or drunk driving could prevent some from crossing borders and flying internationally. As well as bullying, self-reported events such as "I used cocaine on the weekend!" may be enough to freeze education, employment, travel, and applying for citizenship opportunities. Making political statements on social media could have much the same result.

Electronic bullying starts at a very early age. Elementary students may be called fat pigs or whores online. In previous years, if a student was being bullied at school, it could have been possible to be transferred to a different school. Now, victims can be bullied electronically from anywhere by anyone, anytime. Bullying can be directed through multiple social media formats.

Questions

- Have you ever been bullied in person or electronically?
- When did this happen and who was doing this?
- Have you ever engaged in electronic bullying of others?
- Have you been a focus of revenge?

Photographic Images

Photographic images appear in various formats. They are seen electronically on TV, the internet, or on digital devices as well as in print form such as magazines, posters, newspapers, books, and photo albums.

Photographs are an excellent way to freeze an image in time. Before the digital age photographs were taken with relatively large and bulky cameras where images were recorded onto film that had to be professionally processed to create printed pictures. It could take a week or longer to see the final photograph plus film, and printing was quite expensive. Today, photo images can be instantly recorded and viewed at no extra cost above monthly cell phone bills. Thousands of photos can be taken, stored and viewed from a single cell phone or tablet. Though dedicated digital cameras still exist, they are being replaced by the much more versatile multipurpose cellular phone. It used to be that the photographer had to be skilled in order to acquire a photograph that was in focus and properly exposed with precise contrast. Professional quality prints could cost as high as $50 a piece. Today digital images are very high quality, essentially perfectly focused and exposed and can be printed in high quality for pennies with digital printers. The cost of film and printed photographs very much limited how many pictures could be taken. Now an endless number of photographs can be taken of a given subject, so the chance of getting the best image is more certain. Since computers, cell phones, and notepads display very high resolution images, there is no real need to print them anymore. Being able to send high resolution images almost instantly to others with digital devices makes photography a near-effortless process. The cell phone camera is now ubiquitous and is a primary tool used by those with eating disorders. Could use of the cell phone become the number one eating disorder behavior to scrutinize body image? It likely already is.

Photographic images play a major role in body awareness. Photos can do the following:

- Freeze an image immediately of any part of the body, including the whole body.
- Create an image that can be looked at in the future.
- Be used to compare a set of before and after weight-change images.
- Be compared to body images of others.
- Punish or reward one's self.

Selfies

Selfies are photographs taken by individuals of themselves (McLean, Paxton, Wertheim & Masters, 2015). These photos are taken to have available instant images of oneself to determine if one likes what one sees or not. They can be viewed instantly or saved to be viewed in the future, often to gauge how one looks now compared to previously. Taking selfies can be an obsession leading to literally thousands of photos. They, of course, can be shared with others.

Thinspirational Photos

Thinspirational photos can be any photograph used to inspire or motivate one to keep engaging in eating disorder behaviors (Talbot, Gavin, van Steen & Morey, 2017). They originally were photos of people downloaded from the internet that could be viewed on the computer video screen or printed. The printed images were used in different ways. The prints could be stored in thinspirational scrapbooks to build a growing collection of photos to be referenced anytime. Prints could be placed on the fridge to discourage one from eating. Thinspirational photos may be of animals such as pigs, elephants, or hippopotamuses. These too can be displayed on fridges, storage cupboards for food, or on food packages.

Thinspirational photographs of people may be of emaciated or cachectic woman. They may be of famous models or other celebrities who are profoundly thin. These may be images of those someone wishes to emulate. There are also photos of morbidly obese women, often presented in an unflattering and even degrading way. These too can be printed and put on the fridge or put in a book as examples of negative body images, reminding people of what they do not want to look like and will look like if they open the fridge to find food to eat.

Photographic images of *dead anorexics* taken from the internet are used to display an end goal or ultimate achievement for weight loss. Images of *dead bulimics* serve a similar purpose. Though they may truly provide motivation for a genuine death wish, others view them as a sort of macabre interest, and others will hope they meet their weight loss or body image goal just shy of death. "I'll quit my eating disorder just before this happens!" Selfies are a reliable source of thinspirational photos. Cellular phones have the capability to download and store an ocean of thinspirational images.

Old Photos

Old photos may be found in family photo albums and in digital form. They are used to compare what one used to look like compared to how someone looks today. They may be viewed to feel good about how successful at weight loss they have been or to be made to feel bad because body image desires have not been met. Treatment goals should be to separate the individual from all triggering photographs—much the same advice given for those who use the scale, mirrors, or clothing to evaluate body image.

Questions

- Do photographs play a part in your eating disorder, and how?
- How do you acquire photographic images?
- Do you take photos of others to compare your body with?
- Do you take selfies, and if you do, do you do this to scrutinize your body?
- Do you print photos of yourself or others and place them in various parts of your home, such as on the fridge or food cupboard?
- Do you have old photographs of yourself that you compare to current images?
- Do you view photographs of those you have no relationship with found on the internet and compare their bodies to your own?

- Do you look for those with very thin bodies or those that are majorly overweight?
- Do you view internet images of dead anorexics or bulimics, and why?

Nonhuman Photographic Images

As touched on in the section on "Thinspirational Photos," photos or drawings of animals have a powerful emotional and, therefore, motivational effect. The images elicit negative emotions and have derogatory intent. Images of pigs, cows, hippopotamuses, or elephants are typically used. Each brings its own eating or body image-shaming message.

Pigs are seen as fat, "piggish" indiscriminate and noisy eaters that will eat anything no matter how disgusting and will even roll around in their own filth—a very humiliating image to compare one's self to.

Elephants are seen as "humungous" but not necessarily big eaters and are smart. Hippos are seen as humungous as well but also gross and cartoonish in their behavior. Cows are seen as large and stupid and graze all day. Grazing is viewed as a form of endless eating, with a "I don't give a damn and I'll eat anything I want anytime" attitude.

Questions

- Why do you choose this animal to compare yourself and others too?
- Do different animal images have their own specific meaning, or do they all serve the same purpose?

Photographic images of animals may be stored in scrapbooks, in computers or cell phones, or on the internet. These images may be shared through social media. They may be shared with others with eating disorders to encourage their weight loss ventures as well.

Animation

There are many media sources that can sensitize us to our bodies. Animation can implant the concept of an idealized or desired body image from a very early age. Animated movies depict images of young women and girls in the context of a princess, mermaid, or Snow White displaying exceptionally thin bodies including waistlines. They portray girls and women in even a more extreme and unrealistically thin image than advertisements of fashion models. The imprinting of this desired body happens as young as 5 years of age, or possibly younger. Female characters are presented with excessively skinny legs and arms, a smaller than size zero waist, and unrealistically tiny feet. Images may be sexualized by presenting the protagonist scantily clad.

Dance

Dance has been a classic trigger for needing to control body image, including weight loss (Arcelus, Witcomb & Mitchell, 2014). Whether someone is 3 years old or a teenager taking modern or ballet dance lessons, he or she is exposed to strict body image scrutiny. The scrutiny may come from dance teachers who comment regarding a student's need to lose weight in order to fit the dance image ideal. Teachers may request parents have their daughters go on a diet to meet this end. Students may, themselves, compare their body shape to other dancers, feeling they should be thinner themselves. Students may make "fat" comments to each other. Being allowed to perform on stage can depend on students losing weight; otherwise, they may be denied performing. The modern body image adopted for ballet comes from the choreographer George Balanchine, the father of American ballet style. His expectation of dancers was to present "a perilously thin, desperately beautiful, gracefully elongated girl who was pale as the driven snow"—the Balanchine Body. He felt that a more lithe or slender and taller body better suited the artistic integrity of the art.

The body image scrutiny that has its beginnings in dance schools follows into professional dance and may be even harsher. Maintaining a very thin body beginning in youth will likely be more difficult to maintain in adulthood. In recent years there have been efforts to prevent dancers with severely low weight from dancing. Dancers will be expected to be followed closely medically.

Questions

- Have you ever been a dancer?
- How old were you when you started, and do you currently dance?
- Were you professionally trained to dance?
- What kinds of dance were you trained in?
- Where there any expectations of body shape or weight by your teacher?
- Have you ever been intimidated by other dancers who you perceive were thinner than you are?
- If you still dance and need to maintain an excessively trim body, should you get out of dance to help you with recovery?

Idols and Other People

Some will wish to emulate the body of others. This could be family members, friends or coworkers, teammates or celebrities. Even inanimate objects such as the Barbie doll possess sought after body shapes. Celebrity mentors may include actors, music idols, and models. Other mentors may include those with eating disorders observed in the media, whether celebrities or those with eating disorders sensationalized by the media. These can be very powerful attractions to want to pursue weight control goals. Coincidentally, the lifestyles of celebrities and not just their body image may also be copied. Drug, alcohol, and sexual practices may be emulated. Family, friends, and school- and teammates as well as coworkers may be sources of body envy.

Questions

- Is there anyone who you wish to look like?
- Is there anyone you are trying to look like?
- What is the attraction for wanting to look like them especially?
- Do you think they might have an eating disorder as well so that they are able to maintain the body type you admire in them?

Competition

> *"Growing up I had been really involved in competitive riding, but one of my only and definitely the most vivid memory of the most important show of my life is trying to decide when to eat my half energy bar that day."*

Those with eating disorders will have many opportunities to be competitive with others. This competitiveness may start at a very young age. Competition to be better or the best at swimming, dance, playing violin, or academic marks are examples. The desire to have the thinnest body or be the most attractive may have been seeded in early childhood. Competition may be among peers, teammates, or family on one or possibly several fronts.

Low Self-Esteem

> *"Following the onset of my eating disorder I developed anxiety, depression, and very low self-esteem and confidence."*

> *"I was a shell, simply trying to fill my time between when I was allowed to eat."*

Poor esteem is a powerful driving force for those with eating disorders (Raykos, McEvoy & Fursland, 2017). In the face of all objective evidence, a pervasive feeling of lack of worth, the inability to achieve anything useful, and feeling like a total failure is believed to be replaceable by the successes of weight loss and sense of being good at least at one thing.

12 Introduction

Superiority to Others

Regardless of self-doubts, people-pleasing tendencies, and emotional sensitivities, a few with eating disorders state they wish to feel superior to others and not just to live up to what they think others expect of them. They want an upper hand. This may be with regard to body image but also with other attributes such as being more successful generally as well as being seen as smarter or confident. When asked about what her quest for achieving an ideal body image was about, one young woman said, "When I walk into a room full of people, I evaluate every woman there and compare myself to them. I want to be the thinnest, most confident, and successful woman in the place."

Fit in, Conform, Belong

Some have a need to fit in, conform, or belong. Eating disorders, similar to drug or alcohol use, can result from a wish to have something in common with peers. In some social settings such as boarding schools, it is a requirement to be included.

Control

If there were one word and one word only that we had to choose to describe what eating disorders is about, it would not be food or body image. It would be *control*. Those with eating disorders almost ubiquitously have issues with control. Control of what? Well, just about anything. Control drives may be weight- and body image-focused or may be with regard to other life experiences. Often control issues present on several fronts.

When asked regarding the reasons for control in one's life, the following items may arise.

Control of:

- Any emotion
- Feelings of low esteem
- Weight and body image
- Just one thing or everything in life

Questions

- Do you feel you have a need for control in your life?
- Do you feel you have control in your life?
- Do you feel you do not have control in your life?
- What areas of your life do you want control of or do not have control of?

- Do you really think that you can obtain control of the things you want control of?
- Do you think others have control in their lives?
- Do you think that control could be just a mythical concept?
- How would your life be different or better if you were in control?
- How does the eating disorder bring a sense of control when dealing with emotions generated from past experiences of sexual abuse?
- How does controlling your weight bring a sense of control to your life?
- Is it possible that success with losing weight is because you do not have control of the eating disorder but that is has been controlling you?
- When you achieved a weight you thought would give you control, have you ever felt betrayed by the eating disorder because any fleeting sense of control evaporated and left you just as powerless or even more so than before you set out to lose weight?
- Do you want control of just one thing or everything in your life?

Excuse to Fail

Recovery puts several demands on individuals. Responsibilities such as attending school, work, or engaging with family and friends will have been avoided due to consequences of the eating disorder—medical instability, depression, anxiety and isolation being a few. Active involvement in the eating disorder provides a pass on life tasks.

Punish Others

The eating disorder may be used as a tool to punish others. Refusing to eat and persisting to binge and vomit or to continue weight loss deliberately is very hurtful to family and friends. Professional caregivers may be the target of one's wrath as well.

Slow Suicide

Some view the eating disorder as a slow suicide. When enquiring regarding suicidal thoughts, a comment such as "I would never deliberately kill myself, but if I die from the eating disorder it would be OK" is not that uncommon.

Gender Dysphoria

Some are not happy with their genetically determined gender or the expected role they portray to meet societal gender identity (Feder, Isserlin, Seale, Hammond & Norris, 2017). Efforts to change body shape come into play in order to deal with gender dissatisfaction. Through weight loss, breast size and natural body curves can be diminished to a degree. This may result in an androgynous or even genderless image. Weight gain, on the other hand, may create a more female or womanly form. Those who are *gender fluid*, meaning wishing to be more masculine or more female depending on their desires, use weight control methods to assist with this.

Gender dysphoria can lead to other body-altering methods such as the use of surgery. Surgery can be used to augment breast size or reduce it. As well, total removal of breast tissue or top surgery may be desired. Genital surgical alteration may also be an option. Hormonal alteration with the use of medication administration further aids in the gender transition process.

It becomes important to determine whether any or all of the body-altering methods incorporated to deal with gender issues are blended with eating disorder objectives.

Maintain Medical Instability

Maintaining medical instability is a measure of success with regard to eating disorder achievements. Becoming healthier may be deemed becoming a failure or losing control with regard to meeting eating disorder goals. It may serve as a signal to family and caregivers that this individual is not well enough to move on with life and pursue academic or career objectives.

Negative Dialogue

Many describe experiencing negative dialogue in their head. The dialogue may be interpreted as between the eating disorder self and "the real me" or between an angel on one shoulder and devil on the other. The negative dialogue supports eating disorder objectives, and individuals will state that the negative voice becomes louder and more derogatory the more they wished to make efforts to recover. The *eating disorder voice* can be a brutal taskmaster.

Questions

- Do you ever have dialogue in your head?
- Who is the dialogue between?
- Is the dialogue negative supporting more weight loss?
- What does the negative voice say?
- Do the voices tell you to harm or kill yourself?
- Why do you pay attention to the voices?
- Why do you pay attention to the voices when you know they are destructive and not of real people?

- Do the voices become louder and more abusive when you try to make recovery efforts such as eating more or wanting to not lose more weight?

Stay in Hospital

For some who have been hospitalized, they do not wish to be discharged. The reasons for this are numerous, including:

- Not wanting to have to face contact with family.
- Not wanting to have to deal with the expectation of having to eat at home and face consternation from parents or partners with regard to resisting eating or contain purging behaviors.
- Not having to face expectations of going back to school or to get a job.
- Not admitting they may be getting better enough to not require hospitalization.
- Not admitting that treatment in the hospital is not helpful and being seen as a failure or not trying to recover.
- Fear of losing the support they have been receiving in the hospital regarding nutrition support and avoidance of engaging in other eating disorder behaviors aside from restricting. They may feel they will crash and burn after leaving the hospital and regress.
- Being afraid to lose their social interactions with staff and other patients. The interaction with caregivers and patients becomes deemed a meaningful and caring environment that they will lose once discharged. The ward provides clear daily structure and expectations. Food is provided without having to face shopping for food or having to make decisions about what will be eaten or whether they will eat at all. Treatment directives are clear and usually not very flexible with regard to refusing food intake.
- Receiving validation for pursuing eating disorder objectives from others with eating disorders. Treatment programs are rife with clusters of patients with eating disorders working together to undermine treatment objectives including weight loss and maintaining purging behaviors. As well, support around drug and alcohol use may be in place. The water bottles individuals bring to groups may be filled with vodka—a way to stick it to the system and provide a method of making it through treatments they have no intention of following. A powerful comradery can develop that creates a toxic vortex that others trying to recover can find impossible to resist.

The ways individuals can help to ensure they will not be discharges are to escalate eating disorder behaviors to increase potential medical risks if they were to leave the hospital, show an increase of depressive symptoms or serious self-harm behaviors.

16 Introduction

If a person is already discharged and wants to return to hospital, a suicide attempt or significant drop in weight and possibly overt medical symptoms may aid in this objective. Depending on the expectations of emergency room and ward treatment programs, however, these methods may backfire. Suicidal behavior and the escalation of eating disorder behaviors including medical risks may exclude individuals from being accepted back into treatment. Emergency room staff are usually the gatekeepers to ward and hospital-based programs.

Questions

- How do you feel about leaving the hospital and why?
- Will you miss anything about the treatment, staff, or other patients?
- Are you not doing well with treatment to avoid having to be discharged and go home?
- Are there other patients who are not wanting to recover and are undoing recovery options?
- Are you not wanting to recover? And if not, why?
- Is there anything about your treatment that would be more helpful to help you want to pursue recovery goals?
- What are you afraid of after being discharged?
- What are your plans once discharged with regard to recovery or life plans in general?
- What support will you have after being released both at home and with regard to recovery?

Stay on Disability Insurance

Those who are receiving disability insurance have motivation to keep receiving financial benefit. Being deemed to have recovered enough to return to work would put them at risk of losing disability benefits and making them return to a job they cannot mentally or physically handle. It will help to put them back into the same work environment that may have contributed to worsening of the eating disorder or drug and alcohol use. To some losing disability insurance, this could be devastating financially. Without this source of income, they could become destitute, putting some at risk of having to live on the street, return to the sex trade, or live in squalor.

Questions

- When you go off of disability, how will you cope financially?
- Will you have financial support from family or your partner, or do you have savings to draw from?

Introduction   17

- When you come off of disability support, how will this affect you emotionally?
- Will not having this financial source have a negative or positive effect on your eating disorder or drug and alcohol use, and why?
- Will you be ready to return to work?
- Will you be able to return to work and keep momentum with your recovery?
- Is your disability insurance limited as to how long you can draw from it?

Student Loans

Some will wish to be seen as not recovering and, therefore, not be expected to enter the work-force, as they will have to start paying back student loans in a timely manner. With sometimes tens of thousands if not hundreds of thousands of dollars in loans to pay back, the prospect of having to do so can be deemed insurmountable. Other owed money such as to pay back credit card debt, bank loans, or loans from parents compounds the problem.

Questions

- How much do you owe in student loans?
- What would your monthly payments be?
- When would you have to begin or resume paying back student loans?
- Would consolidating debts and amortizing payments over an extended period of time help?
- Have you considered bankruptcy?

Qualifying for student loans may have the opposite effect from avoiding paying them back. If individuals are receiving student loans, they may avoid leaving university to accept much-needed treatment for their eating disorder or drug and alcohol addictions. This will aid in denying themselves treatment options and help to keep them ill. Funds for apartment rental, car payments, gasoline, food, and other expenses could be put at risk. Compounding this is the desire to stay in school as well. They will not want to be seen as a failure for not completing university or not want to get behind in attaining their education and career aspirations.

Questions

- What can you do to financially support yourself without student loans in the meantime?

18   Introduction

- Are you not afraid of what may be the result of not receiving treatment at this time?
- What will be the consequences of you not putting your education on hold for now with regard to the eating disorder as well as mental and physical health?
- Do you not think that if you do not accept treatment now that you may never ever be able to finish your education and career goals? An ounce of prevention. . .

Fear of Losing Partner If Weight Gained

As some will want to be trim in order to get into a relationship, those who already are may want to not gain weight or will even lose weight to keep a relationship. This could be for someone who already has an eating disorder or who does not.

Sensitivities to one's weight may be aggravated by her partners bantering about how fat others look or possibly how she looks and comments such as "Should you be eating that? You don't want to get fat" or "You don't want to look like your mother, do you?" add pressure to remain trim or to become trim. If a partner has a swivel head while driving in a car and ogles women on the street for their beauty, that gives signals that her partner has an established standard of attractiveness that she may feel she has to live up to.

Unspoken body language and loose body image related comments may send very powerful messages.

To Keep the Family Together

When parents are considering separating or divorcing, the one with the eating disorder brings attention to herself from parents as well as siblings. As parents want to provide the most dedicated and supportive care possible, they may agree to work together for the health of their child. However, recovery may be felt to be a threat to family unity, and the one with the eating disorder may feel the need to remain ill or even decline in health. Ironically, the stress in the family created by the eating disorder may instead fracture the family further. Remaining unwell may be a way of punishing the family by not allowing a reprieve from worry.

Attention Seeking

One thing that those with eating disorders are accused of is wanting to get attention. For the most part, this is never the original reason for taking on an eating disorder. The opposite is usually the case. The last thing anyone desires is to be noticed. Most just want people to leave them alone and not bug them about weight loss or their eating disorder behaviors. The satisfaction they receive with weight loss comes from internal drives and not to receive accolades for their success in becoming thin. The eating disorder is typically an intensely personal and intimate experience. Fulfillment comes from within.

While this is true, those with eating disorders often receive copious quantities of attention not asked for or wanted. With time this unwanted attention becomes a source of hoped for and expected attention for various reasons. Though the attention is perceived as usually negative or critical, especially initially, it is often the first time they have had such constant and intense attention. Even though it is attention for an illness, they may crave it if it is gone. They may feel abandoned or that people don't care about them anymore if the attention wanes. A lack of attention may be wrongly perceived that others think they are getting better. This can make them believe that they are gaining weight and have to do more to control it. The attention gives them a *special status*. They may feel special, and others may feel that they indeed are given special attention. This special status can be resented by siblings, as they feel that the spotlight has been taken away from them. This special status or attention getting may be a reason to want to keep the eating disorder alive and well. Anyone seeking attention very well may require it.

Questions

- Does the eating disorder bring you attention from others?
- Is it desired or unwanted attention?
- What kind of attention are you receiving?
- Do you crave attention and why?
- Are you afraid of losing this attention?
- Do you think the eating disorder makes you feel special?
- Do you think others see you as special?
- Does this specialness cause problems for you?
- What is your fear if you lose the attention or specialness?

Control Acne

Individuals who are hypersensitive about body shape are likely sensitive about any body imperfections. Acne is a common source of discontent (Strumia, 2005). Acne has been well established to have its origins in hormonal status. The hormone shift that comes with going through puberty and becoming an adolescent is often a time acne develops. Acne can, however, develop later in the teen years, twenties and later. Acne may develop spontaneously anytime or be triggered by specific situations. Discontinuing the combined oral contraceptive pill, NuvaRing or patch, which

20   Introduction

usually decreases or inhibits the development of acne, may reverse this protective hormonal defense, allowing acne to develop. The addition of progesterone-only birth control methods can stimulate acne. These progesterone methods are the progesterone-only pill, Depo-Provera injection, birth control implants and any hormonal intrauterine devices, such as the Mirena, Kyleena, and Jaydess intrauterine systems. Some believe by losing weight and eliminating periods, the body adapts a hormonal state that may aggravate acne. Some will adapt strict diets in the hope of suppressing acne and, as a result, develop a severe eating disorder

Should someone develop acne spontaneously, abnormal hormonal states may need to be investigated. Polycystic ovarian syndrome is a condition that can have an androgenizing effect resulting in acne, oily skin, abnormal hair growth, and hair loss. Quick weight gain is often associated. Blood testing looking for an altered hormone state helps to make the diagnosis. Hypothyroidism should be considered as well.

Lifeline

Some view the eating disorder as a lifeline. That is, without it they may parish through suicide or destructive behaviors such as accidental overdoses with alcohol and drug abuse. Before attempting to help individuals recover from an eating disorder, determine that their eating disorder involvement is not the only thing keeping them alive.

Questions

*   Do you feel the eating disorder is a lifeline?
*   What would happen in this lifeline was removed?
*   Would you make efforts to attempt suicide if you lost this lifeline?

Coping With Abuse and Neglect

As referred to multiple times in this text, abuse issues are rampant. The carnage they amass and the importance the eating disorder plays in coping cannot be overstated.

Media

The media have always been and are still very much a source of body imagery. Classically, photographic images of fashion models and movie stars were displayed in women's magazines, including fashion magazines as well as tabloid newspapers. Similar images are presented on the TV as well as in music and fashion videos viewed on the computer. Commercial clothing stores also display large advertisements showing glamorous fashion models or movie stars with idealized bodies and beauty features.

The media also display other messages that compound our discontent for our bodies. Printed, television, and computer media present restaurant and other food ads followed by diet ads. The diet ads plant messages of discontent with our bodies, compelling some to want to themselves lose weight. The most dangerous thing about these ads is that they make us believe we can be successful with achieving significant weight loss.

The media also brings personal discontent when they show very successful people as just ordinary people who worked hard and became successful. These personal stories can make us feel inadequate because we do not have their talent or we are not working hard enough to achieve the kind of success we want. Low self-worth for any reason will often manifest in body image discontent. The media also hints at other ways we can improve ourselves by suggesting we need new clothes, a new haircut, or different nail polish.

In the age of computers, images of anything, including humans, can be altered by computers. Photos of famous people and models are typically altered to better present the ideal image the advertiser or magazine editor wants. This then displays an impossible image that none can live up to. Tall, thin men model women's clothing just to show an even more lithe fashion image. In an age of social acceptability for those that cross-dress, are gender fluid, or transgender, the sky's the limit for providing a wide range of body imagery that may or may not play into individuals' discontents.

Modeling

Modeling is a career purveying exceptional body images. For those entering the modeling business from a very young age to later in adulthood, there are often unrealistic weight and body shape expectations (Preti, Usai, Miotto, Petretto & Masala, 2008). The very tall and thin images desired are unobtainable for most of society. Out of the tens of thousands of those who feel they could be model material, only four or five of these will be deemed supermodel eligible by modeling agencies. These photo images of models are then subject to computer alterations. Models are subject to sexual exploitation by disreputable modeling agencies. They may be expected to serve as escorts for customers.

Questions

- Have you ever been a model?
- How did this affect your drive to be thin?

- Has this had an effect on your eating disorder?
- If modeling is keeping you engaged in the eating disorder, have you thought about quitting?
- Have you ever been put in a position of unwanted sexual advances or sexual exploitation?

Food Allergies

When enquiring regarding allergies in the medical history, we want to know about all known allergies, including food allergies. Food allergies or sensitivities may or may not play a part in someone's eating disorder. Those with gluten or lactose intolerances or egg, nut, or sea food allergies are forced to limit food choices. The requisite elimination of food types readily plays into eating disorder mentality. It becomes an excuse to restrict foods based on health reasons.

Sometimes some believe they have food allergies based on allergy testing. There are reputable and questionable allergy testing methods. Some tested will say they have been told they have as many as 48 food allergies. This pretty much eliminates most foods in all food groups. When individuals have fixed beliefs of food allergies, even if likely false, it may become very hard to navigate refeeding programs.

Focuses of Body Image

> *"For the most part, it began in what many consider a "normal" or "expected" way . . . when I was young, I was a gymnast. When I was in high school, I was part of the lightweight rowing team. I took a year off before university and did some modeling. After my year and a half in university, I became an exotic dancer. All these things are what people typically associate with body image, that is, low weight, low BMI, judged on how you look, always being scrutinized for your body."*

Eating disorders are, in part, driven by body image concerns. Though fear of weight gain, being fat, or becoming fat are hallmarks of body image dissatisfaction, there are other sources of body image dissatisfaction that may be as pertinent. A few include blemishes, stature, gender dysphoria, and esteem issues. They may be in addition to weight related body image concerns or be the primary or only focus.

The reason for knowing what the body image focus is, is that each can have its own driving force or engine that can lead to consequences favored by the individual. Each may have its own meaning. Some body image focuses may not be as important as others or may take priority. Some body image concerns may not be alterable, and as a result, the individual has a sense of having to live with them for the rest of their lives, leading to feel resolved to a life of doom. Sometimes different words with different literal meanings may be used loosely to refer to a different word that, to them, has the same meaning. As an example, if individuals say that they want to be thin, they may actually mean they want to lose weight. Ask as to whether the words they chose are what they really mean.

Body Images Not Desired

Fat

Fat is likely the most common term used to define how people do not want to look—comments such as "I don't want to look fat!" or "I don't want to become fat just like my mother!" It is unfortunate that the word for being overweight is the same word for the nutrient fat in foods. When trying to get someone to eat foods that are satiating, such as proteins or food fats, individuals can project that they are being expected to eat a food that will make them fat. The word fat used to describe a liquid fat such as olive oil is the same word to describe a 400 lb. person. Trying to encourage individuals to add fats to their diet often comes with a degree of consternation.

Questions

- What do you mean by fat?
- Are you worried about becoming fat generally, or are you worried about parts of your body becoming fat?
- Is there a certain weight that will say you are fat?
- Who do you know who you think is fat, and why?
- Have you ever been fat, or are you just afraid of becoming fat?
- Do you use other words to describe when someone is fat—large, gross, humungous, obese or any other word? Are these words interchangeable?
- If you use different words to describe your "fat feeling," why is this, and when would you use one over the other?
- Do you see others who are your weight as fat or normal?

Gross

The word likely refers to being overweight but has the added inflection of one being repulsive or repugnant. It is more of a derogatory term than the word fat. Individuals could use gross in reference to themselves because they are comparing themselves to something else they see as gross, such as a cow or hippopotamus. Gross may be interchangeable for the terms dirty or filthy. The word gross can also refer to someone being excessively thin or cachectic. The individual may use this term to describe themselves; parents and friends may use the same term as well. It can mean someone looks grossly ill, as would someone who has advanced cancer or AIDS.

Questions

- Why do you think you are gross?
- What about you do you think is gross?
- Are you comparing yourself to something that you feel is gross, too?
- Do you use other words in place of gross to describe yourself, and why?

Large or Big

The words large or big may be used in place of the word fat or any other negative descriptors, as it may be felt to be a slightly less demeaning choice of word than any of the others. It may be seen as the last step before becoming fat. Large or big may also imply being taller as well as over-weight. Large and big may not necessarily be synonymous.

Questions

- Why do you think you are large?
- What do you mean by being large?
- When did you first start to feel large, and why?

Obese

Obese is more of a technical health or medical term to describe being overweight. This is a scientific descriptor, as determined from medical weight or body mass index (BMI) weight or BMI charts. An individual may use this word because nutritionists or medical clinicians have used it to describe them. Health and fitness magazines report weight and height values for obese individuals.

Questions

- Why do you think you are obese?
- How do you describe someone who is obese?
- Are you using this work in reference to weight, diet, or BMI charts?

Humungous

The word humungous implies a feeling of being over the top or excessively overweight or large.

There are gradations of the fat feeling. Some will feel a little fat, very fat, or humungous. They may use their own language to describe this. Some will feel "more fat" or "more obese," depending on triggers. Weight increases could cause this. Not being able to exercise or vomit more when hoping to or becoming depressed may amplify worse body images.

Questions

- When do you feel humungous as opposed to just feeling overweight?
- What triggers you to feel humungous as opposed to any other body size?
- Does the humungous feeling increase even if you have not gained weight, and why do you think so?

Flabby

Flabby implies having loose muscle or fat. People will often grab the underside of their upper arm, abdominal fat, or legs when discussing this. They may or may not necessarily feel fat. They may see being flabby as a precursor to becoming fat or as a warning that they are going to become fat and better get fit soon. Flabbiness could imply to them that they have too much fat in proportion to lean muscle mass.

Questions

- Why do you think you are flabby?
- What parts of your body do think are flabby?
- Do you think you are overweight because of this or afraid you will become overweight?
- How do you plan on remedying this? (Increasing exercise is often the method used to prevent flabbiness.)

Out of Shape

Out of shape is a loose term to describe a lack of physical fitness. It may be seen as a stepping-stone to becoming flabby or fat. Exercise is likely being considered to deal with this.

All of these negative body image terms may be used by anyone of any body shape or weight. Someone 20 years old, 5'5" who is 82 lbs. and visibly emaciated could describe themselves using these terms. They may feel this way currently or are afraid of becoming any one of these descriptors. As mentioned earlier, these terms may be used interchangeably or have unique meanings. Any term may have a different meaning at various times for different reasons. Any of these terms may also be synonymous with non-body image feelings such as feeling anxious, depressed, lonely, exhausted, abandoned, and possibly others.

Question

- Can you give another word to describe the word you use?

Body Images Desired

Some desired body images may be specifically defined by weight goals alone while others are images hoped to be achieved as a result of weight loss.

Thin, Trim and Slight

These are body images aimed for as a direct result of weight loss. Weight loss is an end in itself. Certainly, any other desired body image may be a goal as well.

Low Weight or Underweight

As with being thin, trim, and slight, becoming low weight or underweight may be desired. Weight goals may be more important than achieving body shape changes.

Anorexic

The anorexic look is one of illness. It is beyond thin or being just under-weight. Other terms for this look are emaciated or cachectic. It is a look that says either "I'm successful" or "I've given up." It may convey a message of total hopelessness, helplessness, or total resolution to the eating disorder, either deliberately or after giving in to it. It is the ultimate visual expression of an eating disorder. Either attempts to further hide the eating disorder have failed or it is an in-your-face "this is the way it is" monument to its success. This image just might imply "Go away and leave me alone."

Beautiful or Pretty

Beautiful and pretty are not words very often used to describe the body image one wishes to achieve. Other words identifying how one wishes to look may mean the same thing to some.

Questions

- Is your goal to look beautiful or pretty?
- Do you have other words to describe how you wish your body to look?

Powerful

The look of thinness may not be seen by others as one of power, but to individuals with an eating disorder, it may give them a sense of power. The feeling of power may come from being successful with weight loss or that they will have more confidence from being thin in a culture that associates thinness with power, success, intelligence, and beauty. Powerful people are deemed as being *in control*, possibly the ultimate goal of those pursuing an eating disorder.

Looking Hot

To *look hot* suggests sexual attractiveness. Sexual attractiveness is almost never the answer anyone with eating disorders would give as their primary goal or ever a goal. Looking asexual or non-feminine would be more commonly desired.

Buff, Athletic, Toned, Healthy

The hope of having an athletic or buff body is engrained in our social consciousness. Fitness, gyms, and yoga parlors are agents of achieving this goal. The attaining of an athletic body may or may not be the precursor to an eating disorder. It may be an innocent stepping-stone in its evolution. What tips the scales of reaching for a toned body into becoming an eating disorder is the degree to which someone pursues this end. Toned is not enough, as it does not get rid of the fat feeling for long, and more efforts to reshape the body become essential.

Invisible

Invisible describes the goal some with an eating disorder want to achieve. This likely comes from a very low self-worth. It may be that they do not want to be noticed for any reason, including the eating disorder. An invisible person does not have any responsibilities and can't be expected to do anything.

Focused Body Areas

Face

Of all of the parts of the body one may want to change to become thinner, the face is likely the hardest to have success with. The whole rest of the body may be emaciated, yet the face is often the least affected by weight loss measures and can look normal. As clinicians we usually are only exposed to someone's face and hands, as most of the body will be covered by clothing. We, therefore, may acquire a false impression that individuals are better nourished than what they really are. While pretty much the rest of the body can be somewhat hidden by clothing, the face is always exposed. Those who hate how their face looks due to the perception that it is too fat may feel the most inescapably exposed fat person to others. As a weight on a scale or the ability to fit into size 00 or XXS clothing is the ultimate measure of success for weight control for many, a thin facial image may be the ultimate measure for some. All engaged eating disorder behaviors are employed to meet this end.

The face is often the most noticeable part of the body to show increased fullness with refeeding, and thus the development of what is perceived as a "fat face" becomes a major hindrance to recovery.

Prominent Bones

Some may have a goal to look bony generally, while others desire specific parts of the body to look bony. Exposed or bony hips, clavicles, elbows, knees, ribs, and spine are enviable weight loss goals to many. Individuals may spend much time in front of a mirror watching and rubbing bony body parts as a kind of trophy. Bony looking wrists, hands, and feet may be coveted weight loss goals as well.

Exposed bones—those that have become prominent due to major fat and muscle wasting—can create problems when coming in contact with pressure. The ischial tuberosities, the bony prominences we all sit on that are part of the hip bones, can become painful with sitting. Chronic pain of these bones can develop where individuals can never sit normally. Due to the lack of muscle and subcutaneous tissue to protect these bones from excessive pressure, skin sores can develop as well, making it even more difficult to sit. Also, exposed spinal prominences can make it hard for someone to lean against a chair back or lay on the floor while doing floor exercises due to pain. Again, skin sores can develop over spinal points of contact with furniture.

Thighs

Large or big thighs are a major focus of concern for many. A major fear is that thighs touch each other. This can be a mortifying experience. Dieting and exercising to tone up the thigh muscles may be deemed remedies for this malady. There can be conflicting attitudes toward using exercising to control thigh size. Exercise has the potential to increase muscle mass, therefore increasing thigh size. It depends on the belief system of the individual whether exercise is seen as the fixer or an aggravator of thigh size management.

Abdomen

Probably the greatest focus of desired weight change is to reduce the size of "the stomach" or abdomen. Many commercial weight loss advertisements focus on size reduction of the abdomen. Before and after photos of those who have successfully lost abdominal girth are used as the major selling feature of their diet plan.

Prominent and redundant abdominal skin and fat are referred to as love handles. These are targets of abdominal shape reduction.

While restricting and exercising as well as many other eating disorder behaviors can be engaged, surgery has a major part to play for some. Tummy tucks are a common surgical solution to reducing abdominal size.

As the rest of the body loses weight and size, the abdominal girth may remain the same. This results in the abdomen becoming disproportionately larger in proportion to the rest of the body. If the most important goal is reducing abdominal size, losing weight may indeed make body image worse.

Buttocks

As with the abdomen, the buttocks are at the top of the list that many wish to reduce in size. In recent years there has been a trend to increase buttock size, with the goal to create a large "booty."

Arms

The distribution of fat and muscle is quite variable between individuals. Fat is sometimes distributed disproportionately to the upper arms, a fairly exposed part of the body. The upper arm skin and fat tissue may be perceived as flabby—loose and hanging.

Breasts and Gender, Sexuality, Availability

Breast size and shape can have a significant influence on body image. Breast augmentation and reduction surgery are common surgical procedures, not necessarily of eating disorder origin, but they may be.

Breast reduction may be desired for many reasons. Breasts may be seen as a source of undesired weight, fat, or bigness. Weight reduction methods may be deemed a way of dealing with this. The breasts, as with the face, may be the hardest body part to reduce using an eating disorder. Similar to abdominal size reduction, as the rest of the body reduces in size, the breasts may be minimally affected, resulting in the individuals feeling breasts look even bigger in proportion to the rest of the body than they did before. This

30 Introduction

may or may not be a wanted effect. Though breast size reduction may be a goal for many with eating disorders, increased breast size may be preferred.

Efforts to changes breast size and shape may be driven by typical eating disorder weight loss and body image drives, but there may be other motivations. These motivations may be separate from the eating disorder or blend in well with eating disorder goals.

Breasts play an important role in gender identity. Altering breast size can have an influence on one's own gender identity or how others perceive them. Some chose to want to be seen as a typical woman in society or may wish to be identified as a typical male. Some are gender fluid and wish to choose their identity as the mood moves them. Reducing breast size through weight loss or surgery can lead to more of an androgynous look, a child's look or masculine look. An absent breast profile can give the individual a sense of not being sexually available or being asexual.

A history of sexual assault can play a part in one's awareness of their breasts and importance in sexuality.

Knees

Prominent, knobby, or bony-appearing knees are a hallmark of the anorexic look. The visible distinctiveness of the knees is, in part, the result of the reduction of subcutaneous fat tissue as well as wasting of calf and thigh muscles.

Blemishes

Any blemish may be a source of body image dissatisfaction—a little or a lot. Blemishes come in several forms. Though blemishes are not usually the result of weight issues, they can result in self-loathing and contempt for one's body. This will add to any other body image dissatisfactions from other sources. They only compound the discontent and have an additive effect. "Just one more thing to hate about my body."

There are naturally occurring blemishes such as moles, acne, and unsightly hair growth. Blemishes caused by trauma may result in scars or creases in skin. Surgery may also cause scars as well result in unwanted outcomes.

Though weight loss measures will not correct blemishes, the eating disorder can become a way of coping with negative feelings overall from any source.

Physical Deformities

Physical deformities caused from genetic or congenital etiology, trauma, surgery, or acquired illness may bring further body image discontent.

Neurofibromatosis may create unsightly disfiguring tumors and is associated with short stature, another undesirable physical attribute.

Physical Disabilities

Physical disabilities from many causes can add to body image discontent. Charcot-Marie-Tooth syndrome results in weakness of the limbs. Leg and foot weakness will result in feet being noticeably toed in and deemed a possibly unattractive attribute.

Distorted Body Image

> *"To me, that mentality of not being thin enough to even ask for help was one of the biggest obstacles to accepting treatment."*

The concept of a distorted body image is very real (Molbert et al., 2017). A reason to seek a trimmer body is sometimes based on an incorrect belief that one's body is too large in spite of objective evidence to the contrary. For those of us who observe those with normal, thin, or even emaciated bodies, it is difficult to understand how they could feel that they are overweight.

> *"When I was admitted into the adolescent eating disorders program after emergency intervention due to critically low electrolyte levels, I still maintained that because of my weight, I wasn't sick enough to have an eating disorder."*

Although a distorted body image is common in the eating disorder world, it is not always the case. Some with anorexia nervosa know very well how they look and either want to maintain this appearance or with best efforts can't escape it. Individuals can know exactly how they look and still feel 300 lbs.

Body image distortion may be made worse with any stress, depression, or anxiety. Academic or work pressures, sleeplessness, and exhaustion are also contributors. Certainly, failing to meet eating disorder goals doesn't help. Others with identical body shape and weight as themselves can be seen as healthy or trim, but they only see themselves as overweight.

We think of those with a distorted body image as only those with eating disorders. Once, when I was visiting an eating disorder hospital ward, I glanced around the room and accidently saw a patient of mine who I had been treating for anorexia nervosa. I was shocked by what I had seen in that moment. I became aware that this person was far more emaciated than I had been perceiving her. I had come accustomed to seeing her and

32 Introduction

normalized her body image to some degree because of our frequent contact. This taught me a lesson about my own body image perception of others and to check my own assumptions regarding this.

I remember talking to a colleague years ago who said that when he was seeing a 12-year-old girl for anorexia nervosa she would always ask him to go through doors before her. One day he asked her why she wanted him to go first. She said "If you can make it through the door so can I!"

When doing body image work with a group of those with an eating disorder, we would do an exercise where they would draw on a sheet of paper on the wall what shape they likely are. While someone else would trace the individual's body accurately, the individual's real size was usually smaller than their own imagined one.

Questions

- Do you think you see your body accurately?
- Do others make comments about your body that you disagree with, and what comments are these?
- Why do you think there is a difference between how you see yourself and what others see?
- Do you think you are in denial of how you really look?

Personality Triad

Though everyone with an eating disorder cannot be generalized to be the same, there is a *personality triad* that seems to be common to many. This triad includes being *people pleasers*, *perfectionists*, and *hypersensitive*. Each trait can be a vulnerability or strength depending how each is expressed. They may be opposite sides of the same coin. Though each of these traits in limited capacity may not cause problems, there is a point where they can be problematic.

People Pleasing

People pleasing is a trait where individuals make significant effort to ingratiate themselves to others, avoid disapproval, and not wish to hurt others. It is also a way to avoid interpersonal conflict.

A consequence of people pleasing is that individuals tend to put others first at the expense of their own wishes. This can lead to a perpetual drive to please others that they can never really fulfill. They seem to not get that others cannot be pleased much of the time anyway. This leads to a repeated lack of reward for their effort. One can feel like a doormat. Patterns of always seeking approval develop. Constant approval seeking can be very wearying to family and others as her need for approval never seems to be satiated. It's never enough. The perpetual need to show approval is draining on others.

Many with eating disorders wonder why they end up having to cover other's shifts at work or work harder than others, with no rewards for their extra efforts. They are doing favors for others, but favors are not returned. Someone will wonder why others take advantage of her. What is happening is that her pattern of doing favors for others teaches others how to treat her. They know she will cover shifts without refusing, so they know they can depend on her to repeatedly do this. There can be a fear of saying no, as others may feel disappointed or hurt. People pleasing can be prominent in certain situations or permeate every aspect of an individual's life.

People pleasers tend to be good listeners. This results in others depending on someone to listen to their most intimate concerns. There may even be an expectation for her to come up with plausible solutions to others' problems. She becomes the listening post for others, but the favor may not be returned. She then takes on the weight of the world of these individuals without them supporting her. Because this emotional support is a one-way street, she will not want to bother others with her own problems. Letting others know she has emotional stresses may cause her to feel vulnerable and may let others know she is not as strong or competent as she would like.

While individuals are hoping to gain respect or possibly praise, or to get people to like them or not hate them, they are creating the opposite effect. Kowtowing to others and not standing up for themselves lets others know they can be taken advantage of. This leads to others acting disrespectful toward them. They may be perceived as weak and lacking self-respect. They need to know that the word "No" can be a powerful tool to gain respect from others. Others may not like that they have said no to giving car rides or covering their Friday night shift, but they will respect it. People pleasers need to learn to not care what others think. They need to know you do not have to explain why you won't do something.

Questions

- Do you think that you are a people pleaser?
- What do you do or say that makes you a people pleaser?
- Why are you a people pleaser?
- Does people pleasing get you what you want?
- Does people pleasing ever make you feel inadequate or bad about yourself, and why?
- Do you think others take advantage of you, and in what situations does this happen?
- Can you say no?
- What would happen if you said what you really meant?

34 Introduction

- What do you think of others who say what they mean and stand up for themselves?
- Can you see a positive side to pleasing people that is constructive?

Perfectionism

The definition of perfectionism is "The refusal to accept any standard short of perfection." Perfectionistic traits tend to transcend multiple aspects of one's life, and not just with regard to eating disorders. There tends to be a desire to attain or expect perfection with regard to academic grades, career goals, athletics, interpersonal skills, and others. Excessive effort and time may be put in for very little in return. This can lead to mental exhaustion and sleep deprivation. Perfection may be a necessary part of feeling like a worthwhile and purposeful individual (Levinson et al., 2017).

Because perfection is impossible to maintain for long or even in the first place, individuals are constantly disappointing themselves. There can be a perpetual sense of failing. The same may be expected of others as well. Everyone seems to disappoint them on a regular basis.

When is perfectionism just a trait or tendency that does not get someone into trouble versus becoming a consuming objective that has negative consequences? What is the difference between perfectionistic pursuits and obsessive-compulsive traits? Where are the boundaries between OCD, anxiety, perfectionism, and pressures to perform at work or at school? There is a fine line that should be delineated between these traits so as to better understand their origin and possibly how to deal with them. Is there actually a bit of any or all of these conditions that blur the borders? OCD, anxiety, and perfectionism can all fan the flames of each other. Treatment options for each condition may vary drastically. The incorrect treatment could bring the individual harm and delay appropriate treatment. Giving a medication to treat what has been incorrectly diagnosed as OCD will not help the individual's perfectionistic goals to meet the impossibly high standards of an employer, professor, or themselves.

When are perfectionistic traits not a problem? Those who wish to achieve high marks or move up in their career and work extra hard to achieve these things are not necessarily hard-core perfectionists. If their efforts seem reasonable for achieving their goals and do not result in wasted time or result in feelings of a total lack of self-worth if goals are not achieved, then they may have a healthy and useful drive to achieve. If worsening of the eating disorder, drug or alcohol use, or depressive and self-harm trends do not follow, then there will be no need to intervene.

In regards to school, with hard work, high levels of achievement may be able to be met on a somewhat predictable basis. The more one studies, the likelihood of obtaining high marks increases. However, in the work world and attending university where individuals are not told what they should know and there are not rules of life to follow, the perfectionist may not be able to thrive. Not achieving one's level of perfection may aggravate depression and anxiety and escalate eating disorder behaviors.

Questions

- Are your expectations realistic or not?
- Are your perfectionistic pursuits only body image focused, or do they extend into other areas of your life?
- Does your hope for perfection cause you any problems?
- Are you afraid to make mistakes?
- How does it make you feel when you do not meet your expectations?
- Even when you do meet your standard, how does it make you feel, and for how long? Would an A+ make you feel happy or just prevent you from feeling bad about yourself if you had not succeeded in your goal?
- If you meet your goal, do you feel you earned it, or do you feel that you got lucky or the task was easy in the first place?
- Do you think very successful people score high on perfectionistic traits?
- What is the worst consequence of doing just "OK"?
- Do you see your pursuit of perfectionism as a waste of time?
- Does it prevent you from enjoying life, including having meaningful interaction with friends and family?
- Do others comment on your perfectionistic drives, and what do they say?

Perfectionistic tendencies may be based, at least in part, on family influences—both behavioral (nurture) and genetic (nature).

Questions

- Are there any others in your family who are perfectionists?
- How do they display their perfectionism?
- Do you think that their own expectations of themselves are also expected of yourself, and in what way?

Perfectionists tend to be procrastinators. Because of the fear that they will not complete a project with excellence, such as academic or work assignments, they delay progressing with their work. Some will finish their work on time, while others will have to ask for extensions on assignments and may actually never finish them, resulting in failing grades, delaying graduating, or risk of losing their job. For those looking for work, they may not be able to complete a resume, as they feel that their accomplishments have not been adequate enough to include in their resume. Even if given a job interview, they may not attend due to believing that they will fail the interview because they are not good enough. If they have been accepted for a job, they may not show up at work due to their fear that they will not be able to perform as expected and that they are frauds. Procrastination creates a reinforcing, self-fulfilling prophecy that they are failures.

Questions

- Do you think that you are a procrastinator?
- How do you procrastinate?
- Does it ever get you into trouble?
- What would be the result of you completing projects on time and accepting them as is?
- Do you really think anyone cares if you are perfect at the things you do?
- Do you think others like people who have it all or are great achievers? (The high achievement of some may make others feel inadequate and not likely endear anyone to them. Others tend to resent those who are more accomplished or are better off.)
- Do you know anyone whom you envy who has crashed and burned in their lives?

Hypersensitivity

Many with eating disorders are perceived to be hypersensitive. That is, it takes little to upset them or hurt them emotionally. They do not tolerate criticism well and are easily hurt by it. There may be great efforts to avoid interpersonal conflict. This trait may have its origin in genetics, at least in part. Parents, grandparents, and siblings may be similarly sensitivity.

As a result of this heightened sensitivity, others go out of their way to avoid upsetting them—they feel they have to walk on eggshells. They feel that they are damned if they do and damned if they don't say or do things.

This tendency to be easily hurt can be observed from a very early age. Even as a toddler. Parents will say that they raised all four girls the same, but "this one" couldn't take the slightest criticism or even a change in tone of the voice without becoming upset. This same child may very well be the one who was always seeking attention or approval.

Questions

- Do you think that you are overly sensitive or hypersensitive?
- Do others comment on this?
- In what situations do you think that you are overly sensitive?

Introduction 37

- Does this prevent you from doing things or cause you to avoid certain situations?
- Does this contribute to your isolation?
- How does this sensitivity affect you?
- Is there anyone in your family who is as sensitive as you?
- Does it ever get you into trouble, and how?
- Are others offended by your responses to their comments or actions?

Food Sources

In order for someone to binge or eat at all, there must be sources of food. The acquisition of food may be an easy task or a very complex one. Food that is readily available in the home often provides a reliable source. Often parents purchase food, or the individuals themselves stock enough food to last for a while. Roommates and partners may do the same.

The point of purchase is a major issue. There are many commercial sources of food, grocery stores and convenience stores being popular ones. Other sources of food are restaurants where one can stay and eat or offer takeout. Those who work in restaurants may either purchase food or steal food for binge eating purposes. Some who work for hotels or caterers may consume food remaining from banquets or smorgasbords. There is often an ocean of free food left over from these functions, and they are easily taken advantage of. One does not have to work for the hotels or caterers to access this food. Some search the internet to locate banquet venues and their time of events, including university campuses, where faculty hold lunch or dinner meetings, after which individuals show up to binge on leftover food. Taking uneaten food from trays in cafeterias or food courts occurs. Other food sources may be garbage cans or dumpsters. See "Dumpster Diving" in Chapter 4. Some take food from pets. Those who work as caregivers to the elderly or disabled may take their client's food.

Transportation

For someone to engage in many eating disorder behaviors, transportation may play an important role. For those who have food readily available in the home provided by parents or partners, then transportation is not much of an issue. Most, however, need to acquire food using some method of transportation. When transportation options are not available, then there can be a significant impact on that person's ability to engage in the eating disorder.

Financial Costs

There may be multiple financial costs required to maintain one's eating disorder.

Food is usually the main expense. Some will not expend funds for food, including food for bingeing, as food will already be purchased and supplied in the home by others such as parents, partners, or roommates. Other sources of freely available food may also be available. Much of the time funds are required for purchasing relatively small to exorbitant quantities of food. Some report that they may spend from about $5 daily to up to $400 a day—an expense rivaling the most demanding narcotic addictions.

Other costs can include the purchasing of laxatives, suppositories, diet pills, gym memberships, fees for personal trainers, plastic surgery, Botox injections, therapist fees, and the added expense of having a single occupancy dwelling in order to have a space to engage in eating disorder behaviors without interruptions or scrutiny.

Some will have spent upwards of $100,000 for treatment of the eating disorder by a private therapist and other coexisting concerns such as depression, anxiety, family issues, and drug and alcohol dependency, as well as others. Some will have spent several hundreds of thousands of dollars for hospital or residential treatments. Sources for such large sums may come from inheritances or relatively well-off parents. Some families may sell their homes to fund these stunning costs. Too often, large amounts of funds go to failed treatment in the end, and individuals and families will lose everything. Colossal debt may follow. Those with excellent health coverage, either through private insurers or government-sponsored programs, will be spared these expenses.

Taking time from work to attend hospital or residential treatment incurs added costs, often leading to more debt. Having to pay for monthly rent and care of pets prohibits many from accepting these treatment options.

Sometimes large future expenses loom for other health maintenance concerns such as dental care. Some may owe tens of thousands of dollars for dental work due to enamel erosion, cavities or gum recession caused by stomach acid as a result of vomiting. Some will be on their second or third set of crowns, caps or veneers in their early twenties.

What must be appreciated is that these eating disorder-driven expenses are compounded onto other day-to-day expenses. Funds for rent, transportation including monthly payments for a car, gasoline, insurance and repairs or bus fare, pet care, and cellular phone and internet costs, as well as entertainment, are only a few. Student loans are a major financial burden to many. Other expenses are demanded for those who take care of children, especially single mothers. Food, clothing, day care, and extracurricular activities such as music, dance or horseback riding or sports are only a few to mention.

Money Sources

> *"Despite the income I was making from escorting, I still literally ate through all my money. I barely had enough to pay the rent. Food was another story. I bought groceries on a day-to-day basis and often maxed out my credit cards on takeout and delivery. But occasionally, I wouldn't have enough for food, and I remember sitting on my kitchen floor, opening a can of cat food and taking a bite. I knew I had sunk as low as I could."*

Sources of money including stealing money, filling up credit cards, draining the partner's accounts, and spending whole savings, including inheritances, as well as taking out loans have been touched on elsewhere. A financial resource for some is to be involved in the sex trade.

Sex Trade

> *"In the 25+ years that I have been fighting this, I have been through a lot . . . overdosing twice on Tylenol and sleeping pills, admitted to in-patient units, hitting rock bottom, crying all the time, feeling that there was no hope, facing extremely low potassium levels, abusing laxatives, being completely broke, turning to prostitution (or escorting)."*

Women and men will enter the sex trade for various reasons. For those with eating disorders, it may serve multiple purposes. The obvious reason is to make enough money to purchase food for binge eating, laxatives, diet pills or a membership to a gym. The hours are often flexible, including allowing for evening or night work, so individuals can make money after a day of other work. Pay will usually be much better than the average day job. Money is also not declared for taxes.

Working as an escort will also be a source of extra money or even the only source of income for all other financial needs. A single mother taking care of three children who has a minimum wage job or is on social assistance can find sex trade work an attractive way to make a living. Some find this option a form of excitement in their lives. This is a common way for some to purchase street drugs or alcohol to feed an addiction.

There are multiple risks to being in the sex trade. One is the risk of acquiring sexually transmitted infections. Another may be an unexpected or unwanted pregnancy. Having another child to take care of becomes yet another financial and emotional burden. A potential for physical violence by employers or clients looms. Some will be left with a reputation that can harm relationships with partners, neighbors, friends, family, and coworkers. If the law finds out about them making illegal money, charges can be made. As well, social workers may be involved to assess the fitness of the mother to take care of their children. The use of their sexuality in this way can provide a sense of being worthwhile or needed. It becomes a powerful tool for obtaining a sense of control in their lives. In some communities, there are resources provided by government or nonprofit societies to help individuals get out of the trade and learn better coping skills and trade skills and improve self-esteem.

References

Arcelus, J., Witcomb, G. L., & Mitchell, A. (2014). Prevalence of eating disorders amongst dancers: A systemic review and meta-analysis. *Eur Eat Disord Rev*, 22(2): 92–101. doi: 10.1002/erv.2271. Epub 2013 Nov 26. Review.

Fairweather-Schmidt, A. K., & Wade, T. D. (2017). Weight-related peer-teasing moderates genetic and environmental risk and disordered eating: Twin study. *Br J Psychiatry*, 210(5): 350–355. doi: 10.1192/bjp.bp.116.184648. Epub 2016 Dec 15.

Feder, S., Isserlin, L., Seale, E., Hammond, N., & Norris, M. L. (2017). Exploring the association between eating disorders and gender dysphoria in youth. *Eat Disord*, 25(4): 310–317. doi: 10.1080/10640266.2017.1297112. Epub 2017 Mar 10.

Levinson, C. A., Brosof, L. C., Vanzhula, I. A., Bumberry, L., Zerwas, S., & Bulik, C. M. (2017). Perfectionism group treatment for eating disorders in an inpatient, partial hospitalization, and outpatient setting. *Eur Eat Disord Rev*, 25(6): 579–585. doi: 10.1002/erv.2557.

Lladó, G., González-Soltero, R., & Blanco Fernández de Valderrama, M. J. (2017). Anorexia and bulimia nervosa: Virtual diffusion of the disease as a lifestyle. *Nutr Hosp*, 34(3): 693–701. doi: 10.20960/nh.469. Spanish.

McLean, S. A., Paxton, S. J., Wertheim, E. H., & Masters, J. (2015). Photoshopping the selfie: Self photo editing and photo investment are associated with body dissatisfaction in adolescent girls. *Int Journal Eat Disord*, 48(8): 1132–1140.

Mingoia, J., Hutchinson, A. D., Wilson, C., & Gleaves, D. H. (2017). The relationship between social networking site use and the internalization of a thin ideal in females: A meta-analytic review. *Front Psychol*, 8: 1351. doi: 10.3389/fpsyg.2017.01351. eCollection 2017. Review. 8. Format: Summary.

Mölbert, S. C., Thaler, A., Mohler, B. J., Streuber, S., Romero, J., Black, M. J., et al. (2017). Assessing body image in anorexia nervosa using biometric self-avatars in virtual reality: Attitudinal components rather than visual body size estimation are distorted. *Psychol Med*, 26: 1–12. doi: 10.1017/S0033291717002008. [Epub ahead of print].

Preti, A., Usai, A., Miotto, P., Petretto, D. R., & Masala, C. (2008). Eating disorders among professional fashion models. *Psychiatry Res*, 159(1–2): 86–94. doi: 10.1016/j.psychres.2005.07.040. Epub 2008 Mar 19.

Raykos, B. C., McEvoy, P. M., & Fursland, A. (2017). Socializing problems and low self-esteem enhance interpersonal models of eating disorders: Evidence from a clinical sample. *Int Journal Eat Disord*, 50(9): 1075–1083. doi: 10.1002/eat.22740. Epub 2017 Jun 26.

Rodgers, R. F., Lowy, A. S., Halperin, D. M., & Franko, D. L. (2016). A meta-analysis examining the influence of pro-eating disorder websites on body image and eating pathology. *Eur Eat Disord Rev*, 24(1): 3–8. doi: 10.1002/erv.2390. Epub 2015 Jul 31. Review.

Strumia, R. (2005). Dermatologic signs in patients with eating disorders. *Am J Clin Dermatol*, 6(3): 165–173. Review.

Talbot, C. V., Gavin, J., van Steen, T., & Morey, Y. (2017). A content analysis of thinspiration, fitspiration, and bonespiration imagery on social media. *J Eat Disord*, 5: 40. doi: 10.1186/s40337-017-0170-2. eCollection 2017.

Tan, T., Kuek, A., Goh, S. E., Lee, E. L., & Kwok, V. (2016). Internet and smartphone application usage in eating disorders: A descriptive study in Singapore. *Asian J Psychiatry*, 19: 50–55. doi: 10.1016/j.ajp.2015.11.007. Epub 2015 Dec 15.

Chapter 2

Fundamentals of Taking a Detailed Eating Disorder History

"The advice I have for professionals working with other persons struggling with an eating disorder is to increase staff sensitivity with this illness and to promote honesty in the patient by addressing underlying fears related to telling the truth."

Why Take a Detailed Eating Disorder History?

A detailed eating disorder history has many advantages over a shorter one. Some of the advantages are as follows:

- It can help to identify *all* dangerous eating disorder behaviors and attitudes. There are over 150 behaviors used for eating disorder purposes, with hundreds of permutations and combinations of their use. Some individuals use 30 or more eating disorder behaviors at any one time and may use another dozen or so at other times.
- It can help to identify all non-eating disorder risks such as medical, psychological, or social risks.
- It can help to identify problems that may be keeping a person locked in the eating disorder.
- A therapist who can ask very detailed histories demonstrates a deeper understanding of eating disorders than previous clinicians may have, and this can help win over the client's confidence, as she may, for the first time, feel she is being heard and understood.
- It helps to identify previously unsuccessful or even harmful treatment and can help the new eating disorder treatment team avoid failed treatment.
- A detailed history, even if it takes several hours, will be cost effective. Since many with eating disorders have a longstanding condition, often utilizing hundreds if not thousands of hours of clinical treatment time costing hundreds of thousands of dollars, a good history is a good investment.
- It can help determine non-eating disorder diagnoses such as gallbladder disease or cancer, when previously believed to be due to anorexia

nervosa or bulimia. Brief histories, often influenced by previous consultation reports, can erroneously lead to incorrect diagnoses. Someone treated for an incorrectly diagnosed eating disorder can create mistrusting clients and parents. Some will waste years in unnecessary and sometimes costly treatment. Rarely, an incorrect diagnosis can lead to death.

- A dictated detailed eating disorder history can help educate other clinicians who have read it as to how to take a good eating disorder history.
- It can identify triggers and ongoing life situations that contribute to eating disorder attitudes and behaviors.
- It can eke out various loci for change such as motivations for recovery.

Who Should Have a Detailed Eating Disorder History Taken?

Because those with eating disorders often have a long-term (chronic) and sometimes severe and life-threatening condition, most will need a detailed history at some time in their treatment. Earlier the better.

The detailed eating disorder history is needed for:

- Anyone not improving with current or past treatments.
- Anyone whose eating disorder behaviors, physical, or mental health is progressively getting worse.
- Anyone who is not able to be discharged from hospital due to lack of progress.
- Anyone who has chronic or severe medical issues as a consequence of their eating disorder.
- Unexplained weight loss and metabolic or cardiac health issues that the current understanding of the eating disorder cannot explain.
- Individuals who are progressing adequately with eating disorder recovery but who are not able to move forward with other life challenges such as education, employment, mood stabilization, relationships, or recovery from drug and alcohol addictions.
- Those with more extreme eating disorder behaviors such as those who binge eat and vomit 20–40 times daily.

People rarely tell us everything spontaneously and will usually only give us information about the eating disorder when directly asked. Many eating disorder behaviors, such as using a scale or mirror, are deemed to be par for the course but the importance of their use is underestimated. A scale or mirror can be the most toxic trigger for engaging in compensatory behaviors. They can lead to the worst emotional consequences such as severe depression, anxiety, drug abuse, and suicidal thoughts and actions.

44 Fundamentals of Taking a Detailed History

The first interview is primarily to triage and establish rapport. This history screens for overt or primary eating disorder behaviors as well as for emotional and medical risks. There will seldom be enough time to do a complete eating disorder history at one sitting. It can take from two to four or more hours to take a detailed history. A complete history includes interviewing family, partners, friends, and clinicians.

When to Take a Brief Eating Disorder History

Detailed histories are important but can utilize much time. Several interviewing sessions may be needed.

Brief eating disorder histories are appropriate in the following situations

- Emergency room visits.
- Typical office visits for therapists, nutritionists, family physicians, and pediatricians.
- The client has limited time during the initial session.
- The clinician has limited time during the initial session.
- Evaluating the likely low-risk client.
- When others are present during the interview and confidential topics need to be addressed later.
- Other issues are more salient or present serious risk such as drug overdoses, major depressive episode, alcohol intoxication, and serious medical problems.
- Other clinicians are waiting to interview the client.
- Non-eating disorder specific consultations such as for maternity, surgery or internal medicine are urgently being requested.
- If another clinician has taken a recent detailed eating disorder assessment.
- To triage urgent versus less acute concerns.

Engaging

Engaging is the primary goal of a history after triaging for serious risks. The clinician may need to engage with someone else other than the one with the eating disorder such as a parent, partner, or friend who may be inquiring on behalf of the individual. The inquirer may be the one to be convinced that you or your program have something important to offer. The initial contact may take place with a phone call or in-office visit for an *intake assessment.*

The chance of engaging increases with the following:

- Offering something the individual needs to hear, such as hope for recovery; a way out of a current situation such as the likelihood of hospitalization; getting parents "off their back"; the prospect of their life getting better; the program will accept the client in whatever stage of change or readiness they present; treatment will not be forced upon them; and that you will listen and provide information as well as maintain confidentiality and demonstrate compassion and understanding. Essentially, you make it clear you are their *advocate*!

- The individual takes medical risks seriously or that hospitalization is a possibility and that you are there to help filter access by family and friends.
- Ask their opinions, ask them to educate you on a subject, ask their permission to pursue sensitive topics.
- Any effort that brings some peace of mind and a sense of safety.

Once individuals show interest in any of these options, then discuss them further until they believe you have something to offer.

Clients and parents need to know that you do have some expertise. Taking a thorough history and expressing eating disorder specific knowledge allows you to demonstrate this. Most clinicians will not have the eating disorder related expertise you have, and this helps to set you apart and gives promise of a more knowledgeable expert. Knowledge is power in this situation. You don't have to say you are the expert, as others will sense it. Maintain good eye contact and listen carefully.

When Someone Will Not Engage

Once you have done what you can to offer individuals choices, but they will still not engage, there is little else yet to do. Sometimes all that is needed is for them to just think about what has been discussed, and they will sooner or later decide they will wish for further contact.

If the person needs urgent attention, then further efforts may be necessary. Contact by phone to just see how things are going is usually met with appreciation. Regular phone contact will reinforce your genuine concern yet demonstrate your willingness to wait for further commitment. You can answer any questions, restate your concern regarding risks, and encourage them to see their doctor and have lab work done as well as to reconnect with family or friends. Even if individuals are not ready to focus on eating disorder recovery, they are usually concerned about any medical risks. They carry major guilt for what they have "done to themselves." You can allay fears that permanent damage is unlikely and that if they attend to the eating disorder now they can avoid serious, long lasting health issues. Meeting with them somewhere in the community first may be a stepping-stone to program commitment. Contact with their physicians may be necessary.

I usually ask if I may call them back, and they often say yes. If they say "no," then, barring life-threatening risks, all you can do is wait. Telephone

46 Fundamentals of Taking a Detailed History

calls allow you to show your stripes regarding attitude, respect, and willingness to listen yet not force issues. *Text messaging* short notes may work better than trying phone contact, as you won't have to play telephone tag or face a full voicemail inbox. *Email* contact may work if they say this form of communication is alright.

Document everything you and the client say for future reference so that you can be reminded of what has been discussed. This will also be a legal document.

How to Have Someone Feel at Ease

Part of what allows someone to feel at ease with your involvement is suggested in the sections in this chapter on "Engaging," "When Someone Will Not Engage," and "The Art of Give and Take."

Once someone is available in person then there are other things that can help the engaging process.

The *interviewer's attitude is everything*! The initial contact, whether by phone or in person, is designed to acquire important information and ensure a return visit. To help ensure someone will return for further visits, the person must be at ease in your company, trust your integrity, and be offered reasons to return.

Individuals can be made to feel at ease by:

- Not sounding like a therapist
- Limiting the using of active listening language
- Keeping good eye contact without staring
- Listening fully then responding only if appropriate—*interactive listening*
- Letting them speak about what they are comfortable with
- Answering questions directly and honestly
- Dressing casually
- Addressing note taking as a necessary evil and by saying that note taking will be much more limited in the future
- Putting the pen down during serious discourse
- Using humor
- Validating feelings and experiences
- Introducing yourself with the least official title or name unless you feel an official title helps to allow a sensed desire for lack of familiarity
- Offering a reason to return by explaining that you are their advocate, providing hope for recovery, further kindness, understanding, promising likely helpful medications, being given a chance to be believed, and being available to parents and other loved ones
- Knowing when not to say anything
- Being honest

Fundamentals of Taking a Detailed History 47

- Being kind and respectful
- Explaining your reasons for suggesting treatment options
- Sounding knowledgeable with regard to eating disorders
- Giving homework: eating activity records, reading material, a meal plan
- Being a referral source for other resources: nutrition, psychiatry, and drug and alcohol and family counseling
- Stating you take an individual approach to treatment
- Showing interest in their personal interests
- Letting them educate you: "Tell me what Spain was like. I've never been there"
- Aligning with their inadequacies or vulnerabilities: "I was never good at math either"
- Being direct and saying what you mean when necessary
- Talking about your own outside interests
- Speaking positively and optimistically when appropriate
- Consulting with them: "What is your opinion?"
- Asking them what they want from you or the program
- Letting them vent . . . to a degree
- Helping them to decrease anxiety and bring temporary peace of mind: "It's OK"
- Showing concern
- Offering a sense that you will stick with them
- Accepting them with any level of motivation

The Art of Give and Take

Interviewing requires skill and some art. Unless the client is 100% forthcoming, we cannot rely on mechanical history taking skills alone. We need to know when to persist, wait, or allow some slack and back away. A rigid and dogmatic approach may encourage the individual to not return, clam up, or fabricate. Clients need to be given permission to keep things to themselves or to tell little white lies yet given the opportunity to fess up at a later date without the threat of repercussion. Trust and control issues are so central to the person with the eating disorder that *leeway is the only way.*

- Take time out. Offer a hiatus from active treatment or hospital outings.
- Change the subject from the eating disorder to something else.
- "Let's continue this discussion next week if you like."
- Follow their line of thought.
- Move laterally in treatment if they can't move forward—focus on other eating disorder topics.
- If safe to do, give a trial period of the client's own recovery plan to prove to them that their ideas may or may not be sound.

48 Fundamentals of Taking a Detailed History

- Agree to disagree.
- Allow some digressions in conversation.
- Validate and comfort through difficult times.
- Try to look for viable treatments together.
- Have sessions outside of the office. I have seen clients in a community or university coffee shop if it was their choice. I arranged clinical session at a 460-acre farm dedicated to mental health treatment. We had to dodge wandering horses, though.
- Help to bring resolve to non-eating disorder life issues first such as family strife, anxiety, or depression.

The Language Used in an Interview

Whether we are talking to someone on the phone or in person, our language helps to set the tone of the interview and can either work with or against our goals. Active listening language, if not tempered, helps to give the impression that we are textbook professionals, and some complain it makes us "sound like a therapist" and like all other therapists before us. The best compliment a client can give us is to say "You don't sound like a therapist." Active listening techniques are a set of training wheels to be used only until the therapist becomes skilled in the use of common language and subtle, non-intrusive professional language.

How to Ask Questions

The same question can be asked many ways. How we phrase a question, the context in which it is used, the terminology, and whether the questions are direct, specific, or open-ended can influence the answer given. A question that is poorly understood or deemed threatening may provide erroneous and useless information. Terminology is important in communication. It is necessary to make sure we know that the client understands our language and, as important, we understand their terminology.

With regard to eating disorder language, eating disorder terms are often misused. As an example, an individual may say she binges but may think that bingeing really means vomiting. Bingeing to some means both bingeing and vomiting, and unless we know for sure how they use these works, we can be misled.

- The word vomit may be interpreted as spitting and chewing.
- The word vomit may be interpreted as bingeing and vomiting.
- The word purging may be interpreted as bingeing.
- The word purging may be mistaken to mean vomiting when other forms of purging were intended. Laxative or emetic use may incorrectly not be deemed as purging.

Fundamentals of Taking a Detailed History   49

- Exercise may be seen as a form of purging.
- "Eating enough" may be thought of as any quantity of food, including eating two crackers as a meal.
- A meal may be interpreted as any quantity of food. Eating an apple may be deemed a meal.
- A binge may be interpreted as being any quantity of food eaten. Eating a sandwich may be perceived as a binge.
- The term "diet pills" may be seen to cover the spectrum of any pill that may be used for weight loss control such as laxatives, diuretics, emetics, appetite suppressants, metabolic boosters, and stimulants. Be very specific when asking about these substances. Ask the exact drug name or what the drug is expected to do in order to help confirm you understand what the client means.
- Ask what the word "diet" means to someone. It could mean fasting, restricting, cutting out, and limiting, or refer to a brand name diet. Exercising, vomiting, laxatives, and diuretic and emetic use may be incorrectly believed to be kinds of dieting.
- Sexual abuse has many meanings depending on the individual. One client, when asked if she had ever been sexually assaulted, answered "no." With rephrasing the question, "Have you ever experienced any unwanted sexual contact?" she said "You don't mean rape, do you?" It turns out she had been raped, and she was currently involved in a lawsuit regarding this. The words "sexual assault" and "rape" were not synonymous in her or her mother's mind. Clarity with regard to sexual assault is essential.

Questions may be asked using very specific or direct language. Examples are "Do you throw up?" or "Are you still trying to lose weight?" Alternatively, questions may be asked in an open-ended fashion and allow a freer flow of ideas at times.

Examples of *open-ended questions* are:

- Is there anything else that you do or think that is a part of your eating disorder or helps you to lose weight?
- What other "tricks" do you use to lose weight?
- Is there anything more I should know about you or your eating disorder?
- What do you mean by sexual assault?

Questions such as these may be interpreted as being less threatening than more direct questions and allow an opportunity for individuals to provide further useful information. A combination of *direct* and *open-ended questions* will usually yield the best histories. It's important to remember that if you don't ask a specific question, you may not get the

50 Fundamentals of Taking a Detailed History

answers you are looking for. *Never assume anything*. Confirm with a clear, thorough history.

Let Them Speak

We want useful information from interviews, but sometimes the client just wants to have their own say without interruption, unsolicited comments, or judgments. Even if the person is trying to convince us that there is not a problem, we can receive useful information about their attitudes toward the eating disorder. This approach allows them to vent and get things off their chest, often for the first time. This shows that we are able to listen and are not judgmental or fixed in our approach. *Venting* individuals can help to set our priorities in therapy, as they tell us what is important to them.

Do Not Be Afraid

Do not be afraid to ask questions about suicidality, sexual abuse, or any other potentially sensitive topic. Be sensitive and respectful when pursuing questioning and look for untoward reactions to questioning. Ask permission to enquire regarding past events that are potentially traumatic. Individuals are surprisingly up front and willing to discuss difficult topics. If you touch on a subject that they are overtly uncomfortable with, they will not be offended or not wish to see you again. There will be a "no harm done" consequence, and you both can move on with other discussions.

You can open with "I'd like to ask if there have been any experiences regarding sexual abuse? If you would rather not discuss this at this time, then that's certainly OK with me." Asking questions about sexual abuse, with a general regard, will not likely be traumatizing or trigger depression or self-harm. You may be the first person they have ever disclosed this with. Allow the client to call off questioning. Defer to more expert therapists who deal with trauma when appropriate.

Questions to Leave Out

Some questions may need to be avoided, at least for the moment.

- Avoid pursuing questions that may be too sensitive. Any question that leads or may lead to significant emotional stress should be deferred to another day. When readdressing a sensitive topic ask the client's permission if you may pursue this line of questioning. Sentences such as these are helpful: "Are you OK with me asking these questions?" "Do you want me to stop?" "Stop me if these questions are too difficult for you?"

Fundamentals of Taking a Detailed History   51

- Avoid questions that may give new ideas to those vulnerable, usually young clients. We can educate some to consider new eating disorder behaviors that had not yet been thought of. Asking questions such as "Do you use a spoon to trigger vomiting?" or "Do you cruise the pro-anorexia websites?" may encourage a few to do just these things. Open-ended questions are best for those who are vulnerable. Questions such as "You told me that you vomit to lose weight. How do you make yourself vomit?" or "Where did you find out how to lose weight?" may be better lines of questioning.
- Avoid questions that you suspect raise anger and resentment in clients. Ask clients what they have not liked being questioned about by previous therapists, and this will help to give you the heads up.
- Do not ask questions in front of parents or others that you have not been given permission to discuss. Commonly, clients have not let parents or partners know what they have told you about the eating disorder or other subjects. There may be opportunities for loved ones to be better informed at a later date if the client likes.

Motivation for Change

Do not assume individuals' motivation for change from a single interview. They will need to be convinced that you have something constructive to offer or be given a reason to want to change before a more accurate assessment of motivation is possible. It may take some time before the client comes onboard enough before we see motivational change. Therapy can help motivation along. Don't wait for motivation to improve before therapy starts.

Individuals are not either motivated or unmotivated to change. There is not just one overriding motivation. There are multiple *motivational focuses*. Each eating disorder behavior has its own motivational barometer. If you ask clients if they want to work on the eating disorder, they may say no, likely due to fear of weight gain. If various potential focuses for change have been identified, ask individuals if they would choose one they might want to work on. As an example, if eating disorder behaviors include bingeing, vomiting, over-exercising, restricting, and laxative misuse, you can ask which one of these behaviors the client would be willing to first try to diminish. She may consider decreasing laxative use as a starting point due to this being seen as a less threatening behavior to give up. This provides an "in" to starting the recovery process. If someone does not want to work on any eating disorder behavior, she may be willing to work on a drug or alcohol addiction or anxiety disorder. At some level, it doesn't matter much where a window of opportunity presents itself; getting started anywhere opens the gate to further recovery commitments.

Stages of Change

The *Stages of Change* model proposed by Prochaska and DiClemente (Prochaska, DiClemente & Norcross, 1992) is useful in the assessment and treatment of eating disorders. It is well recognized that an individual who is not in action mode, that is, not ready to make changes with their eating disorder, is not going to respond to an action directed treatment plan. When it comes to using this model with someone who has an eating disorder, we must be careful not to assume, however, that if someone is in one stage with one area of her eating disorder that she is in the same stage with all aspects of the eating disorder. As an example, if someone is aware she vomits as part of the eating disorder but does not want to stop, she is in precontemplation. She may not think that there is a problem in the first place. This does not mean, however, that she is in precontemplation with other areas of the eating disorder. She may be willing to dedicate to decreasing using the scale, having advanced to contemplation, and possibly be able to move on to action mode with this one eating disorder behavior.

Even if individuals are in the precontemplative or contemplative stage with the entire eating disorder, it does not mean that they are going to be unwilling or unable to work on other issues such as drug or alcohol abuse, self-esteem, or family dynamics.

Stages of change should be expected to shift. This is normal. Backtracking for a period of time should be viewed as an inevitable phase in recovery. At the same time, someone may be becoming resistant in one area of treatment and become ready for action in another area.

Be careful not to judge someone's likelihood or predictability for positive change based on stages of change or perceived lack of motivation. They are not necessarily linked.

Individuals often *plateau* after a period of positive change. That is, they have made gains with decreasing an eating disorder behavior but have come to a point where they are not able to make further gains. They are, however, able to maintain a new level of improvement without losing ground. This too is an expected phase of recovery. It should not be viewed as treatment resistance or that they are being uncooperative or that it is a form of backsliding.

Recovery History

> *"Today, I am proud of where I am in my recovery. I feel stronger most days, but there are still days where I struggle with food and my weight."*

> *"It has taken me 17 years to get to where I am today."*

Even if you believe in recovery it does not mean that anyone else does, including the client, family, partner, or friends. Other caregivers may not

Fundamentals of Taking a Detailed History   53

as well. Asking individuals what they think about recovery will help give you the opportunity to plant the seed that *recovery is possible*. You can ask:

- What do you know about recovery?
- Do you believe in recovery and why or why not?
- Do you know someone who has recovered or has not?
- What do others say about your chances of recovering?
- What have you read or hear in the media about recovery?
- What do you think makes recovery possible?
- What has given you evidence of recovery or that recovery is possible in your own treatment?
- What is recovery? What does recovery mean to you?
- Who do you think recovers and why?
- Who do you think does not recover and why?
- What have other caregivers said about recovery? Have they ever talked about it?

After some questioning, talk a bit about what you think recovery is about and reinforce the prospect that recovery is indeed doable.

What Gets in the Way of a Good History

The concept of the ideal detailed history is a noble one, but there can and will be roadblocks that interfere with this end. We cannot control every situation that may prevent an ideal history, but we can avoid what we are able to and then accept what limitations are inevitable. The following points identify some of these concerns.

- Not enough time to take a history
- Client is unrevealing due to being in denial, is not trustful, or is fearful
- Others are present during the interview
- Client does not show up for sessions
- The interviewer is impatient
- The interviewer is perceived as arrogant, opinionated or too professional, disrespectful, inexperienced, or unknowledgeable
- Previously experienced negative attitudes of other health care staff
- A history of punitive treatment
- Previous unsuccessful treatment
- Negative, disruptive, or controlling attitudes of family or partners during the session
- Active drug and alcohol abuse
- The education level of the client
- The mental development of the client
- The client lives in another city and can't make appointments regularly

54 Fundamentals of Taking a Detailed History

- The client is too malnourished
- The client is taking medications that sedate her or lead her to "zone out"
- Depression
- Anxiety
- Exhaustion
- Sleep deprivation
- Clinician asks the wrong questions or not enough questions, or questions have been worded incorrectly or misinterpreted by the client
- Perceived age or gender gap by client or interviewer
- Sessions are hurried or pressured or interrupted
- Client feels she will not be believed or heard
- Impersonal methods of history acquisition such as the use of questionnaires or computers
- The interview is perceived as too personal; a questionnaire or computer may be better in this situation
- The purpose of questions or methods of treatment offered are not understood
- A feeling that questions "must" be answered; therefore, any answer will do
- Being afraid to give wrong answers
- Shame and guilt
- Lack of skill of an interviewer to take a good history

Age or Developmental Related History

Questioning needs to be directed toward the development or vulnerability risk of the individual. Older clients and others who have had an eating disorder for a long time will likely not be as susceptible to learning new eating disorder behaviors during questioning as those who are younger. Most come for help because they feel they already realize the negative impact of the eating disorder and, to some degree, want it to be gone. They are more likely to shun the prospects of new ways of losing weight. Younger clients, new to eating disorder ways, often feel that they have been dragged to see professionals against their will and have no intention of giving up the eating disorder and also may wish to acquire improved eating disorder behaviors.

When taking a history from the vulnerable, ask questions regarding behaviors you already have been informed of via the intake history, conversations with referring parties or loved ones, consult reports, and discharge histories. You may want to ask if individuals vomit, but do not ask about the many ways vomiting can be induced, as they may learn from this line of questioning. Leading questions such as "Are there any other ways you try to control weight, body image, or food?" or "Are there any other tricks you use to lose weight?" or "Anything else I should know?" are safe to ask.

If behaviors you have been informed of cannot explain the disproportionate degree of weight loss or metabolic abnormalities, then explain this concern. You may ask, "Thank you for being up-front with me about your eating disorder, but these eating disorder behaviors do not explain the degree to which you have lost weight. Is there anything else I should know? Are there other ways you are losing weight, or are you using the eating disorder behaviors you have told me about more often than you've already said?"

Reviewing the history at a later date when the individual trusts you more may help acquire more accurate data. A second interviewer may be helpful. Sometimes nutritionists learn about other eating disorder behaviors that the therapist was unable to elicit. The reverse may be true as well. Interviewing with a parent, partner, or school counselor present may help the client to be more honest, as these people may know quite a bit about the eating disorder from firsthand knowledge. A collateral history may be the most reliable. Others in the interview may be able to speak for your client when she is too shy, disgruntled, or withdrawn.

Who Should Be at the First Interview

A basic rule as to who should be at the first interview is whoever the client will allow in the interview is the right person. Usually it is a parent or partner. It could also be a school counselor or a private therapist. Sometimes a friend will be asked to sit in. At times, clients will not come to a session unless they have been accompanied by a significant other. Having this other person in the initial interview helps with collateral information. Also, the other person may have a good memory regarding times and places. The dual interview also allows you the see some of the dynamics between them. We may witness supportive interaction, while other times we see power struggles and counterproductive communication. We need to know either way.

Often the supportive person can give a more realistic interpretation of what the client is really doing with or thinking about the eating disorder. Meal sizes and whether the person is really eating what she says she is eating can be very different from what you have heard from the client herself.

It is important to discuss confidentiality with those present and that during future sessions one-on-one therapy will be expected most of the time. Young adolescents or children may not be given the option of not having parents present in order to ensure accuracy of history and observe family dynamics. This gives you the opportunity to educate parents and let them ask questions and begin to feel comfortable with your involvement

56 Fundamentals of Taking a Detailed History

with their child. It provides an opportunity to explain who is responsible for what aspects of care of the child.

Individuals may insist that they be interviewed alone. Allow this even if they are very young. You may access more honest information right away. Significant others can be present subsequently.

Personal Writing

Personal writing can be a source of information that helps in therapy. Past writing can be a good historic documentation of the eating disorder and of someone's life. It can be a good memory jog. It can help to compare the current status of the eating disorder versus past experiences. It can document attitude and behaviors over time.

Ask if clients journal, and do they journal regarding the eating disorder? How long have they been journaling, and do they still? Will they show you any writings? Why did they start journaling? If someone is new to journaling, then explain why journaling can be helpful. Individuals can document eating activities, eating disorder behaviors, and feelings surrounding body image, weight, and food. They also can document anything else experienced in their life, as well.

Reconnecting

Sometimes clients do not return for booked appointments or rebook when they said they would. This may happen for brief or long-term periods. Recontacting may be necessary and appropriate. At times it may not be. Discretion is required.

Reconnecting may take place by phone, texting, postal mail, or email. Contacting parents or the family physician to help arrange your client reconnecting with you may be helpful.

When reconnecting there needs to be a clearly stated reason for the contact—reasons such as:

- I just want to find out how you are doing?
- Is there anything I can do?
- I need to close your file if you are not returning.
- Are you wanting to return to the eating disorder program?
- Are you taking your medications and seeing your family doctor?

Certification Driven Histories

Histories can only be competently done based on our training and clinical experiences. If you are not trained in the medical field, then a detailed medical history is not required by you. If you do ask questions beyond the scope of your training, then you may be responsible for proper follow-up. As an example, if you ask if someone has chest pain and she answers "yes," the interviewer will be responsible for transfer of care to medical staff. A medically trained person may be able to rule out serious chest pain symptoms.

Medical doctors, including psychiatrists or family physicians, gynecologists, pediatricians, and internists, are in a position to examine the patient and order diagnostic tests such as blood work, urinalysis, and imaging procedures. They will also be expected to provide proper follow-up including immediate transfer to emergency services if a definitive medical diagnosis is not possible in the office situation. Similarly, accurately diagnosing psychological disorders will be limited by our training and experience. Some clinicians have a legal right and obligation to diagnose and treat mental health disorders, while other do not. Some have a legal right to prescribe medications and are responsible for consequences, including side effects. Any non-medically trained clinician knowing of adverse reactions to medications is responsible for encouraging follow-up with medically trained personnel.

Taking Notes

Taking and recording a detailed history is important. Taking notes while doing the interview is the most reliable way of recording accurate information. The actual act of note taking can, however, seem impersonal and limit the degree of intimacy desired. Recording a history then becomes a balance between meeting clinical and legal requirements as well as maintaining personal connection. During the first interview, I usually tell clients I need to take notes so that the information they provide me is accurate and that I do not usually take notes nearly as much after the first and second sessions. I sometimes put the pen down if I want to show that I am really paying attention or am very concerned. It is okay to rely on memory for short periods of time and then document accurately immediately after.

Because there is so much information that may be needed to be recorded, shortcuts to notation are usually necessary. Shorthand abbreviations to record eating disorder behaviors can save time and help to ensure accurate recording of the client's words.

Such abbreviations could be:

V = vomiting
B = bingeing
R = restricting
Ex = exercise
Lax = laxatives
Fl = fluid loading
D/A = drugs and alcohol

58 Fundamentals of Taking a Detailed History

Often clinicians have a standardized form with which to record data in a specific order and format. Have blank sheets of paper with which to record here-and-now data. Unless there is some urgency to acquire a very directed history, allow it to flow in the direction it seems to want to take. Cutting someone off to redirect conversation may block that avenue of conversation later, and both of you may forget a particular train of thought.

Updated Histories and Review of Chart

Over time, individuals' lives change, and we lose track of originally identified concerns. It is expedient to do an updated eating disorder history to refresh our impression of the eating disorder. We sometimes lose track of some eating disorder behaviors and other issues such as drug and alcohol use or suicidal thoughts when we do not update. Reviewing the whole chart briefly can be a useful memory jog, and we can add forgotten items to our weekly checklist. Updating regarding employment, living situations, relationships, education, medications, drug and alcohol use, and mood status may be necessary so that we do not make incorrect assumptions about them.

Breakdown of Weekly Interviews

Sometimes, with many topics to follow on a weekly basis as well as changes that happen between weekly visits, some form of systematic follow-up is needed. The following is one version that helps to make each session efficient and productive.

There are five main categories a therapy session may incorporate.

- Catch-up time
- Venting time
- Safety screening
- Focused time
- Fielding new concerns

Catch-up

Catch-up time provides an opportunity for your client to tell you about their week in a non-structured way. A question such as "How was your week?" is a good generic opening line. Preparing a *review checklist* prior to the session will help further to recall specific topics or issues that are discussed week to week. The list may include eating disorder or non-eating disorder topics.

An example of a review list that itemizes the previous week's topic of discussion is as follows:

1 vomiting
2 laxative use
3 daily food intake
4 fainting symptoms
5 alcohol use
6 fighting between parents
7 signed up for college yet?
8 seen GP in last week and had lab work done?
9 moods
10 suicidal thoughts or plans

Venting Time

I would never ask someone to vent, but if instigated by catch-up questioning, allow some brief time for someone to vent. A minute or two to allow clients to get things off of their chest may be all the therapy they need surrounding some concerns. If talk becomes too negative, then distract the person by focusing on helpful specific therapy topics or non-emotional chit-chat. Venting may bring forward important, urgent concerns that need addressing right away that routine conversation in sessions may not.

Safety Screening

Make sure any safety issues—medical or psychological—pertinent in the last therapy session are addressed in the following sessions. Drug or alcohol abuse, suicidal thoughts, violence, and family crisis topics need to be followed closely. A brief update is crucial.

Focused Time

The bulk of therapy should be spent on relevant eating disorder or non-eating disorder issues. Salient, important ongoing issues will need most of the session time.

Field New Concerns

Sometimes there are new issues that need attention immediately and require that the usual weekly topics be tabled. Add the new issue to the review list for the next session if needed.

Key Interviewing Points

Never Assume. Always Ask. Always Know.

When we interview someone, it is too easy to assume we know what someone means, or we just make assumptions without any enquiry ahead of time. As examples, we likely assume when clients says they are dealing with bulimia that when they say they vomit it is for body image control reasons. Most of the time we will be right. However, we don't know for sure unless we question further.

If individuals admit to vomiting, we need to ask specifically "Why do you vomit?" Likely they will give the reason as being to control weight. We then need to ask further, "Are there any other reasons you vomit?" They may give other reasons such as to deal with stress, punish themselves, purge negative emotions, or to get rid of abdominal cramps from eating. There may be several reasons for engaging in any one eating disorder behavior.

Another example is if individuals say that they need more time to write exams and they have given a history of ADHD, we may assume the extra time is for coping with difficulties in concentration. If asked, "Why do you need more time to write exams?" the client may give a different answer than the one we assumed, such as "I have multiple sclerosis and my hand coordination is poor and slows my writing down." Reasons may be that both ADHD and multiple sclerosis affect her capacity to finish exams in the usual time frame.

The diagnosis of multiple sclerosis should have been identified as an ongoing health issue during the initial assessment or even before, during the intake history. How could this have been missed? Sometimes individuals genuinely forget to include health or other relevant concerns during an interview or chose not to state them for any number of reasons. Reviewing a medical history with individuals or any other history topic including substance abuse or self-harm risks may bring to light previously missed items. Spending more time on each topic at a later date may be the key to acquiring a more thorough and accurate history. Intake and assessment histories attempt to cover large quantities of information often in rather rushed conditions due to time restraints.

One More Question

When enquiring about any topic, we need to continue to ask more questions until we arrive at an overt reason to discontinue questioning. Just because someone says "no" to a given question or gives a single answer, this does not mean there are necessarily no more further answers. Reframing questions may bring new, enlightening answers.

Frame the Question to Be More Inclusive

Instead of asking "Do you take laxatives?" frame the question to be broader and more inclusive, such as "Do you or have you ever taken laxatives?" If individuals say they don't and have never taken laxatives for eating disorder purposes, ask another question: "Have you ever, even once. . . ?"

The following is a line of questioning where asking one more question and more inclusive questions may be helpful. "Have you ever vomited to control your weight or how you look?" The answer is "No." "Have you ever, even once, made yourself vomit?" The answer is, again "No." "Have you ever even attempted to make yourself vomit?" The answer is now "Yes." "When was this and why did you try? When you tried were you successful with inducing vomiting?" She then gives a helpful reply such as "I first attempted to vomit in Grade 11 but could not. I later became successful at vomiting during first year university." "Your mother says that she sees vomit under the toilet seat and around the base of the toilet bowl. Is there any chance that you have been vomiting recently?" She then fesses up to this. Give her accolades for her honesty.

Reference

Prochaska, J. O., DiClemente, C. C., & Norcross, J. C. (1992). In search of how people change: Applications to the addictive behaviors. *American Psychologist*, 47: 1102–1114.

Chapter 3

General Eating Disorder History

"Learning how to eat again after my eating disorder was the hardest part. I still don't know how to do it after almost 10 years of trying to recover."

A general eating disorder history can be broken down into various subsections. It might also be called a complete or thorough history and will attempt to gather as much information as possible about eating disorder specifics such as eating disorder behaviors, attitudes, and dynamics, as well as demographic, psychological, developmental, medical, family, abuse, and social histories.

Demographics and Contact Information

When enquiring regarding contact information, be as thorough as you can. In emergency situations, accurate, up-to-date data may be crucial and assist in life-threatening situations.

Critical emergency situations where immediate access to contact information is crucial are when someone is acutely suicidal or has life-threatening medical risks. We become ethically and legally responsible for dealing with critical situations where we:

- Answer our phone from a suicidal person
- Receive a text message or email from a suicidal person
- Have been contacted by another person regarding a suicidal person—family, friends, partners, and professionals such as nurses, social workers, caseworkers
- Suspect someone is suicidal
- Are with a suicidal person and she flees our office
- We receive critical laboratory or ECG reports from medical laboratories
- The client calls or texts that she is falling or experiencing a racing heart, shortness of breath or chest pain

General Eating Disorder History 63

- Parents, a partner or friend calls to say she has been falling, fainting or experiencing any of the other above symptoms

In these situations, we may need to connect with the suicidal person and determine the relative risk of suicide and try to coach them through the acute impulsive phase of suicidal drives. At this point we become a lifeline and can buy time while we try to sooth the suicidal urges and bring some resolve, enough to decrease serious risk and provide options for viable support systems. We may determine there is not any lessening of risk and hopefully have time to build a crisis management plan.

We may need to contact family, partners, friends, or bosses regarding the whereabouts of individuals if they might know and possibly inform them of the suicidal or even medical emergency. At this point we will need access to any and all contacts that may be of use to help save the individual's life.

I have needed to contact a number of crucial individuals and services to help thwart a suicide attempt, including the police, ambulance, hospital ward staff and therapists; I have needed their assistance in helping to find the suicidal person and bring her to a safe place, such as the emergency room. I have done the same for medical emergencies. Contacting family, partners, or friends may also be invaluable in locating the person, giving her support, or transporting her to the hospital for evaluation of the suicidal or medical risks by professionals. Other contact numbers should include the emergency wards and hospital wards where the patient may have been admitted as well as laboratory services where critical lab work may be accessed.

Contact information needs to be up to date. Clients change living addresses, email addresses, and phone numbers, and so do family, friends, and partners. Updating contact information needs to be an ongoing task.

Contact data needs to be easily accessed. Having this data only in our office, where we may not be during a crisis situation, is of no use. We need to have the information with us, and it must be mobile. This pretty much means it needs to be in our phones and possibly also in our computers and tablets. If we are actively engaged in a mobile phone call with the patient, family, or police, a second source of contact information such as a computer or tablet may be useful.

If you are speaking to the patient or others on your mobile phone and the contact numbers are in the phone, contact data may be accessed while speaking to someone. Determine if your phone has this ability, and practice talking to someone on the phone while trying to access the data so the first time you have to test this isn't with a suicidal person.

Another reason for having easily accessible contact numbers is if you receive critical lab results and need to inform the patient or family directly by phone. You may not be able to contact the person with critical lab results yourself, but family or others might be able to. Someone's contact

64 General Eating Disorder History

information is invaluable, but you must know more details about the person's circumstances. Trying to contact someone with critical lab results who lives in her car and has an uncharged cellular phone is a nightmare for a clinician. Emergency services and significant others contact information can be lifesaving in situations like this.

Name(s)

First names, middle names, if they exist, and last names need to be recorded. Determine the client's legal names as well as nicknames or aliases. Name changes for marital purposes need to be noted. Legal names are usually used for legal documents such as birth certificate, driver's license, passports, and credit cards as well as medical and insurance purposes. Ambulance, police, laboratory, pharmacy, and hospital contact information will likely record legal names. Contacts such as friends, coworkers, or peers may not be aware of legal names. When communicating with others, our credibility slides when we do not even know the names used by individuals. As a result, they may not want to share information with us.

Another concern is that people change their legal names but do not have them changed on their credit cards or other identification. This creates problems when systems do not have legal names in their systems. The individual may need to provide proof of a legal name change before systems will allow them to make transactions.

Determine why someone will use different names in different situations. It might be helpful to determine why individuals have changed their name. An answer might be given such as "I was abused by my grandfather and do not want to be associated with his last name." Another reason given could be "I want to forget the person I was before and start a new life." They may want to adopt the name of a mentor such as a grandmother or celebrity to give a rebirth to their identity.

Date of Birth and Age

For contacting health or emergency services, we may need to have the person's birthdate as well as legal and other known names before information will be shared over the phone. The age of the person may be requested, and it is good to know this.

Narrowing Down Contact Reliability

Knowing all of the individual's names, residence address, birthdate, and possibly health insurance numbers better narrows down the likelihood that the right individual is being discussed with others. Many have the same name, and the identifiers listed can bring precise identification in systems with large collections of data of people. Again, this brings more credibility that you have legitimacy in sharing information.

If requesting the results of medical testing such as medical imaging, ECGs, or chemistry, it may help to know the precise investigations ordered and the dates the tests were ordered or carried out before information may be allowed to be shared.

Phone Numbers

Phone numbers are the most important tool with regard to dealing with crisis situations. The phone numbers that need to be recorded include their personal mobile and home phone or landline if one exists. Their private and general office work numbers should be included as well. Collect all phone numbers of those who are connected with the individual's life in some significant way. This includes mobile and landline numbers of family, friends, and partners as well as their work phone numbers. Landlines are particularly useful when individual's mobile phones are off, not charged, or in a different location. They are useful to contact significant others for the same reasons. They are also useful for leaving voice messages when mobile phone voice messaging systems are full, shut off, being ignored, or the battery is dead.

Contact information for emergency mental health services or campus security should also be recorded. Police and ambulance services can be contacted at 911 or other phone numbers, depending on the country.

A major advantage of having cell phone numbers is that contacts can be text messaged. Many respond to texts when they will not answer the phone or review voice messages. This provides a 100% chance the message has been sent and received. It also serves as a legal record of exactly what was stated by yourself and the responder or that there indeed was not a response. The precise time of messaging is recorded to the second. Text messages can be printed and included in client records.

Record phone numbers of the emergency department or hospital ward, should the person be under hospital care. Patients flee wards and clinicians' offices, so close communication with hospital staff may need to be frequent and easy. It's nice to know when a patient has returned to the ward as soon as possible so you can stop worrying. Also, family and emergency services can stop looking for and worrying about them, too. Cellular phones also may have GPS capacity to help locate an individual's location. Keep old numbers including addresses as well, as individuals may return to places they have been before.

Addresses

Know the individual's own residential address as well as those of others she may stay with. In particular, family, partner, and close friend addresses may be of assistance. These other addresses may be of use, as a suicidal person may be calling from her partner's or family's home. Phone messages may be left on home answering machines for family and others to notice. Police, ambulance services, or emergency mental health services will need this information to provide safe support on location. Individuals may stay with close friends or relatives from time to time, and their addresses should be recorded. The address of employment should be recorded as well.

Some may live temporarily at locations out of town for extended periods of time. This is true of those who go to university or spend summers away. The contact numbers and address of the places they will be staying at should be recorded, as emergency services may need to be provided out of town. Suicidal calls can come from 3,000 miles away as easily as locally. We need to be just as prepared. As people move, update addresses as needed.

Email Addresses

Email contact seems to be of less importance than it used to be for personal communication. Texting, mobile phone, Twitter, and other apps used for social media are better responded to. Ask individuals how they prefer to be contacted. Regardless of this, email communication may have a use. Like texting, the email message arrives for sure, the precise time it was sent is recorded, and it can be printed as a legal document. Personal and work email addresses of all significant others should be recorded. Some only view email messages when traveling, as they may not take their phones or may shut them off to avoid roaming costs. Also, email messages can be fanned out to several concerned others at the same time. Ask significant others the best way to contact them in an emergency. Know when email addresses have been changed.

Contact Person

Regardless of whether you have several contact numbers and email addresses, there needs to be one contact who would be the first contact for most situations. This should be the most responsible and reliably accessed person. He or she needs to be informed that he or she is the main contact. Ask about the favored method of contact that he or she is most likely to pay attention to.

Living Arrangements

Living arrangements have an influence on people's lives. The dynamics of living with others can vary greatly. Living alone has its own dynamics as well.

General Eating Disorder History   67

Questions

- Why are you living alone?
- What is living alone like for you?
- Does it pose advantages, disadvantages, or both?
- What are the advantages?
- What are the disadvantages?
- Would you prefer to live alone or with others?
- Does living alone help to perpetuate the eating disorder, or not?
- Should you live alone or not, and why?
- Does loneliness become an issue for you?
- Do you get depressed because you are alone?
- Does it allow you to do drugs or use alcohol in excess?
- Do visitors do drugs, and do they influence your drug use?
- Do you feel safe where you live?
- Does living alone feed into feelings of helplessness and hopelessness, or not?
- Does it contribute to isolation?
- Do you have enough social contact?
- Are you looking for a roommate?
- Do you have a partner whom you stay with, or does you partner stay with you?

For those living with others, we need to know many things. The consequences of living with others depend on multiple factors. The dynamics of living with others can have a significant influence on eating disorder behaviors and attitudes—both positive and negative. Living with family will have a different set of influences than living with college roommates, close friends, or a partner. The gender of roommates can change dynamics. Moods, body image issues, self-esteem, and drugs and alcohol as well as sexual pressures may come into play for the individual with the eating disorder.

Questions

- How many people do you live with?
- Do you live with family, others, or both?
- What gender are they?
- Do any have body image issues or possibly have an eating disorder?
- Do you have a close relationship with any of them?
- Do their behaviors affect your moods, eating disorder, or drug or alcohol use?
- Are they respectful of your space and personal belongings and clean up after themselves, or not?
- Are they critical of you, abusive, or supportive?

- Does their presence affect whether you can engage in your eating disorder?
- What do you do about the eating disorder if you cannot binge or vomit?
- Do any depend on you for emotional support, and is this a burden for you?
- Would you rather live alone or with others?
- Is your partner upset because you live with others you could potentially have sex with?
- Do you depend on others for transportation, or are you the driver for others?

Caregivers

Caregiver contact information should be obtained. Caregivers include family, family physician, therapist or mental health caseworkers, medical specialists such as internists, and pediatricians (Stefanini et al., 2018).

Therapists, including psychiatrists, may be the most influential caregivers. They may or may not be available for quick contact. Obtain written permission to speak with them and work out how they want to be involved. Find out if there is anyone else to contact if they are not available. School counselors are sometimes the most involved with school-age clients. They tend to like to keep close tabs on management. Community mental health workers will have some degree of availability, but there will be hours of operation and rules for involving their services. Drug and alcohol therapy workers are also key players in the care of your patients.

Internists may be involved for the management of cardiac or metabolic abnormalities resulting from eating disorder behaviors or chronic conditions such as Crohn's disease. They also will be involved for management of insulin-dependent diabetes, a life-threatening condition when not properly controlled. It is a good idea to have written permission for you to contact them whenever necessary. They may have updated information regarding the management of these health risks and possibly give advice as to how best to support your patient. They will likely want to know about any difficulties you have come across so they have the heads up. Any number of other important health issues may need close monitoring by medical specialists. Multiple sclerosis, migraine headaches, and hypothyroidism are a few.

Questions

- Who are your caregivers?
- How do they support you?
- Can you gather all contact information—phone numbers, email addresses, and work address—please?

- Who would be the best and most reliable contact and why?
- Will you give written permission to allow sharing of information?
- Will you allow me to contact them anytime I see fit, or only with permission?
- Who else can be contacted when these are not available?
- Do you have a safety net or place to go when these supports are not available?
- Are any contacts not supportive, or do any have a negative influence on your care?
- Do they know their boundaries?
- Do they expect you to do favors for them?
- Are they needy and dependent on you for emotional support?

Determine Alternative Support

Sometimes we rely on specific contacts, whether family or other. When these contacts are not available, individuals may lose the support they need and be at risk of losing ground. When their usual contacts are not available due to holidays or other reasons, we can be left carrying the ball, as it were, and be vulnerable to manage critical situations alone. Arrange with your client well ahead of time other supports to replace the ones that are absent. If there are not any replacements, we need to make it clear the need for emergency health services and limits of our involvement.

Risk Assessment

Arguably, the most important piece of a history has to do with *risk assessment*. All else is secondary. Throughout much of the book, risk is addressed time and time again. Risks come from many fronts. Regardless of the focus of the history, there is the possibility of risk lurking. With health issues, such as an advancing kidney infection, developing risks may be somewhat foreseeable. As individuals get sicker from the infection, they look sicker. We then can predict they may die, thus providing time to intervene with lifesaving treatment. For those with eating disorders, individuals may just drop dead midstride without any perceivable warning signs. This makes risk assessment a very tenuous process. A hyperawareness by professionals of ongoing and potential risk factors along with close monitoring is paramount. Risks can present in various forms. Common risks may include the following.

Medical Risks

Medical risks, discussed in detail elsewhere, mainly arising from eating disorder behaviors, which can lead to metabolic imbalances affecting every system of the body. Electrolyte imbalances, cardiac dysrhythmias, myocardial infarction, and renal failure are a few. Medical risks not of eating disorder origins require close attention as well.

Drug and Alcohol Addictions

Overdoses from drugs and alcohol are of prime concern. Overdoses put individuals at medical risk for respiratory and cardiac arrest, resulting in serious organ damage, including of the brain, and ultimately death. Deaths from substance toxicity may be from a deliberate suicide attempt or result accidently. Sometimes we never know.

Emotional Risks

Growing depression, anxiety, and psychosis may be disabling unto themselves. The most important emotional risk is that of suicidal ideation and attempts (Conti et al., 2017).

Compounding Risk

One risk can easily compound others. There can be a domino effect. As an example, escalation of depression can trigger anxiety, eating disorder behaviors, and suicidal ideation plus substance abuse. This chain reaction can also create feedback loops whereupon evolving anxiety, eating disorder behaviors, or drug abuse can amplify depressive symptoms, and so on.

History of Chief Complaint

The *history of chief complaint* will be on the topic of what the individual presents with in the office or emergency room. This may be with regard to eating disorder, drug and alcohol, or emotional concerns. Certainly, for medical staff, attention will need to be directed toward any medical issue presented.

Previous and Ongoing Eating Disorder Treatment History

> *"I attended three treatment centers and saw multiple mental health professionals in between. I absolutely hated being in treatment."*

> *"I hated being around others like me, being forced to eat food that disgusted me, and being locked out from the bathroom for what felt like an eternity after meals."*

A current and past eating disorder treatment history needs to include both eating disorder and non-eating disorder treatment information. An eating

General Eating Disorder History 71

disorder treatment history should include the following regarding treatment options:

- Community-based programs
- Hospital-based programs
- Medical support
- Nonmedical support
- Psychotherapy
- Occupational therapy
- Physiotherapy
- Medications
- Self-help material
- Family therapy
- Refeeding programs
- Nutrition and weight goals
- Legal certification

Questions

- When did you start treatment?
- How many separate times have you been treated?
- How long was each treatment?
- What were the dates of all treatments?
- What were the reasons for treatment?
- What were or are the goals of treatment?
- What were the results of treatment?
- Are you experiencing benefits still?
- Have you lost ground?
- What worked, and what did not?
- What would help again?
- What do you think will help that has not been tried?
- Which caregivers were helpful, and why?
- Which were not helpful, and why?
- What would you like me to do and not do?
- How do you want to be treated?
- Do you mind if I contact you if I haven't heard from you for a while?
- Do you have any questions of me?
- What is the hardest thing for you to deal with in therapy?
- What do you not want me to talk about?
- What other treatment do you think you need?
- Aside from the eating disorder, what needs attention in your life?
- What non-eating disorder specific treatment have you had, such as for drug and alcohol, family, or sexual assault concerns?
- Have you been treated for any life-threatening conditions?

72 General Eating Disorder History

- What other eating disorder treatment centers have you been treated at?
- What makes treatment difficult?
- What undoes successful treatment?
- Do you sabotage treatment, and why?
- What are your goals for treatment?
- Do medications help?
- Did you do drugs or use alcohol during treatment? Did others in treatment?

Previous Psychiatric Diagnoses

During a psychiatric history ask about any current psychiatric diagnoses as well as any previous psychiatric diagnoses. Also ask about specific disorders such as depression, obsessive-compulsive disorder, anxiety, bipolar disorder, borderline personality disorder, and psychosis. Sometimes clients have been given diagnoses without explanations as to what they really are. They may accept the diagnoses willingly or resent them. They may believe or not believe them. Do not assume any previous diagnosis is accurate until you have confirmed it with an adequate history. In previous years, the standard was that because individuals had an eating disorder, they must also have a borderline personality disorder. Some previous diagnoses may have been accurate when originally made but no longer apply, yet the patient or caregivers still think it is valid. Sometimes diagnoses are bases on behavioral traits that are not truly suggestive of full-blown disorders. Typically, cutting behavior may lead to an erroneous diagnosis of borderline personality disorder. Use as expert advice as can be obtained to confirm an accurate diagnosis.

One of the problems with erroneous diagnoses is that they give inappropriate labels and often deny individuals proper treatment. As an example, once clients are diagnosed with borderline personality disorder, they are seen as incurable or will not respond to treatment for an eating disorder or will be unmanageable on a hospital ward.

Psychological History

> *"I had a hard time engaging in the stuff going on around me because my mind was so full of thoughts about food."*

> *"Good days for me still revolve around food and my body image. A bad day is when my ankles are puffy with fluid when my stomach isn't flat, if I drink too much liquid and feel like my insides are sloshing, when I am constipated, and when my cheeks don't look hollow."*

The assessment of psychological issues will be familiar to therapists. Various psychological topics have been addressed throughout the book.

Developmental History

When determining a *developmental history*, there are a few specific topics to address.

Pregnancy

Questions

- During your mother's pregnancy with you, were there any concerns such as infections or premature rupturing of membranes?
- Were you born term, premature, or late?
- Did your mother smoke or take any medications during the pregnancy?
- Did your mother take any psychotropic or seizure medications or consume alcohol or street drugs during the pregnancy?

Labor and Delivery

- Were there any concerns during labor such as a very short labor with precipitously fast delivery or very prolonged labor?
- Were you delivered vaginally or by cesarean section?
- Why was a C-section performed?
- Did you have good APGAR scores or was there a delay in you responding?
- Were you exposed to streptococcal infection?
- Did you spend time in a neonatal intensive care unit, and why?

Milestones

- Did you meet expected milestones such as when you should be crawling, walking, or talking?

Health Concerns

- Were there any health concerns in your youth such as infections, or did you require surgery?
- Were you told that you had been exposed to a streptococcal infection?
- Were you hospitalized for any health concerns?
- Did you miss school for prolonged periods of time due to health reasons?

Genetics

- Have you been told that you may develop any genetically related health concerns (Huckins et al., 2017)?
- Have there been any genetically related health concerns in your family?

74 General Eating Disorder History

- Do diabetes, thyroid disease, and cardiovascular disease as well as mental illness or substance abuse run in your family?
- Is there a family history of any connective tissue disease such as Marfan syndrome or systemic lupus erythematosus?
- Is there a family history of genetically determined degenerative neurological conditions such as multiple sclerosis, muscular dystrophy, Huntington's chorea or Charcot-Marie-Tooth syndrome?
- Is there a history of early death in the family, and from what health concerns?

Family History

> *"I'm fortunate to have the family support that I do, but I know it caused all of them a lot of struggle themselves."*

> *"I remember one morning my dad made me eat an extra pancake (one that I had made that was low calorie and low in fat) and I cried, telling him he had wrecked my whole day."*

Family will have been and may possibly still be the most influential force in one's life. Whether there are close, remote, or non-existent family dynamics, it all counts. Everyone has been painted by family relationships, and these relationships typically have or have had a strong imprint on individuals' lives. There will be no exceptions. Assessing these family dynamics the best we can is an important part of assisting those with eating disorders.

What needs to be understood is that whether the family interactions are or have been close and supportive or remote or destructive, links between the individual's eating disorder and family influences may not be obvious or even understandable. Those with the most supportive, understanding family can have the most critical disorders, yet some with very toxic families may not. The influences of family members on the individual's life, including the eating disorder, may be the result of the subtlest of dynamics rather than glaring and seemingly disruptive ones. It is important to not read anything into what you observe but to clarify as best you can by talking specifics with your client. Your client may not be aware of family influences, and it is your task to help bring constructive light on these. Regardless of family dynamics, the eating disorder may have a life of its own without much family effect. Even with the best efforts to make salient important family factors, they may exist under the therapeutic radar.

When enquiring regarding family, we need to focus on general family dynamics as well as eating disorder related factors. We want to know which family members are currently involved in the person's life, who comes and goes, and who is not involved, including those who have died. Aside from parents and siblings, others in the family may be depended upon a little or a lot. Some will have a favorite grandparent or aunt or uncle that they can confide in and rely on for emotional and possibly financial support.

Questions

- Who is in your family, including parents, siblings, grandparents, and aunts and uncles, as well as cousins?
- Who lives with you?
- Are there others who are not blood relatives that you consider family, and do they live with you?
- Do you have favorite family members?
- Who do you not have a close or positive relationship with, and why?
- Is there anyone in the family that you are in competition with?

Interviewing Family Members

Some reasons for interviewing family members include:

- Information from family may speed treatment along
- Providing collateral information that may help support what the client has stated or provide a countering perspective
- Providing newer updated information, both eating disorder or other
- Providing historical information for both eating disorder and non-eating disorder related events
- Others can tell you what makes the eating disorder or other issues better or worse
- Identifying eating disorders in other family members
- Identifying dieting, exercise, weight loss, and body image concerns in other family members
- Pointing out the effect of other family members' focus on food, body image, and weight on the individual with the eating disorder and vice versa
- Identifying psychological—depression, bipolar disorders, psychosis—drug and alcohol issues in family members
- Family stresses of financial, marital, illness, or violence origin
- Disclosing the effect of eating disorder on siblings
- Discussing their expectations of treatment and recovery
- Explaining your expectations of treatment and recovery
- Explaining why treatment options are chosen and not chosen
- Suggesting reading material, videos, web pages
- Suggesting possible other resources for marital or drug and alcohol difficulties as well as eating disorder family support groups
- Showing optimism for recovery

76 General Eating Disorder History

- Explaining statistics for recovery
- Explaining eating disorder treatment
- Giving them the opportunity to answer any questions
- Describing the shifting or chameleon-like nature of an eating disorder
- Providing the opportunity to explain how family dynamics are affected by the eating disorder
- Identifying roles of family members, such as "parents are parents and not therapists or nutritionists"
- Normalizing everyone's response to the eating disorder
- Explaining stages of change and how treatment options may be affected by these
- Suggesting "time out" periods from focusing on the eating disorder so the family can focus on being a family
- Suggesting that some family members may need to leave the home for a while to help prevent toxic interactions and give some family members a rest; sometimes it may be a parent, sibling, or the one with the eating disorder who will stay with family friends or relatives for a while
- Identifying danger in the family setting
- Showing the alliance between the client and the therapist or nutritionist
- Identifying loss and grief in family members

Family and Eating Disorder History

Because family is usually the earliest contact, they have the greatest influence on any and all developmental paths. Attitudes toward body image, food, and healthy and unhealthy lifestyles including exercise likely began in the home.

Questions

- Has anyone in the family ever had an eating disorder?
- Is there anyone who you know or suspect has an active eating disorder, and who would this be?
- Do you suspect an eating disorder in a family member?
- Are you intimidated by family members who you feel eat healthier than you do or who are in better physical shape and keep a regular exercise program?
- How long have family members been dieting for?
- What kind of diet or exercise regimes do others in the family have?
- Who is dieting, and using what kinds of diets?
- Do others in your family make it hard for you to focus on recovery and why?
- When you live away from family, is this helpful for you to not engage in your eating disorder, and why?

Family Lineage and Eating Disorders

Body image, food preferences, and attitudes toward health can have a strong basis in family lines. What great-grandparents from both sides of the family felt about these things will have influenced grandparents and possibly one's parents and may have had an effect on individuals with eating disorders. Family ethnicity and religious backgrounds play a part. When parents have food choices and body image attitudes, they may have family-of-origin beginnings. It is also possible that parents and their children have adopted more contemporary attitudes, and family background may not necessarily be a factor.

Basic Food Dynamics in the Family

When assessing family influences on one's eating disorder, we need to acquire basic food related information (Johnson et al., 2017):

Questions

- Who purchases the food for the family?
- Whose money is used to purchase food?
- Do individual family members shop for their own food?
- Do food choices cause strife between family members?
- Does anyone store their own food for themselves?
- What are the kinds of nutrition requirements in the family, such as any food restrictions?
- Are there any food limitations such as vegetarian or vegan choices or gluten and lactose elimination?
- Are food restrictions based on food allergies or other health concerns?
- Are carbohydrate, fat, or protein restrictions of issue to family members?
- Do food preferences create problems with being able to prepare meals or eat with each other?
- Does the family eat together?
- Which family members eat together and which ones don't, and why?
- Do you take other family members food, and does this cause problems?
- Does anyone take your food?
- Is anyone critical of others' food choices?
- What do you think of family members' nutrition and lifestyle choices?
- Do food choices or eating dynamics change when extended family members visit, such as when grandparents, aunts and uncles, or cousins visit?
- Do food choices or eating dynamics change when a sibling returns home?

78 General Eating Disorder History

- What foods are not allowed in the house, and who determines this?
- Do you think the family is held hostage by others' eating preferences, including yourself?
- Do your food choices come largely from your family influences, modern culture, or both?

Family Body Image and Weight Issues

Everyone in the family will likely be aware of their own body shape, size, and weight unless very young. Having said this, very young children are too commonly aware of these body image concerns. It is not much of a surprise that children will be aware of body awareness in other family members.

Questions

- How do other family members see their own body?
- How do they see the body size or shape of others?
- Is anyone particularly weight conscious?
- If so, are they weight conscious of themselves, other family members, or of those in society generally?
- Do any verbalize body dissatisfaction with regard to themselves or others in the family?
- What effect does this have on you or others in the family?
- Does it affect your own body image concerns, and how do you deal with this?
- Is there anyone in your family who is overweight or obese?
- Is there anyone who is underweight, and why?
- How does this affect you?
- Is anyone critical of your body or how you eat or exercise?
- Is there anyone in your family who is thinner, smaller, or weighs less than you who you compare yourself too?
- What is the body size, shape, or weight of those in the family?
- Who is being self-critical of body image and weight?
- Who is critical of others' weights or body size?
- How do these attitudes affect you or others in the family?
- How young do you remember body image talk from other family members?
- Do others' body image attitudes or nutrition and lifestyle patterns cause you to engage more in your eating disorder?

Children

The children of those with eating disorders may have an integral involvement in eating disorder dynamics. Money used to feed and clothe children

General Eating Disorder History   79

or that must be used for medical bills may result in the person with the eating disorder denying themselves funds required to feed themselves. Children may learn eating disorder behaviors from a parent by copycatting behaviors or may use them for deliberate weight and body image control. Siblings of those with eating disorders can learn eating disorder behaviors and attitudes from the one with an eating disorder. For parents fully engaged in their own eating disorder, the strict dedication to eating disorder dictates can lead to neglect of children, especially for those with concurrent drug and alcohol addiction or major depression.

Questions

- Are your children aware of your eating disorder?
- Do you think they are influenced by your body image dissatisfaction or copy eating disorder behaviors, and why do you think so?
- Do any of your children have an eating disorder?
- Do your children complain about their weight, or are they on diets?
- Do you feed your children but not yourself?
- Do you sacrifice providing for your children at your own expense?
- Do you think you are neglecting your children due to focusing on the eating disorder or drug and alcohol use?

Pets

Pets may play an integral part in families. Those with eating disorders seem to be particularly attached to pets. Pets may be a source of comfort and companionship when otherwise there may not have been any. The relationship with the pet or pets needs to be addressed.

The role of pets is fairly obvious, including providing companionship and a sense of being needed or useful with having to take care of them. Pets, however, bring other dynamics. The pet may be the only one in the family that the individual can relate to, rely on, or trust. It may help to relieve loneliness and a sense of isolation within the family structure. Pets also can bring a sense of burden with having to take care of them, as well as guilt for not being a good pet owner. The financial cost of caring for pets may be prohibitive. Parents may berate a teen or adult child for not taking care of the pet, and this itself becomes a source of strife.

Pets may play a significant role in the eating disorder. Pets are used, especially dogs, as a means to encourage excessive exercise. Long walks or runs with a dog may be a deliberate reason to exercise in order to burn calories. Pet owners may have limited funds and will pay for food for the animal, then use this as a reason to not feed themselves. Food may be handed to animals at the dinner table as a way of getting rid of unwanted calories without family members noticing. Some will feed their own vomit

80 General Eating Disorder History

to pets. This brings great shame and regret. Some eat their dog's or cat's food if there is no other readily available food source or possibility as a way to punish themselves. Veterinary bills can be exorbitant and deprive individuals of the funds needed for daily expenses, including purchasing food.

I remember an endearing story of a young woman with bulimia who kept a kitten in her suite in the parent's home. The kitten would jump up and cling onto a nightgown hanging in the closet until the nightgown dropped to the floor. She then would move on to the next one and bring it down as well.

There may be other animals attached to the family such as horses, birds, pigs, or cattle. These animals may or may not be important in someone's life. Horses may be available for show horse riding and bring a focus of competition. These animals may bring a personal responsibility for their care and upkeep and be a source of unwanted stress, including financial demands.

Questions

- Do you have any pets, and what kind?
- Is it the family pet, or just yours?
- How important is this pet to you, and why?
- How does the pet influence your relationship with others in the family?
- Are there any expectations for you to be successful in competitions with these animals such as with show dogs or horse riding?
- Do you take care of the animal, or does someone else?
- Does it provide a burden for you in any way, including bringing financial hardships?
- Have any pets died that have had an impact on you?
- Do they have an influence on your eating disorder and how?
- Do you spend money on your pet that results in you not having funds left over to purchase food?
- Does having to care for your pet prevent you from socializing?
- Do veterinarian bills leave you seriously broke?
- Do you use your pet for exercise?
- Do you feed food to your animals that you should be eating yourself?
- Do you feed vomit to your pet?

Illnesses

Illness affects every family sometime. For those with an eating disorder, this will create an added stress to what is an already stressful life. Several issues come into play.

General Eating Disorder History 81

Because those with eating disorders tend to be people pleasers, there can be an automatic tendency to feel responsible for others' recovery and care. There can be feelings of guilt if they are not involved. They may feel a sense of needing to share the load with a parent who is caregiving, There can be fears that if they aren't involved, the person they are caring for will die or be poorly cared for otherwise.

One may take on the responsible for caring for a family member with a physical disability, mental illness, or alcohol or drug addiction as well as age-related health issues such as dementia, arthritis, or blindness. The ill person may even be dying.

These responsibilities are often time consuming and lead to tiredness or exhaustion. This can come as a cost to academic responsibilities such as attending classes and studying demands. Some need to drop classes or even quit school until they have more of an opportunity to engage in educational ventures. Work may suffer, and there may be a need to quit work for their caregiving duties. This can be frustrating and demoralizing. All of this will add increased stress, where the need to use the eating disorder to cope becomes ramped up.

For those from families where alcoholism, drug addiction, neglect, and various kinds of abuse may have been the case, there can be even more codependence issues that arise. The caregiver becomes the parent of the parent. Sometimes all the efforts of caregiving are not rewarded with appreciating but met with criticism for not meeting someone's needs. The abusive power of a critical, unsupportive parent becomes amplified.

Illnesses affect those with eating disorders as well. There may be mild, short-term health problems such as colds and flus, viral bronchitis, stubbed toes, or fractured collarbones. Other illnesses may be lingering and can be quite disruptive, such as infectious mononucleosis, a broken leg from skiing, or chronic migraine headaches. Other illnesses are permanent, such as multiple sclerosis, arthritis, insulin-dependent diabetes, or some chronic pain syndromes. Any illness may have a little or a lot of effect on the degree to which someone will engage in their eating disorder to deal with the stress. For those who rely heavily on a sense of control in their lives, illness brings a feeling of great uncertainty and lack of control in their lives.

Illness can increase a sense of helplessness and worthlessness, and a void in a purpose in life. There can be a feeling of "This is the last thing I need right now!"

A very few may be at risk of a genetically acquired illness where the "clock is ticking," and there may be little time in their life to feel fulfilled. Cystic fibrosis and Huntington's chorea are examples. Insulin-dependent diabetes mellitus can be genetically determined and can become entwined in eating disorder dynamics.

82 General Eating Disorder History

Mental Health and Drug or Alcohol Use in the Family

Mental health, as well as drug and alcohol concerns, often have a genetic link. Mental health or substance abuse issues in an individual with an eating disorder may be, in part, genetically driven (Kandel, 1990).

Questions

- Is there anyone in your family with mental health issues, and who are they?
- What mental health issues are these?
- Is there anyone in your family with drug or alcohol addictions?
- Do their mental health or drug and alcohol challenges affect you in a negative way?
- Do you access drugs or alcohol from within your family?
- Do you provide drugs or alcohol to others in the family?
- Does their mental health or substance abuse affect your eating disorder, and how?
- Does their mental health or substance abuse make your eating disorder or substance use worse?
- Do you think your mental health or substance abuse has a genetic origin in your family?

Deaths

There are few events in an individual's life that have as much impact on one's life as the death of family members or others. The degree to what effect a death has on someone may range from minimal to profound and life changing. The response to a death will depend, in part, on the role of the family member and their interactions with the individual.

Deaths may have occurred outside of the family such as with friends or mentors including teachers, coaches, caregivers, and others. Sometimes relationships with those beyond the family can be the most profound and should not be underestimated in importance. Some may find the loss of a music teacher more disturbing than the loss of a parent. Others may experience longstanding overwhelming grief over the loss of a pet when compared to people. The only way to assess the impact of the loss of a significant other is by asking, in some detail, what this impact has been.

Deaths play an important role beyond emotional influences. There can be a domino effect or cascade of life changes as a result. They can result in consequences that influence finances, the need to move to a different home, including to another city, as well as employment and academic options. Living arrangements may change, where others may move into the home or may move out. The ripple effect of a death, regardless of whether the deceased was particularly important to someone, can be significant. Deaths can play an important part in the dynamics of what drives one's eating disorder. It is, of course, possible that it has not.

Sibling deaths, including and especially the death of a twin, may have the most brutal influences. The cause of death will also be important in determining the impact one experiences. Death from natural causes such as cancer, heart attack, or stroke may not be as traumatic as those resulting from suicide or murder.

Deaths may bring on added life pressures or actually release one from them. The death of someone who has been abusive or neglectful may be a relief. The death of an alcoholic, abusive grandparent who had been living in the basement may be deemed a blessing. If this same grandparent, however, owned the home and left it and the estate to others, this could lead the family members who depended upon them for free lodgings and financial support to end up becoming destitute.

Questions

- Has anyone close to you died, and who was this?
- Did you have a close relationship, or not?
- What effect has this had on you emotionally, including others in your family?
- Has this death had an influence on your finances or living arrangements?
- Has death affected others in your family in a way that has brought hardship to yourself, such as others relying on you for emotional or financial support?
- Is their death a loss to you, and in what way?
- Is their death a relief for you or others, and why?
- Has this death influenced your eating disorder, and how?
- Did this person make any body image comments about others, themselves, or yourself that could have influenced how you feel about body image, weight, or food?
- Will the loss of this person result in you having to make a shift in employment, career, or academic options, and how?
- Were you financially dependent on this individual, and how?
- Was this person ever abusive to you, and how?
- Does this death prevent closure for unresolved issues such as sexual assault, and how will you be able to eventually bring closure?
- Now that this person is dead, will you tell others in the family about abuses, or do you think it will hurt them or harm your relationship with them?
- Are you worried that if you divulge abuses, you will not be believed or will be ostracized?
- Have there been others in your family who have been abused by the same individual?

Regrets

Regrets can have a significant effect on how individuals feel about themselves and influence eating disorder attitudes and behaviors. Regrets that may seem to be rather minor to others may have a profound influence on a given individual. Regrets come in all sizes and shapes, and there are too many to list here. Regrets may include the loss of relationships and education or career opportunities as well as not meeting personal goals such as athletic goals, including making it on a national Olympic team. Regrets may be the result of things they said or did that bring shame or guilt their way. It is helpful to enquire regarding personal losses. There may be regrets in families.

Losses

Losses to one family member may have a significant effect on others in the family. The loss of family members through death or suicide, the loss of health, or the loss of a job are a few such events. The sense of loss and sadness in one can spread to others. Other losses may come in the form of separation or divorce.

Questions

- Have there been any losses to individuals in the family or losses that affect the whole family, and what are they?
- How do these losses affect you, and in what way?
- Does one person's sadness or sense of helplessness and hopelessness have a negative effect on you?
- Do these individuals rely on you to support them through this difficult period?
- Is this person unkind to you, or does he or she blame you?
- Does the personal loss of others, such as loss of a job or divorce, put you at risk of having to move out of your home or result in you having to live with others?

Moves

Moves can bring major shifts in someone's life. The shifts may be seen as positive, negative, or not of any real concern. Moves can remove some from friend and family ties and disrupt academic or career consistency. Moves may, however, present new opportunities. Because those with eating disorders groom a set of predictable regimes over time, moves can be feared and very disruptive if they do occur.

Questions

- Have you experienced moves that have affected you in a negative or positive way?
- Where did you move from, and where did you move to?
- Did moving affect your eating disorder, and how did it do so?
- Did moving remove you from eating disorder triggers or introduce new ones?
- Did the move remove you from any undesirable pressures or bring new pressures, and what were they?
- Did moving cause loneliness due to the loss of friend interactions?
- Did moving contribute to isolation or possibly improve it?
- Has this move taken you away from drug and alcohol influences or introduced new ones?
- Has the move introduced you to any new toxic environments including the risk of violence, including sexual assault?
- For others who have moved with you—family, friends, or partner—how have they been affected by the move, and has their response had an influence on you?
- Has the move brought new opportunities and become like a fresh start for you?

Living Situation

As mentioned elsewhere, determining who lives in the home, whether long-term or on and off, is important. Though parents and siblings will typically reside in the home, others such as grandparents, aunts, uncles, or cousins may be in the picture as well. Each individual involved with the home may have a significance impact with the person with the eating disorder. Home and family dynamics can be very complicated.

Questions

- Who lives in your home regularly?
- Who comes and goes from the home?
- How do you get along with everyone in the home?
- Are there those that you do not get along with, and why?
- Is anyone abusive to you or others in the home?
- How do individuals affect your eating disorder?
- Is there anyone else who has an eating disorder in the home?
- Does your eating disorder affect your relationship with others?
- Does the coming and going of interim cohabitants affect you in any way?

Social History

Friends and Other Peers

> *"I lost a lot of friendships at the start of my eating disorder, many of them because I hated to be around people."*

Relationships with friends and other peers may be the most important, at least at various times in one's life (Linville, Stice, Gau & O'Neil, 2011). These relationships may be very supportive or destructive. Their influences may affect self-worth, identity, substance use, social interactions, sexuality, competitive drives, and companionship. Concerns regarding bullying, social exclusion or other forms of victimization need to be brought to light.

Questions

- Do you have close friends?
- How would you describe your relationship with them?
- Do they influence how you feel about your body image or support eating disorder attitudes and behaviors?
- Do you find friends or other acquaintances supportive or punitive?
- What affect do they have on drug and alcohol use or sexual interactions?
- Do they take advantage of you, such as borrowing money and not paying you back, or do alcoholic friends ask you to drive them to the liquor store to buy booze? Do they not invite you to join them for social events?
- Do friends share their problems with you and not return the favor?
- Are friends a lifeline for you?

Work

Work experiences can play an important role in one's life. They provide a source of income, but as important or even more so are the interpersonal connections they create. Workplaces may be rife with body image and weight control influences. Some say they work in an environment where "everybody talks about their weight and dieting."

Questions

- Do others at work seem to fuss about their weight?
- Are coworkers on diets?
- Are some coworkers talked about because they are overweight?
- Are you worried you are being gossiped about regarding your weight?

School

Formal education from preschool until graduation takes 13 to 14 years of our lives beginning at quite a young age. This requires a huge amount of dedication for the major part of our youth. These are important formative years that very much ingrain influences from being educated and relationships with peers and teachers. All this happens concurrently while evolving within the family as well as any and all experiences outside of school and the family. Preceding all this is a genetic predisposition that very much influences personality and emotional states upon which family, school, and other experiences are built. By the time someone develops an eating disorder, there have been significant developmental influences.

Questions

- How old were you when you started school?
- Did you start in kindergarten or preschool?
- Did you attend public school or private schools?
- Did you go to a boarding school?
- How did you feel about being sent away to school?
- Did you miss your family and friends?
- Do you have any resentments regarding being sent away?
- How was your relationship with your teachers?
- Were your teachers generally supportive, or were any dismissive or abusive?
- How did your athletic coaches treat you and others on the team?
- Did teachers or coaches ever put pressure on you to look a certain way or suggest that you lose weight?
- Did you experience what you felt was a sexualized relationship with any?
- Did they have a positive or negative influence on your self-worth, and how did this happen?
- Did they have any influence on your eating disorder?
- How was your relationship with peers?
- Did you have good friends?
- Were you ever picked on or bullied in any way, and by whom?
- Were you pressured to engage in drugs or alcohol by peers?
- Did you ever influence others with regard to drug or alcohol use?
- Did you ever go away on a school exchange program?
- How was the eating disorder affected during this exchange?
- Did being away from home allow for an increase in freedom to engage in the eating disorder or put restrictions on it?
- How did you cope with food being provided by the host family or experience local restaurant cuisine?

88 General Eating Disorder History

- Did you gain or lose weight, or did your weight remain stable?
- Did you experience any emotional, physical, or sexual abuse by members of your host family, students, teachers, or others during your time away?
- If you did experience abuse, did you tell your parents or anyone else?
- How have you dealt with this experience, and do you think you need further support?

Dating

Dating and sexual experiences may be pretty much the same thing or possibly not necessarily related at all. As with school and family experiences, they provide a crucible for change.

Questions

- Are your relationships with men, women, both, or those who are trans?
- Have relationships had an effect on your concern with body image or weight?
- How did this come about?
- Have your partners been critical of your weight or others'?
- What effect did this have on your eating disorder?
- Were you ever in competition with your partner for weight, physical fitness, or the degree with which you engaged in exercise or sport?
- Are you currently in a relationship that influences your eating disorder?
- Have relationships made you feel better about your body image or had a positive influence on your eating disorder?
- Have your relationships been generally supportive, or have they ever been abusive, and how?
- Have previous relationship experiences had a negative effect on later relationships, and how?
- What effect did your partner's family have on your relationship with your partner?
- Did they have any influence on how you felt about your relationship with food or body image?
- Did your partner's family expose you to any ethnic food challenges, and how?
- Did this create problems with you being able to eat or engage in your eating disorders?
- Did cultural differences create friction between you and them, either regarding food or any other issues?

Sexual Experiences

Enquire as to any and all sexual encounters from the past as well as ongoing (Palmer, Oppenheimer, Dignon, Chaloner & Howells, 1090). See the later section on "Sexual Abuse" in this chapter.

Gender Orientation

Gender orientation has an influence on identity, self-worth, and body image. Find out if gender orientation has any relevance and whether it plays a positive or negative role in their lives. See "Gender Dysphoria" in Chapter 1.

Drugs and Alcohol

Enquire regarding drug or alcohol use both currently and from the past (Piran & Gadalla, 2007). Drug and alcohol use has been addressed in various locations in this text.

Artistic Activities

Many with eating disorders have artistic talents. These talents may play an integral part of their well-being or be perceived as a burden or an unfulfilled muse. The need for artistic expression may be minimal or at the core of their self-worth. There are many factors that need to come into play before someone is able to be involved artistically.

Some of these factors include:

- Having the finances.
- Having a place to work or practice.
- Having the tools needed.
- Having time enough.
- Having the education to increase artistic skills or provide the academic credentials required to move on in a career.
- Having the confidence to pursue their artistic dreams.
- Having the motivation or mental and physical energy needed to apply themselves.

Finances will be needed for some artistic ventures to be carried out. Expenses may be needed to purchase musical instruments or painting materials, to lease a workspace, pay for private lessons or a college education, to travel, or to pay for rent and food. Artistic activities that used to be able to be engaged in may end when someone goes to university or takes on a full-time day job.

Any musician or visual artist needs a space to work. There needs to be a physical space plus personal space where there are not others whose presence gets in the way. For musicians, there must be tolerant cohabitants and neighbors exposed to sounds from a musical instrument, including the voice. Potters require funds to rent time in a commercial pottery facility where there is access to a pottery wheel, a kiln, and a place to store works. Otherwise they need their own place to work in, including harboring a kiln. On top of this, artists need to have the time available to dedicate to practicing, studying, and creating works. For those who work or attend school full-time or have to raise a family, time dedicated to creativity may be non-existent.

How does this all relate to someone with an eating disorder? For a few, artistic expression is life itself. Without it, there may be a total lack of purpose or meaning in life. A profound lack of self-worth and feelings of anxiety, depression, and despair may engulf the individual. All of these may be triggers for eating disorder attitudes and behaviors as well as self-harm or suicidal risks.

Questions

- Do you or have you ever had any artistic interests, and what were or are they?
- Do you experience pleasure or have a sense of accomplishment with engaging in your art?
- Does your art bring added stress to your life or have a negative influence on the eating disorder, and how?
- Does your art bring important financial obligations, and are you able to meet them?
- Does not having funding to pursue artistic endeavors prevent you from being involved with it?
- How does it make you feel when you are unable to meet artistic needs?
- Do you plan to make a living from your art, and how?
- Do you sell your work currently?
- Do you see involvement with art as a kind of lifeline that helps to keep you sane or safe?
- If you are unable to get involved with art but want to be, what is preventing this, such as a lack of funding, a lack of a place to work, or not having enough time, or are others discouraging you?
- Are there others who support you or that indicate that you do not have the talent to do what you want?
- Do you need more training to improve your skill, and have you been looking into education opportunities?
- Are you not involved with art because you do not have the talent or are not good enough?

General Eating Disorder History 91

- What do others say about your talent?
- How would you be able to afford training programs?
- How much of your identity and self-worth is tied up in your need to realize your artistic muse?

Athletic Activities

Athletic activities have been addressed to some degree in other sections. Many of the comments mentioned under "Artistic Activities" applies to athletic activities, including those addressing finances, time to engage, and self-worth and identity issues (Sundgot-Borgen, Torstveit, & Klungland, 2004). (See "Exercise" in Chapter 4).

Writing

Individuals write for different reasons. Some writing is for personal gratification, such as writing stories or poetry. It may be an artistic outlet. Some write as a form of therapy to record their daily life experiences or help to work through personal problems. Some write to help stay focused on destructive attitudes and behaviors such as those used in an eating disorder or depressive and suicidal visions.

Questions

- Do you like to write?
- What kinds of writing do you engage in?
- Is writing helpful in some way?
- Does writing help you to keep focused on your eating disorder agenda?
- Does writing keep you locked in a negative head space?

Abuse History

A core target of inquiry when compiling information for an eating disorder assessment is regarding experiences of possible emotional, physical, or sexual abuse. Abuse issues may have little effect on one's functioning including dealing with an eating disorder or may have profound and paralyzing consequences. It is essential to determine the kinds of abuse experienced as well as how long the abuse went on for. As well, is the abuse indeed still ongoing?

Because there is a large range of abuse options within each of emotional, physical, and sexual abuses, precise descriptions of these should be elucidated. As an example, within the subject of physical abuse, getting a rap on the fingers by a piano teacher for playing an incorrect note is a kind of physical abuse. Being kicked and beaten and pushed down stairs is also a

92   General Eating Disorder History

form of physical abuse. The effect any abuse has on an individual, however, may not be in relation to the severity of the assault.

How one interprets abuse can be steeped in cultural norms. As clinicians, we have to be very careful to not project our own attitudes regarding abuse onto those we are caring for. We need to collect accurate, factual descriptions of alleged abuses without injecting our own emotional responses to them. Rephrasing questions can aid in bringing forward more detailed and accurate accounts. What may be deemed abusive to one individual may not be by others.

Someone may experience abuses from one individual or several at the same time or at different times from different people. Because memories of abuse may be remote due to having occurred years earlier, we need to direct questions in order to jog memories.

Feelings regarding abuse may be undermined by the individual due to being deemed not serious enough to be concerned about. Responses such as "Others had it far worse than I did" contribute to this minimizing of importance. Abuses may be culturally acceptable and normalized.

With regard to eating disorders, abuses can have a major effect on self-worth and may be triggering for depression, anxiety, and eating disorders as well as substance abuse behaviors.

There are legal definitions for abuses. The legal relevance of abuses will depend on those defined nationally, regionally, or locally. When abuse issues are dealt with within a legal system, clarity of definitions is paramount. The emotional impact abuse has on someone may bear little relationship to its legal importance.

One form of abuse may be indistinguishable as emotional, physical, or sexual abuse. In other words, the same abuse may be an inclusive form of emotional, physical, and sexual abuse.

When sleuthing sources of abuse, the following people may have had an influence on one's life including and contributed to abuses.

- Biological parents
- Stepparents
- Foster parents
- Siblings
- Grandparents
- Aunts or uncles
- Step- or foster siblings
- Baby sitters
- Friends of the family, both of parents and children
- Teachers
- Janitors
- Coaches
- Partners

General Eating Disorder History   93

- Peers
- Police
- Doctors
- Nurses
- Therapists
- Employers
- Coworkers
- Anyone else

An approach to questioning regarding these people is to phrase them as given here.

- How was or is your relationship with this individual?
- Have there ever been or are there currently any negative experiences connected with them?
- Describe these negative experiences?
- Would you describe these experiences as emotional, physical, or sexual abuse?

Emotional Abuse

Emotional abuse covers a vast array of possibilities. Emotional abuse may come from many different sources and come in many forms.

Emotional abuse may come in the form of individuals not being believed with regard to any personal concerns including abuse events. Just as abusive in nature is when significant others who do acknowledge these abuses took place brush it off as not either being very important or that it happened so long ago that the individual is making too much of a deal out of it.

Emotional abuse may not be directly or deliberately delivered but be a consequence of neglect—an absence of emotional support or protection from physical or sexual violence.

Emotional abuse may not necessarily be directed from a given individual but from an institute or bureaucracy. Military bureaucracies that do not respond to allegations of abuse by superiors or peers is a form of abuse itself. Institutionally generated abuses only compound abuse concerns. Individuals treated poorly by hospital staff because of prejudices regarding those with eating disorders, mental illness, or substance abuses are examples of institutionally driven abuse. Physical and sexual abuses should both be included as forms of emotional abuse.

Physical Abuse

As with emotional and sexual abuse, physical abuses come in many forms. Hitting, beating, slapping, biting, and pushing as well as objects being thrown

94 General Eating Disorder History

at someone are a few examples. Physical abuse may not result in any visible physical trauma or may result in life-threatening, disabling consequences. For legal reasons, photographs of injuries and accurate medical reports need to be acquired. As with anything that affects an individual's body image, physical signs of trauma further aggravate negative body self-awareness.

Sexual Abuse

A sexual abuse history is important. Not everyone with an eating disorder has been abused, but many have. Sexual abuse can have a profound effect on someone's life and eating disorder.

Questions

- Have you ever been sexually abused?
- Have you had any regretted sexual experiences, even with consenting sex, due to being compromised from drug or alcohol use?
- Have you exchanged sex for drugs?
- Who were the perpetrators and over what period of time or from what age on?
- How many separate events were there?
- Are sexual abuse experiences of any issue for you these days?
- Have you had any treatment for it, or have you engaged in any self-help work?
- Does the sexual abuse have any effect on body image, weight, or food issues?
- Were police involved?
- How did family or partners respond?
- Who knows about it?
- Have there been any sexualized relationships not involving physical contact?
- Are you in a sexually uncomfortable relationship now?
- Do you feel unsafe?
- Do you experience body memories or flashbacks?
- How has it affected relationships?
- Have you ever been promiscuous?
- Have you ever worked in the sex trade?
- Are there any self-esteem or control issues as a result?
- Have you had a pregnancy as a result?
- What happened with that pregnancy?
- Have you ever had a sexually transmitted infection?
- Are drugs and alcohol a way of coping with sexual assault?
- Have those experiences led to suicidal thoughts, plans, or attempts?
- How does your experience with sexual assault affect getting on in life?

Self-Harm

Self-harm is a term used to describe behaviors used to inflict physical, psychological, or socioeconomic harm to one's self (Koutek, Kocourkova & Dudova, 2016). These may include physical actions that induce pain or create marking of the body. Eating disorder behaviors as well as drug or alcohol use may be forms of self-harm.

Physical actions may include scratching, burning, cutting, hitting, or any act of mutilation. They may be used to cause physical pain in order to punish one's self, to distract from intolerable thoughts or emotions, to "feel something" or to relieve stress. They may be used for all of these reasons together or at different times. They may be used to cause markings or scarring for the same reasons. Cutting, scratching, and burning may be to create random markings or to scribe words or symbols into the skin. Mutilating and other self-harm behaviors may or may not be eating disorder related. With regard to the eating disorder, self-harm may be used to punish, reward, focus, deter, or numb out. Eating disorder attitudes can induce self-harm—"I'm fat, therefore I should be punished"—or self-harm may activate eating disorder thoughts and behaviors—"I've punished myself, therefore I won't binge again."

Self-harm, such as scratching, may present low risks or instead be very dangerous, such as trying to cut the carotid artery or overdosing. Self-harm may be used for a deliberate suicide attempt when it had been previously used for attention getting or other reasons given earlier.

Ask clients if they are doing anything to hide that they have harmed themselves, such as wearing long-sleeved shirts or long pants after cutting their arms or legs. Do they keep wounds from healing by picking at them or re-scratching, burning, or cutting, or are they not using dressings or antibiotics prescribed to help them heal faster?

If individuals have admitted to one self-harm behavior, ask if they have other ones they use or have used. Ask if they have plans for utilizing never previously used self-harm methods. A response may be "I have tubing in the trunk of my car that I can hook up to my car exhaust after I leave your office."

Questions

- What have been the reasons for harming in the past and the consequence of these actions, including hospitalizations?
- Do you have a planned date to act on these self-harm behaviors?
- Where did you learn these behaviors?
- Are there others who are doing the same thing?
- Do you self-harm with others?
- Are you using pro-ana suicide or self-mutilation websites to gain ideas and inspiration?

96 General Eating Disorder History

- How is self-harm related to your eating disorder, if at all?
- Do you use it at different times or for different reasons than for the eating disorder?
- How does it help you cope or not cope with the eating disorder?
- Does self-harm make the eating disorder worse, better, or both?
- What would happen if you were not allowed to or couldn't harm yourself?
- Would you plan more harmful mutilation behaviors, become more depressed, suicidal, use drugs, or escalate eating disorder behaviors?

Accomplishments and Skills

Asking about individuals' sense of accomplishments may have value. Accomplishments may have been in sports, music, arts and crafts, academics, social skills, or anything else they mention. Knowing about accomplishments helps the clinician to identify areas of success, skills, and possible sources of worth as well a source of a sense of failure. Unmet achievements may be devastating to perfectionists and to those whose esteem is dependent on making the mark. Achievements may have personal importance only or be to fulfill what others expect of them.

Questions

- What do you feel you have been accomplished at from as far back as you can remember?
- Are you proud of these accomplishments?
- Do these achievements not make you feel accomplished, and why?
- Do you set high standards for yourself because you are afraid to fail?

Life Goals

Having life goals can be an incentive to wanting to recover from an eating disorder or drug and alcohol addiction. Individuals may already have life goals, while others may not. Some may have had goals but become so wrapped up in ongoing life obligations that they have been forgotten or have seemingly become impossible to achieve. To help some find constructive directions in life, clinicians need to identify already established life goals or help set goals that give individuals a reason to move forward.

Life goals may be directed toward:

- Education
- Recovery from an eating disorder or drug and alcohol addiction
- Coming to terms with abuse issues

- Managing mental health issues
- Resolving family conflicts
- Career
- Artistic or athletic excellence
- Relationships
- Having a family
- Material possessions such as owning a house and property or making money
- Travel
- Achieving humanitarian goals such as working toward world peace, combatting global warming, or feeding the hungry
- Enjoying life
- Owning a pet, having a garden, purchasing wood-working tools

Questions

- What life goals do you currently have?
- What life goals have you had but are now not an option?
- If you do not have life goals, why is this?
- Do you not have life goals because you haven't thought that far ahead or because you don't believe goals can be met anymore?
- Do you think you do not deserve to have your dreams realized and why?
- Are you afraid that if you set out to achieve these goals that you will fail at doing so?
- Do you have a plan B for goals that you may not be able to achieve, and what are they?
- Have you established a plan for meeting these goals?
- If you do not meet goals how important is this to you, and what would you do about it?
- What is getting in the way of meeting your goals, and what could be done about this?
- Can you think of solutions to impediments in achieving these goals?
- Do you have others to support you with your goals?
- Do you have the finances necessary to meet goals?

Failures

Fear of failure is a good motivator to seek excellence and set high standards. What needs to be determined is if fear of failure is a direct result of actual failure to meet expectations previously or is based on fear only. A sense of failure does not necessarily come from unmet grandiose goals but may be from somewhat seemingly insignificant events. Feelings of failure can come from unmet unrealistic goals such as aiming to achieve

98 General Eating Disorder History

100% in every exam. A mark of 99% in an exam could make individuals feel like complete failures.

Questions

* Do you have a fear of failure, and why?
* Have you actually failed at anything, and what was this?
* What is the most important thing you are afraid of failing at?
* Are you afraid to fail because you do not want to disappoint others, and who are they?
* Have you ever experienced consternation from others because you did not meet certain expectations?
* How do you feel if you fail at something?
* What do you do in response to failing?
* Are there any real consequences if you do not meet expectations? An example would be not achieving high enough grades to be accepted into law school.
* Do you think your fear of failure is disproportionate to what would actually occur?
* Have others told you your fears are unwarranted, and with regard to what?
* Have previous failures or fear of failing escalated eating disorder attitudes and behaviors and why?

General Medical History

> *"I passed out in public, likely due to my electrolyte imbalances, at least five times. Each time I was hospitalized. Luckily, I didn't fall into traffic."*

A general medical history needs to include any information regarding eating disorder and non-eating disorder related health concerns.

Height and Weight History

A height and weight history is essential for helping to determine one's attitudes toward eating disorder objectives and assessing medical risks.

Questions

* How tall are you?
* Do you know what percentile you were for height and weight growing up? Parents may have better knowledge of this.

- What is your current weight?
- What was your weight before you began the eating disorder?
- What was the lowest weight you have been since starting the eating disorder?
- What was the maximum weight you have been since starting the eating disorder?
- What is your goal weight?
- Have you achieved this weight previously?
- Do you change what you want to be your goal weight, and why?
- What do you think your *natural* or *biological* weight should be?
- What do you think your *healthy* weight should be?
- What do you feel your *ideal* weight should be?
- What is the difference between what you perceive is a natural, biological, healthy, or ideal weight?
- Does your weight return to the same weight after losing weight?
- Have you tended to gain more weight after having lost weight?
- How much weight have you gained since initiating dieting?
- Why did you choose your specific goal weight?
- Did you determine your ideal weight from fitness magazines, the internet or pro-ana websites?

Current Health Status

> *"On Christmas Eve, my potassium tanked so badly that I was admitted to the hospital. I still remember my doctor came to see me in the middle of the night . . . on Christmas Eve! How selfish was I to take him away from his family? Who does that?"*

We need to know an individual's current or recent health status. We need to ask about general health concerns as well as any that may be eating disorder related.

A set of general health questions is helpful. "Have you ever been hospitalized for anything, including surgery?"

Questions

- Are you dealing with any ongoing health issues?
- Have you had any fairly recent health concerns?
- Are you undergoing any ongoing medical testing or follow-up, and if so, what are these?
- Should you be having any medical follow-up but are declining to have this done, and if so why?

Past Medical History

> *"The first time I passed out, I landed on my chin, cracked a tooth and bit my tongue so badly that I almost cut it in half. The second time I landed on my forehead, resulting in more stitches. I can't imagine how much blood I left behind, as I woke up in the ambulance. Another time I passed out at work and cracked my forehead open yet again. The last time was probably the worst, as I was walking home and fell on the concrete sidewalk."*

Any and all past health information should be acquired. This includes eating disorder related health concerns. Some topics to address are described under separate topics.

Questions

- Have you had any health issues in the past, and what were they?
- Have you ever been hospitalized?
- Have you ever had surgery?
- Are you currently being followed for ongoing health concerns?
- Are you following recommended treatment options?

Medications

A medication history is essential to determine what medications clients are currently taking, what medications they have taken but are not actively taking, and what medications they may require but are avoiding. It is important to ask about specific medications such as birth control pills and asthma medications because they are often not mentioned if we only ask "What medications are you taking?"

Common kinds of medications used are those for contraception, antibiotics, painkillers, psychotropic medications, and asthma. There is a plethora of other medications for many other health issues. There are over-the-counter and prescription medications. Illicit drugs and alcohol are discussed later. *Individuals use drugs and alcohol to "medicate" themselves.*

Aside from medications, nutrition supplements such as minerals and vitamins and protein powders need to be asked about as well.

For those with eating disorders, there may be medications that are either specifically chosen or avoided for weight control purposes. Hormonal birth control methods and psychotropic medications such as antidepressants, antianxiety medications, mood stabilizers, and antipsychotic medications are a few that may be avoided for fear of weight gain. Medications that increase metabolism such as thyroid medication and metabolism boosters may be chosen for weight loss purposes.

Ask about all medications. Ask if any medications are used for treatment of the eating disorder specifically. Are clients using psychiatric medications? Ask about the classifications of medications such as asthma inhalers, oral contraceptives, migraine treatment, and supplements, as many do not think of these as medications. Ask about medications they should be taking but are not. Also ask why they have not begun to take them or why they have discontinued them. Ask what the medications are being taken for. We cannot assume the reason individuals take them, as many medications now are indicated for multiple reasons. As examples, Wellbutrin, an antidepressant, is used to aid smoking cessation, while other antidepressants are also used to treat anxiety and obsessive-compulsive disorders. Another antidepressant, amitriptyline, is used to treat migraine symptoms. Sometimes individuals take the medications not knowing the reason they have been prescribed. They may be taking the wrong dose or taking them at inappropriate times of the day.

Medical staff should ask about side effects of current and discontinued medications. Often medications are discontinued due to side effects. Sometimes they are not taken in the first place due to erroneous fears about the drug. The individual will need more education to help make an informed decision. Ask what happens when medications are discontinued. Coming off of antidepressants may result in increased anxiety and depression.

Questions

- Do you take any over-the-counter, street, and prescription medications, and why?
- Are any drugs abused, overused, or used inappropriately for any reason?
- Are they used for eating disorder purposes?
- Are they used for self-harm purposes such as to punish or kill yourself?
- Do you use them with other medications, alcohol, or street drugs?
- Have you ever been addicted to medications, and which ones?
- Do you borrow medications from others or share medications?
- Do you steal drugs or prescription pads?
- Could you be pregnant or at risk of becoming pregnant? Medications can harm the unborn child or cause premature labor or miscarriage.
- Do you or have you used needle drugs, and do you think you are at risk of acquiring HIV or hepatitis?
- Are other family members using similar medications for similar reasons?

Immunizations

In developed countries there are typically a series of immunizations that begin soon after birth, then on into adulthood. Some are mandatory, as

102 General Eating Disorder History

established by government systems and travel guidelines, while others are optional and a matter of personal choice. Some immunizations that have not been given may need to be suggested to have, as individuals may be at health risks otherwise. Those in work environments that put employees at risk of hepatitis A or B, such as in hospitals or community health clinics, should be encouraged to receive their immunizations. As well, those who travel may be at risk of hepatitis. Because of the near ubiquitous spread of human papilloma viruses (HPV) sexually, vaccines should also be encouraged to help prevent cancers of the cervix, vulva, vagina, and anus. Both women and men should be encouraged. Because the HPV vaccine does not protect against someone already exposed to one or more strains of HPV, immunizations should be begun as soon as possible. For those already exposed to HPV, injections help to build up a stronger immunity against the acquired strains to prevent being reinfected by them in the future.

Questions

- Are your childhood and adult immunizations up to date?
- Have you had the human papilloma virus immunization?
- Have you had a pap smear recently?
- Have you been immunized against hepatitis A and B?
- What immunizations that you should have received did you not have, and why?
- Did your parents refuse to have you immunized when you were younger and why?

Allergies and Sensitivities

Some will have known allergies, and some will not. Even if individuals state they do not have any allergies, it must be acknowledged there indeed could be allergic potential. Even if there aren't any suspected allergies, the potential for developing allergies may arise. Cross-sensitivities between various substances can complicate the allergic picture. Some believe they do have allergies because they get rashes or experience itching, nasal stuffiness, swelling of the face and other parts of the body, or difficulty breathing for no obvious reason. Aside from external allergic sources, there are internal or body-induced allergic sources that include autoimmune diseases, as well as allergies to endogenous hormones.

There are several categories of allergic reactions based on allergy-inducing substances (allergens). Some of these categories include food and medications as well as environmental ones such as insects, animal (dust mites, dander), plant, bacteria, fungi, parasites, and scents—natural and artificial. There may be proven allergies based on proper allergy skin testing or perceived ones based on questionable allergy assessments. A history of real or perceived allergic reactions may play a significant role in one's eating disorder attitudes and behaviors. We need to ask what role, if any, their allergies play a part in the eating disorder. It's important to ask why someone believes they have allergies. There may be overt proof, or there may only be a suspicion that they have built up as being very important, regardless of a lack of evidence.

Food allergies, whether real or perceived, are common triggers for eating disorder attitudes and behaviors. This is similar in kind to food eliminations based on vegetarian diets. They become legitimate reasons for not eating certain foods, such as eggs, peanuts, shellfish, or food with gluten or lactose, or are actually eating disorder reasons for eliminating specific foods or food groups from their diet.

For the person wanting to improve nutrition, food allergies may present a problem, as those with a gluten allergy or even gluten sensitivity find it difficult to find foods without gluten in them.

Some may assume they have allergies, though not proven, or have had "allergy testing" by alternative health practitioners. For a person who believes she has 48 food allergies, it becomes a challenge to try to have her increase her nutrition.

Contraception

Contraception or birth control methods are commonly used by girls and women. Birth control methods include the combined oral contraceptive pill, progesterone-only pill, intrauterine devices, NuvaRing, Depo-Provera injection, condoms, contraceptive patch, withdrawal, rhythm method, basal body temperature measurements, and progesterone implants. There are always new contraceptive methods being developed.

The hormonal methods are commonly feared to cause weight gain and are therefore avoided. This puts women at risk of an unplanned pregnancy. Statistically, hormonal methods do not cause weight gain, and individuals need to be educated about this fact.

Ask if clients intend to become pregnant and when. Do they have any concerns regarding becoming pregnant, being pregnant, the delivery, and what having a baby will possibly do to the course of the eating disorder? A multivitamin with folic acid (folate) should be recommended.

It is important to know the reasons contraceptive methods are currently being or have been previously used. Contraceptive methods may be use for contraception as well as other purposes. Uses for contraceptive methods may be as follows.

- For birth control or contraception
- To regulate periods to cause them to come in a predictable manner

104 General Eating Disorder History

- To control pain or cramps during periods
- To control blood flow in order to decrease the number of days periods last as well as flow volume
- To treat anemia
- To treat menorrhagia
- To skip periods for pain, excessive flow, to avoid having them altogether for any reason, and work schedules
- To treat symptoms of polycystic ovarian syndrome
- To decrease depression associated with periods
- To avoid menstrual headaches
- To control the pain of arthritis
- To help diminish female gender dysphoria
- To treat osteoporosis secondary to amenorrhea caused from the eating disorder or athletics
- To help eliminate evidence of becoming a mature woman while wishing to remain prepubescent, or fear of growing up
- To trigger periods in those who experience amenorrhea

We need to know the reasons birth control methods are being avoided.

- The individual is gay
- She has never been sexually active and is not intending to be so soon
- For religious reasons
- She wants to get pregnant
- There has been a history of blood clots, deep vein thrombosis (DVT), or pulmonary embolism (PE) in the family or herself
- She has migraine with aura and cannot take estrogen
- She has experienced side effects or is afraid of the following:
  - Hormonal contraception can result in acne, depression, breakthrough bleeding, absent periods, body shape or weight increases; the person has gotten pregnant with their use or has heard bad things about them; there is a history of breast cancer in the family; or the person has heard they cause infertility.
  - Copper intrauterine devices cause pain; she has become pregnant with their use, including an ectopic pregnancy; the IUD was ejected; she fears perforation of the uterus; or she thinks IUDs cause infertility and increase the risk of STIs.

Questions

- Why are you using contraceptive methods?
- Are you compliant with their use?

Hormone Treatment

Aside from hormones prescribed for contraception, individuals may be taking hormonal medication for other reasons. Hormonal treatments may be taken for the following reasons.

- To treat thyroid disease
- To increase fertility
- To aid in individuals who are going through sexual reassignment
- To control sexual urges for sex offenders
- To increase libido in men
- To enhance athletic performance

Questions

- Are you taking hormones for any reason other than birth control, and why?
- If you are going through gender reassignment, how will this affect your body image, and what effect might this have on your eating disorder behaviors?

Pregnancy

Pregnancies past or present or that may occur in the future bring profound body image and weight gain fears to those with eating disorders. For individuals who fear even an ounce of weight gain, the thought of needing to gain the expected 25–35 pounds by full term can be overwhelming. Weight changes may be less or more than this range. Anyone who is pregnant or likely to become pregnant will require close support before and during pregnancy, as well as postpartum.

Although most of the weight gain during pregnancy is not due to fat tissue, some have an emotionally hard time accepting any weight gain for any reason. Those expecting to become pregnant as well as those who already are will need to be informed of the several physiological factors that contribute to weight gain.

Feared permanent weight gain during pregnancy may be based on weight gain from previous pregnancies. Individuals may also anticipate weight gain because others such as their mother, sisters, or friends gained weight they could not lose. They need to be reminded that they are not their mother, sisters, or friends and need not concern themselves with the experiences of others.

Physiological factors that contribute to weight gain during pregnancy are:

- The baby.
- Increased blood volume acquired during pregnancy.

106 General Eating Disorder History

- Placental growth.
- Uterine growth.
- Amniotic fluid production.
- Breast enlargement.
- Fluid retention.

The statistical range of normal expected weight gain during pregnancy is between 25 and 35 pounds for an average, healthy weight woman. Women underweight will be expected to gain more, and those overweight may need to gain less. There is no reliable way of determining how much a given individual should or will gain. This uncertainty may bring great anxiety during the whole course of pregnancy.

The struggle individuals have is between desiring not gaining weight at all versus having to gain enough weight for the health of the baby. The desire to be "good for the baby" tends to override realized weight control objectives. However, some will invest great efforts into not gaining any weight but to actually lose weight during pregnancy. These individuals require very close attention for monitoring of the mother and progress in pregnancy.

As much as individuals want to know how much weight they will gain during pregnancy, they very much want to know how much weight they will lose after delivery. This, of course, is an impossible question to answer as well, and they will need to be informed of the factors that cause weight gain during pregnancy and will be reversible to some degree after delivery.

For those who have been pregnant before, a record of the course of previous pregnancies is required. We need to know how many pregnancies there were and the outcome of each. Determine the age of the children. Some pregnancies last to term and some will be premature, while some will result in miscarriage or therapeutic abortion. For those pregnancies that made it to full term, enquire as to how much weight was gained by term and how they dealt with weight gain (see the next section, "Postpartum"). For some, being pregnant is believed to have a protective effect against engaging in eating disorder attitudes and behaviors for unknown reasons, where it becomes easier to step back from eating disorder dictates. Sometimes the greatest risk of an escalation of eating disorder behaviors is not during pregnancy but after delivery, when the mother does not feel she is putting her child at risk. I have found that the postpartum period is when clinicians will notice a ramped-up escalation of eating disorder drives. Be afraid!

For those with eating disorders who will become pregnant or already are, a supportive system should be put into place as soon as possible. This includes family, friends, and their partner as well as health care professionals such as maternity experts, mental health workers, and possibly prenatal medical experts. Arranging preliminary visits with clinicians before there are any health issues is advised.

For those wishing to become pregnant, there may be a fear that they cannot become pregnant due to low weight or being amenorrheic. Though these conditions may result in temporary infertility due to anovulation, some may still be ovulating regardless and be able to become pregnant. For those relying on amenorrhea as a contraceptive method, they need to be informed of pregnancy potential.

Some believe that they should not have a child until they are cured of the eating disorder, as they feel they will not be a capable, responsible parent. They need to be informed that this is not necessarily so.

Questions

- Do you think you are pregnant?
- Are you taking prenatal vitamins with folic acid?
- Have you had a positive pregnancy test recently?
- How long have you been pregnant?
- Are you sure of your dates?
- Are there any non-eating disorder complicating factors in pregnancy such as twins or triplets, diabetes, hypertension, or intrauterine growth retardation?
- Have you seen your doctor for the first prenatal visit?
- What are your plans for the pregnancy? Plans may include carrying the pregnancy to term or ending in termination.
- Was the pregnancy expected?
- Do you want to have a child?
- Are you ready to have a child?
- How is the pregnancy affecting your eating disorder, if at all?
- How will you be able to cope with the natural weight gain in pregnancy?
- Are you taking any medications, and can any of them harm you or your baby?
- Have you been using illicit drugs or alcohol during the pregnancy?
- Do you have any eating disorder associated health problems such as palpitations, fainting, or metabolic abnormalities?
- Have you had any bleeding or spotting during pregnancy?
- What was your weight just prior to pregnancy?
- What was your weight at your first prenatal visit?
- What is your weight now?
- Have you set any weight limitations during this pregnancy?
- When was your last normal menstrual period, and how sure you are that it is accurate?
- Have you missed any periods before your last "normal" period?
- Do you have any symptoms of pregnancy?

108   General Eating Disorder History

- If you are planning to be "good for the baby," what do you mean by this?
- Are you nauseated?
- Does nausea affect how you eat?
- Do you vomit due to nausea?
- Do you use nausea as a reason to restrict now?
- Are you on any medications to control nausea, and do they work?
- Are you taking anti-nausea medications if prescribed them?
- How is the pregnancy affecting your eating disorder, either in a positive or negative way?
- What are your plans for the eating disorder during pregnancy?
- What are your plans for the eating disorder after pregnancy?
- If you have had previous pregnancies, how did you cope with weight gain and the eating disorder?
- How have your moods been during this pregnancy?
- How were your moods during other pregnancies?
- Will you have adequate friend or family support during your pregnancy?

Postpartum

As much as pregnancy brings significant concerns regarding weight gain, the postpartum period brings further significant risks. Our concerns regarding the course of the eating disorder do not end with delivery and may indeed only be the beginning of risks beginning in pregnancy.

After the baby has been born, a full-on, foot-to-the-floor-boards drive to lose weight may develop. At some level, postpartum weight loss efforts may be deemed a rebound response to having to put off eating disorder plans during pregnancy. A sense of having to make up for lost time with achieving eating disorder goals may develop. There is a kind of doubling up of eating disorder motivation, including having to lose the weight gained with pregnancy plus having to achieve pre-pregnancy eating disorder goals. As soon as the clinician is aware of a pregnancy, he or she should determine what the individual is already planning with regard to escalating eating disorder behaviors and hoped-for weight loss targets after delivery (Knoph et al., 2013).

Questions

- What are your plans for the eating disorder and weight control after delivery?
- What are your current eating disorder behaviors?
- If you are breastfeeding, do you use this to control how much you will eat or weigh?

General Eating Disorder History   109

- What is your daily caloric intake if you know?
- Are you calorie counting?
- Do you know how many calories breastfeeding uses daily?
- How long do you plan to breastfeed?
- Do you have a weight goal, or how much weight do you want to lose and over what period of time?
- Are you taking any medications, and can they be transported to the baby through breastfeeding?
- How did you deal with the eating disorder postpartum after previous deliveries?
- How are your moods now?
- Have you ever had postpartum depression?
- If so, did you have any treatment for it, including medications?
- Who supports you currently?
- Are you afraid that your child will acquire an eating disorder from you?

Surgery

When taking a surgical history, we want to know what surgery individuals have already had, of any upcoming surgery, and any surgical procedures recommended but not yet booked. We need to ask specifically what surgery they may have had, as dental surgery including wisdom teeth extraction and gum grafting or mole removal may not be seen as important enough to report, as they do not typically require a general anesthetic. Therapeutic abortions or dilatations and curettages (D &C) are often not reported as well. Similarly, biopsies of the skin and breast or of the uterine cervix are not seen as important enough to mention at times, again, because they do not usually require a general anesthetic.

Aside from cosmetic surgery there may be other surgery that has an effect on eating disorders. Jaw surgery can cause someone to be able to eat little due to jaw wiring, and also pain allowing only the ability to drink fluids. This can result in weight loss, leading to accolades from others, instilling a wish to maintain a lower weight.

For those who have bulimia, there can be an increased risk of spontaneous vomiting during or after surgery due to having a lower threshold for inducing vomiting. With the likelihood of delayed gastric emptying in patients with eating disorders, it should be assumed they could have stomach contents remaining even after not eating for several hours prior to surgery. This could also be putting them at risk of regurgitation during and after surgery.

For those with Crohn's disease, surgery may present other problems. In extreme forms of Crohn's disease, removal of much of the intestines, including the whole stomach and esophagus, can prohibit any oral

110   General Eating Disorder History

consumption of nutrition for the rest of their lives. Those with eating disorders may choose to eat regardless, causing serious exacerbation of the remaining Crohn's disease of the throat.

Other surgery can cause further dissatisfaction in one's body image. The surgical removal of tumors, such as for the treatment of neurofibromatosis, can lead to an individual wanting to cover all parts of their body where surgery has taken place because of scars that develop. Some surgery plays into eating disorder body image and weight control mentality, as discussed in "Surgery and Other Cosmetic Altering Methods" in Chapter 4.

Infectious Diseases

Ask about any history of infections. Common childhood infections could include ear, throat, or lung infections as well as chicken pox and impetigo. Infectious mononucleosis as well as global influenzas, urinary tract infections, pneumonias, and pelvic infections are worth enquiring about. Ask about potentially serious infections such as meningitis, blood infections, and rheumatic fever as well as gastrointestinal infections, including bowel abscesses.

Infectious diseases can have a profound effect on the evolution of an eating disorder. A major consequence of any long-term infections is that they may significantly disrupt an individual's life plans. Infectious mononucleosis is a common example of a prolonged debilitating infection. This can prevent someone from finishing school terms or may result in not being able to attend work. Extended loss of work can result in serious financial problems. This can contribute to depression, anxiety, and low esteem and aggravate the eating disorder. Infections make people feel sick. That is, they can feel severely lethargic, exhausted, nauseated, or feverish or have headaches. Infections can suppress appetite or cause nausea. This contributes to the difficulties of trying to eat. Significant weight loss can result very quickly, thus triggering a further spiral into the eating disorder. An increased lack of motivation to recover can set in. Any gains in nutrition and weight can quickly be reversed. This may feed into the person's weight loss mentality or contribute to the frustration of trying to recover.

Streptococcal pyogenes infections can lead to serious health issues. It is the cause of rheumatic fever that results in heart valve damage. This heart valve damage can be minimal or lead to heart valve replacement. Heart valve damage can create a heart murmur or swooshing sound when the physician listens to the heart. With a history of streptococcal infection or heart murmur, a thorough investigation of the heart is required. Heart valve damage-induced health risks can be increased in those with anorexia nervosa due to weight loss and compromised electrolyte values. Opportunistic gut infections such as clostridium difficile are life threatening, especially to an already medically compromised individual. Infections are a major cause of death in those with eating disorders.

Pediatric autoimmune neuropsychiatric disorders associated with streptococcal infections, or *PANDAS syndrome*, is caused by group A streptococcal infections. The infection may harbor in the throat, sinuses, or skin. It may become bloodborne and infect any other part of the body. This condition has been linked to the development of anorexia nervosa, PANDAS-anorexia nervosa (PANDAS-AN).

Questions

- Have you ever had a serious infectious disease?
- What was the infectious disease?
- Did this impact on you in any important way?
- Have you ever had a strep infection?
- Do you know how or where you got the infection?
- Could you have spread this to anyone else, including children?
- Did the infection result in you having to drop out of school or leave work, or did it interfere with plans such as traveling?
- Did the infection have an effect on your eating disorder, and how?
- Did the infection affect your ability or desire to eat?
- Did you lose weight, and if you did, how much?
- Were you hospitalized for it?
- What treatment did you receive?
- Did the infection have an effect on your moods?
- Did your eating disorder begin after an infectious disease?
- Have you ever had a sexually transmitted infection and if so, was it treated?
- Do you get flus or colds frequently?

Menstrual History

A menstrual history used to be essential for making a diagnosis of anorexia nervosa. A criterion for having anorexia nervosa used to be that a woman did not have three menstrual periods or more in a row—amenorrhea. Today, this is not a specific criterion. Regardless, periods can be affected, and a loss of periods may be attributed to the eating disorder, possibly due to weight loss and stress.

Amenorrhea has importance, as it may be an indicator of decreasing nutrition and weight loss. It may also be a result of extreme exercise such as experienced by athletes. It may be the result of both. Certainly, pregnancy has to be considered. Prolonged amenorrhea may lead to osteopenia and eventually osteoporosis. Bone loss may not be recoverable even if adequate nutrition, weight normalization, and the return of periods occurs.

112 General Eating Disorder History

Individuals likely are not ovulating and therefore not likely to be fertile, an issue for those wishing to conceive. A caution to patients is that those who experience amenorrhea may actually be ovulating and can, indeed, become pregnant. It is not a reliable contraceptive method.

Other factors that cause amenorrhea are the use of hormonal contraceptive methods. Progesterone-only contraceptive methods such as the hormonal intrauterine devices, progesterone-only pill and progesterone injection (Depo-Provera) may eradicate periods. A phenomenon called *post-pill amenorrhea* results after discontinuing the contraceptive pill and may last for many months. Taking the combined estrogen and progesterone contraceptive methods in tandem and skipping the usual seven days of not taking any hormones sometimes eliminates periods, though not reliably in some.

The combined hormonal contraceptive methods such as the combined oral contraceptive pill, NuvaRing, or Evra patch will usually artificially trigger periods in those who would otherwise experience amenorrhea. Endocrine-altering disorders such as polycystic ovarian syndrome or thyroid disease can affect periods.

There are surgical causes of amenorrhea such as hysterectomies and oophorectomies. Ovarian and brain tumors as well as some cancers may result in a loss of periods. Some pharmaceutical drugs also have to be considered.

Periods may be irregular but not absent. The reasons for this are multifold. Similar to amenorrhea, weight loss, excessive exercise, stress, and medications as well as metabolic conditions may result in irregular periods. It may be of genetic origin as well.

Periods may return, if only briefly, with sexual arousal in those with anorexia nervosa.

Questions

- When was your last normal menstrual period?
- Are your periods regular?
- If so, how often do you get your periods?
- How long do your periods last?
- Are your periods irregular?
- Has there been any change in regularity such as days between periods, days of flow, or amount of flow?
- What do you think might be the reason for the changes?
- Do you think that your nutrition or weight has any influence on this?
- Are you using any contraceptive methods that could alter periods?
- Are there any non-contraceptive methods that could be altering your periods?
- When did this irregularity start?

General Eating Disorder History   113

- Has it ever happened before, why, and for how long?
- Could you be pregnant?
- Are you using birth control methods, and what kind and how regularly?
- Do you want to have periods, or not and why?
- If you miss periods, how many have you missed that you expected, or how many months do they disappear for?
- Do you have any medical conditions that could contribute to irregular or missed periods?
- Have you had any gynecological operations, and if so what kind?
- Do you think stress may be having an effect on your periods, and why?
- Are you taking hormones for gender reassignment?

Ethnicity

Some will have grown up in an ethnically defined environment, and others will not. We cannot assume that because individuals have an Italian-, Korean-, or Ukrainian-sounding last name that they necessarily identify with those cultures. We need to ask if they have any sense of ethnicity. If they do, we can ask about that. Even if they do not identify themselves or think they have been affected by ethnic influences, we need to ask. Ethnicity can have a significant influence on individuals' eating disorders, even without them being aware of it. We need to find out how.

Ethnic influences affect religion, one's relationship with food, family dynamics and expectations, education standards, work ethic, and ideological beliefs. Ethnic influences on food and body image can be extensive.

Food choices, meal quantities, the time of day when meals are expected to be eaten, importance of family eating together, saying of grace, what are considered healthy foods, religious associations of food, or the use of alcoholic beverages all factor in.

Meal times can be a nightmare for foreign students who attend private schools or universities or who are on student exchanges. This may be so whether someone has an eating disorder or not. Some may develop an eating disorder due to restricting because there are few foods they like to eat, and as a result they lose weight inadvertently. The same is true for anyone dropped into an unfamiliar culture for any reason, including those immigrating to a new country. Food odors and textures play a part.

The preparation and presentation of food can influence how food is received. One culture may typically prepare a whole cooked fish with the head, eyes, tail, skin, bones, and intestines intact, while another may have all evidence of these body items totally stripped away, leaving only the meat visible on the plate, such as fish and chips being an example.

A Taiwanese student who is used to fish, rice, and lentils for a typical home-cooked meal may have genuine difficulty with having to eat bratwurst or poutine and French fries from a private school cafeteria. When individuals with an eating disorder complain they can't eat the food in a new cultural environment, this may be a very real concern and not a ploy to restrict.

Ethnicity influences those with eating disorders who are away from their own culture at times (Sala, Reyes-Rodriguez, Bulik & Bardone-Cone, 2013). An exchange student from North America going to Japan faces cultural expectations to eat foods of the host family. Often there is more food than the visitor wants to eat, but having to be polite and eat everything she is presented with can result in unwanted weight gain. There is much fear of insulting the host family by turning down food, and this may be a very real pressure.

Loud slurping sounds created while eating is a sign of enjoyment and approval of the food prepared in some Asian cultures. This loud slurping sound can be annoying or revolting to someone not used to it. This can prevent those with eating disorders from eating with others, as they are put off their food.

The following quote says it all regarding ethnicity in food and eating. "I believe that most or all Scottish cuisine is based on a dare." This quote is taken from the movie *So I Married an Axe Murderer* and has been quoted by the comedian Mike Myers. Haggis and black pudding (blood pudding) are a couple of examples of food to be dared.

A kosher or Hebrew culture forbids products from pigs such as bacon and ham. Because, as Jay Leno once said, "Bacon is a taste worth dying for," there may be cheating on Jewish diets from time to time.

There can be cultural, ethnic, or religious food-related issues that arise in partner and marriage relationships. These issues can have a profound stress on these relationships. Stresses come from deciding on food choices, when to eat, amounts of food, and what is a healthy diet. More stress can develop when having family dinners such as eating with parents and siblings.

Religion

Most of the influences of religion and food and eating have been identified in the "Ethnicity" section. Guilt and shame as well as whether there may be life after death are part of the equation. Food is often a part of religious ceremonies.

References

Conti, C., Lanzara, R., Scipioni, M., Iasenza, M., Guagnano, M. T., & Fulcheri, M. (2017). The relationship between binge eating disorder and suicidality: A systematic review. *Front Psychol*, 00: 2125. doi: 10.3389/fpsyg.2017.02125. eCollection 2017. Review.

Huckins, L. M., Hatzikotoulas, K., Southam, L., Thornton, L. M., Steinberg, J., Aguilera-McKay, F., et al. (2017). Investigation of common, low-frequency and rare genome-wide variation in anorexia nervosa. *Mol Psychiatry*, 25. doi: 10.1038/mp.2017.88.

Johnson, C. M., Henderson, M. S., Tripicchio, G., Rozin, P., Heo, M., Pietrobelli, A., et al. (2017). Observed parent-child feeding dynamics in relation to child body mass index and adiposity. *Pediatr Obes*, 10. doi: 10.1111/ijpo.12209.

Kandel, D. B. (1990). Parenting styles, drug use, and children's adjustment in families of young adults. *Journal of Marriage and Family*, 52(1): 183–196.

Knoph, C., Von Holle, A., Zerwas, S., Torgersen, L., Tambs, K., Stoltenberg, C., et al. (2013). Course and predictors of maternal eating disorders in the postpartum period. *Int Journal Eat Disord*, 46(4): 355–368. Published online 2013, 11. doi: 10.1002/eat.22088.

Koutek, J., Kocourkova, J., & Dudova, I. (2016). Suicidal behavior and self-harm in girls with eating disorders. *Neuropsychiatr Dis Treat*, 12: 787–793.

Linville, D., Stice, E., Gau, J., & O'Neil, M. (2011). Predictive effects of mother and peer influences on increases in adolescent eating disorder risk factors and symptoms: A 3-year longitudinal study. *Int Journal Eat Disord*, 44(8): 745–751. doi: 10.1002/eat.20907.

Palmer, R. L., Oppenheimer, R., Dignon, A., Chaloner, D. A., & Howells, K. (1990). Childhood sexual experiences with adults reported by women with eating disorders: An extended series. *The British Journal of Psychiatry*, 156(5): 699–703. doi: 10.1192/bjp.156.5.699.

Piran, N., Gadalla, T. (2007). Eating disorders and substance abuse in Canadian women: A national study. *Addiction*, 102(1): 105–113.

Sala, M., Reyes-Rodríguez, M. L., Bulik, C. M., & Bardone-Cone, A. S. (2013). Race, ethnicity, and eating disorder recognition by peers. *Eat Disord*, 21(5): 423–436. doi: 10.1080/10640266.2013.827540.

Stefanini, M. C., Troiani, M. R., Caselli, M., Dirindelli, P., Lucarelli, S., Caini, S., & Martinetti, M. G. (2018). Living with someone with an eating disorder: Factors affecting the caregivers' burden. *Eat Weight Disord*, 24. doi: 10.1007/s40519-018-0480-7.

Sundgot-Borgen, J., Torstveit, M. K., & Klungland, M. (2004). Prevalence of eating disorders in elite athletes Is higher than in the general population. *Clinical Journal of Sport Medicine*, 14(1): 25–32.

Chapter 4

Eating Disorder Behaviors

"It is an illness that affects millions of women and men worldwide."

A core necessity of being able to take a detailed eating disorder focused history is being informed about as many specific eating disorder behaviors as possible. As well, we need to know about any and all of the various ways of carrying out given behaviors. As an example, there are over a dozen alternate ways for someone to induce vomiting. Each alternate method should be considered a separate eating disorder behavior, as there may be very different consequences including life-threatening outcomes depending on methods used. Someone using one finger to induce vomiting is likely at a different risk than someone who drinks toxic floor cleaner to deliver the same result.

Current diagnostic criteria for eating disorders include about 15 behaviors used by those with eating disorders. There will be over 150 behaviors used by those with eating disorders, including variations, many of which have been mentioned in this book.

Eating disorder behaviors have been grouped, as they serve a common purpose. The sections in this chapter include:

- Purging Behaviors
- Calorie Burning and Metabolism Altering Behaviors
- Body Gauging Behaviors
- Binge Eating and Related Behaviors
- Restricting Eating Behaviors
- False Information
- Organizing Behaviors
- Symptom Management Behaviors
- Surgery and Other Cosmetic Altering Behaviors
- Substance Use

The eating disorder behaviors discussed here have been described as separate entities. However, there are numerous permutations and combinations of

Purging Behaviors

Vomiting

Vomiting is a common behavior used in bulimia but may also be used in anorexia nervosa or variations of these conditions. Vomiting can be a very complicated behavior to assess due to the many ways it may present and its connections with other eating disorder behaviors, most notably bingeing and vomiting. It is a behavior as addicting as crack cocaine—some only have to try it once and they are hooked. Vomiting is a behavior that may start for many reasons. Some reasons may be to control body image, and some may not be.

The methods by which individuals vomit present numerous possibilities. The most common method is by using fingers. It is important to ask what hand and what fingers they use. This may vary from time to time. If someone uses two fingers such as the second and third finger of their left hand, inquire if they use other fingers at different times and why. If they say they use three or even four fingers, this likely means that they are unable to trigger the gag reflex easily and may even be unsuccessful with all efforts. Some will try to use their whole fist in a losing attempt to induce vomiting. Why is this important? If someone relies on vomiting heavily for weight control but is unable to vomit, they very likely will rely on another eating disorder behavior to compensate. Some compensatory behaviors may be minor, such as restricting or increasing exercise the next day; however, they may be very dangerous, such as drinking hydrogen peroxide to induce vomiting.

Other methods of inducing vomiting may be the use of spoons, spatulas, and a paperclip on the end of a string or emetics. Some will change body position, such as supporting themselves upside down in a chair with the hope gravity will aid in their venture. Using spoons, spatulas, or other objects may result in them being caught in the throat, and they may need to be removed by an emergency physician. Objects lodged in the throat could lead to fatalities.

Some are so adept at vomiting that they do not need to trigger vomiting with fingers or objects. They can vomit spontaneously. They just think about it or will it, and it happens. Sometimes just bending over a toilet or garbage can assist in their quest. A frightening possibility is that some will vomit spontaneously in their sleep. This can be very dangerous and even cause death by choking.

118 Eating Disorder Behaviors

Where do people vomit? Anywhere you can imagine. People may vomit in their homes but may also have several options of where they vomit in their home. They may vomit in the bathroom, usually in the toilet, but may also vomit down the shower drain while taking a shower or even in the sink. Some are less discrete and may vomit around the toilet, where others may become vividly aware this practice is going on. Some vomit into the garbage disposal in the kitchen.

They can vomit in their bedrooms so others do not become suspicious. They may vomit into bags, plastic food storage containers, cups, or other receptacles then transport the vomit to the toilet, where it is flushed. Alternatively, they may take it outside of the home and get rid of it in the garbage cans, garden, or flowerbeds. Though likely rare, some will eat their own vomit or give their vomit to their pets to eat. Vomit may be mixed in with other food or put on a pizza, then consumed this way. Some will eat their vomit because they have run out of food or as a way of punishing themselves.

Most of the time we think of our clients as likely vomiting at home, but unless we ask we could be wrong. They can vomit anywhere else in the community. They may vomit at their parents', friends' or partners' homes. They may vomit at school or university or in the work place. Vomiting may occur in a car, where they will vomit into bags or even open the car door at a stoplight and vomit onto the street. They also may vomit in airplanes or buses.

> *"I flunked out of an in-patent unit because I kept sneaking to the bathroom to purge."*

> *"While living with a family, food was still my priority, and I would wake up in the middle of the night and sneak food and purge."*

Hiding vomiting behavior can be tricky, and creative options will come to light as mentioned earlier. Other methods may include using air freshener in the restroom, bedroom, or any other space vomiting occurs to hide the smell. Windows may be left open and the restroom fan turned on to help dissipate the smell of vomit.

What do people vomit? This may seem an odd question, because we usually think of food as the obvious answer. However, individuals may vomit water, bile, air, "markers," blood, or any substances ingested.

When associated with vomiting, fluids are used to thin or liquefy food in the stomach. This will allow the stomach contents to be eliminated with relative ease. Tea, coffee, milk, juices, or pop provide an arsenal of liquid choices. Fluids serve another function as well. Clear fluids, especially water, are commonly used as an indicator that the stomach has been completely emptied of all food. That is, the individual will keep drinking clear fluids and vomit continuously until only clear fluid returns. In theory, this may work quite well to rid the stomach of all food, but some report that even after they do this, they may be able to still vomit food.

From a medical perspective, excessive water intake can lead to serious and even lethal consequences. Brain swelling may occur and cause seizures or death. Electrolyte abnormalities may develop as well.

Eliminating air from the stomach is an extreme attempt to deal with body image dissatisfaction. Possibly the most focused-upon body area that individuals loath and want to change is their "stomach." They can't stand a protruding abdomen. Vomiting food, restricting intake, excessive exercising, and other behaviors used in eating disorders are typical methods attempted to decrease abdominal distention or prevent it from increasing.

Markers are ingested substances, usually food, that do not change much in appearance after being eaten. Examples are licorice, lettuce, red peppers, chocolate, Cheetos, brightly colored sweet or sour candies including, gummies, and carrots. The thought is if someone eats a marker first then sees the marker return during a session of vomiting, they will have purged all of the food eaten after to the marker. To some this is felt to be a reliable method of telling when all of the food in the stomach has come up, while others know it may not be. The stomach typically churns food after receiving it and so may mix the marker with the food and make the process unreliable. However, in many with eating disorders, the gastrointestinal system experiences the *intestinal motility disorder*. This is when the stomach and the intestines significantly slow peristalsis to the point where some say they will vomit food they had eaten 12 hours earlier. Food should usually leave the stomach within an hour. It is conceivable that markers may have some degree of reliability in a few.

It is important to ask why someone stops a vomiting session. There are several reasons for stopping a vomiting episode. The expected and usual reason is they feel they have rid the stomach of most if not all of their food. Sometimes other reasons prevail. Some will stop or interrupt vomiting due to an anticipated or hoped for end point. They will stop vomiting if they see blood, bile, markers, or clear water as indicators the stomach is empty. Other reasons for discontinuing vomiting may be out of fear when they see blood, experience chest pain, or vomit to the point of exhaustion. When seeing blood or experiencing chest pain, they may fear rupturing the stomach or esophagus, which can be fatal. Binge eating and vomiting can be fast and furious, setting the stage for choking on either food or vomit, thus providing another indicator to stop.

Non-body image reasons for vomiting may be due to gastrointestinal conditions such as traveler's diarrhea associated with vomiting, "stomach flu," food aversion, or difficulty swallowing and vomiting in order to get rid of the "full feeling" or cramping after eating. Some may vomit to relieve anxiety, including coping with emotions surrounding sexual abuse.

120 Eating Disorder Behaviors

Emetics are ingested substances that induce vomiting (Steffen, Mitchell, Roerig & Lancaster, 2007). They include synthetic chemicals or normally ingested substances such as salt, spices, and alcohol. They will likely be used when it is difficult or impossible to induce vomiting by other means. Floor cleaners have been tried as well. Emetics may be very dangerous. One common commercial emetic, *ipecac*, contains the chemical emetine that is absorbed into muscle including heart muscle and can cause heart swelling, or cardiomegaly, and cardiomyopathies that induce irregular cardiac rhythms or dysrhythmias leading to sudden cardiac death. Ipecac is lethal in as little as two vials a week, yet some will take six vials daily, a very dangerous enterprise. Another life-threatening consequence of using ipecac is that it can cause such harsh or violent contractions of the stomach that the stomach lining or esophagus can tear and cause bleeding, even to the point of death. Because bleeding from either site is internal, catastrophic bleeds leading to death can develop unnoticed. *Salt* mixed with water may be ingested to induce severe nausea, resulting in vomiting. *Hot spices* placed on or in food can also do the same.

When can people vomit? The answer is anytime . . . anytime they have the availability, that is. The opportunity to vomit may be denied when others are around. Individuals become so adept at vomiting they can manage to vomit while others are present in some situations. Restaurant workers only have to lean over a garbage can while appearing to change a garbage bag and effectively vomit into the bag unsuspected. As mentioned earlier, others may vomit into coffee cups while appearing to be drinking or leave the house and vomit outside into planters, garden, or garbage cans while giving the appearance of going for a stroll.

The clinician needs to know whether vomiting behaviors are relatively *constant, increasing, or decreasing.* The reasons for this may be revealing. Increasing the frequency may indicate a franticness to lose more weight or stop weight gain. If vomiting is on the increase, ask if any other eating disorder behaviors are also increasing or being introduced. Decreasing or stopping vomiting may imply they are working on recovery, or they may have become fearful because of experiencing chest pain or seeing blood. It may also be that they have achieved a comfortable low weight or vomiting is not working well enough for weight loss.

Questions

- What triggered you to vomit in the first place?
- Did you start vomiting and continue vomiting to control body image or weight?
- How old were you?
- Where did you learn to use vomiting for body image or weight control?

Eating Disorder Behaviors   121

- How did you first induce vomiting?
- Where were you then?
- Why did you not stop vomiting after this?
- Were there any other eating disorder behaviors that you were involved with before introducing vomiting, and what were they?
- Have you added any other eating disorder behaviors since vomiting began, and what are or were they?
- What motivated you to continue to vomit?
- Currently or recently, are you or have you been vomiting, and why?
- What is your goal with vomiting?
- How many sessions of vomiting do you do in a day?
- How many times during each session of vomiting do you vomit?
- How many days of the week or month do you induce vomiting?
- What is the range of vomiting sessions in a day, and what would be the average or typical number in a day of vomiting?
- Is vomiting linked or associated with another eating disorder behaviors, and why?
- Are there eating disorder behaviors you never engage in if you use vomiting, and why?
- Is vomiting easy or difficult, and why do you think so?
- Does vomiting become easier or more difficult the more you do it, and why do you think so?
- Are there extended periods of time when you do not vomit, and why?
- Do you engage in other eating disorder behaviors to compensate for not vomiting?
- If vomiting becomes more difficult or does not work at all, what do you do instead?
- Where do you vomit? Possibilities are at home, school, work, in the car, at your parents' or friends' homes, and elsewhere.
- What receptacles do you vomit into?
- Do you carry vomit with you, and why?
- Do you store or hoard vomit, and why?
- What do you do to make vomiting easier, such as eat food that is easy to vomit or drink fluids to liquefy stomach contents?
- What foods are difficult to vomit?
- Has your method of vomiting changed over time, and why?
- Why do you end a vomiting session? What is the end point?
- Do you or have you ever used markers?
- Do you or have you ever used emetics?
- Have you ever used any tools such as spoons or spatulas or other aids to induce vomiting?
- What do you do to hide evidence of vomiting?
- Have you ever vomited in your sleep?

- Have you ever choked while vomiting?
- Have you ever seen blood during vomiting sessions?
- What do you do if you do see blood?
- Have you ever had abdominal or chest pains during or after vomiting?
- What do you do when this happens?
- Does seeing blood or experiencing chest or abdominal pains cause you to be afraid?
- Are you aware of any potential physical risks with vomiting, such as choking or bleeding to death?
- Does not being able to vomit cause you to panic or become depressed or suicidal or lead to any form of self-harm including cutting, burning, hitting, or drug and alcohol use?
- Does vomiting lead to guilt or shame?
- Do you avoid contact with others or isolate in order to have the opportunity to vomit?
- What situations interfere with you being able to vomit?
- Do you eat your own vomit?
- Do you leave vomit in plain sight of others to find, and why?
- Do you feed vomit to pets?
- Does your cat vomit?

Laxatives

> *"Taking that many laxatives would also make me very nauseous. One night, when I was working an overnight front desk shift at a hotel, I was curled up in a ball behind the desk throwing up into a paper cup. I couldn't leave the front desk unattended, and that was all I had. At the same time, I desperately needed to use the washroom. When my coworker finally stopped by the desk, I made a run for the washroom up a flight of stairs and didn't make it in time. The rest of the shift was very uncomfortable."*

Laxatives are substances ingested for the purpose of relieving symptoms of constipation. For those with eating disorders, they are used for this same purpose at times but also with the hope of increasing the rate that food is transported through the gut, expecting food will not be digested and nutrients will not be absorbed that could cause weight gain (Elran-Barak, 2017). The gut is generally so efficient at absorbing food that increased gut activity will likely not decrease nutrient absorption. Some, however, say that they can see undigested food in their stool as a result of laxative use.

> *"If I took enough pills, the food would just pass through me undigested."*

Eating Disorder Behaviors 123

There are several categories of laxatives. There are bulk-forming laxatives, stool softeners, lubricant laxatives, stimulant laxatives, saline laxatives, and hyperosmotic laxatives. Some are more dangerous than others.

Bulk-forming laxatives just absorb water, creating a loose but bulky substance that increases peristalsis. Water must be taken with the bulk laxative to prevent stool from becoming hard, creating further feelings of bloating, cramping, and constipation. Psyllium and bran are in this category. Psyllium tends to work better.

Stimulant laxatives (Ex-Lax, senna) work by chemically irritating the bowel to stimulate contractions and water production. This is akin to you putting dish soap in your eyes and creating tearing and inflammation. Because the bowel is essentially free of pain sensation, this inflammation is not noticed. These laxatives can be dangerous because they can cause damage to the bowel. They can destroy the villi of the lining of the bowel that allow absorption of nutrients, thus resulting in a malabsorption syndrome. They also can poison the two nerve plexuses between the three layers of muscles of the gut. This nervous system is what triggers the contractions of the muscles and can become paralyzed by laxatives, causing bowel obstructions. Sections of bowel may need to be removed surgically to prevent obstructions.

Laxatives may cause problems socially. Because they induce diarrhea, individuals need to be near a restroom. Diarrhea can strike anywhere, including while driving in a car as well as riding on a bus, subway, or airplane. To hide the use of laxatives, some will defecate down a shower drain to hide odor or prevent flushing the toilet that others may hear. This can create much embarrassment when a plumber is called to unplug the shower drain and reports the cause of the blockage.

The bowel tends to habituate quickly to laxative use. Initially, one or two tablets can stimulate a strong urge, but often more laxative is required to have the same effect. Laxative doses increase when smaller doses that used to work well do not anymore, often resulting in dependency. Quantities of 300 laxative tablets a day have been reported.

> *"I remember being warned that my bowels would eventually stop working on their own, and then I would have real issues. That never stopped me. The desire to get rid of food from my body was too great."*

Decreasing and discontinuing laxatives creates problems as well. Because the gut gets "used to" laxatives, decreasing them results in a slowing down of the gut, resulting in severe constipation, abdominal cramps, and bloating. Body image concerns are ramped up because of feeling "fat," triggered by bloating and feeling stuffed. Individuals need to be informed of this phenomenon so they are psychologically prepared. Sometimes tapering laxative use helps while at the same time introducing less stimulating and

124　Eating Disorder Behaviors

safer laxatives temporarily. Laxative use can be very expensive. Some will order them online in bulk to reduce cost. Sometimes the cost is shared with someone else who is using them for the same reason.

> *"I abused laxatives throughout my journey with my eating disorder.*
> *I still do to some extent. At first it was a purging method."*

Informing clients that laxatives do not typically work to lose weight, cost a lot of money, are psychologically addicting, and only lead to more cramping and bloating may help them work on eliminating their use. If there is weight loss, it will be most likely be due to stool and water loss—not fat loss. Electrolyte problems may develop due to a loss of potassium and sodium. Fatal metabolic conditions can arise.

Questions

- Do you use laxatives, and why?
- Do you use them to relieve constipation?
- Do you use them to lose weight?
- If you use them to lose weight, are you expecting to lose weight due to stool evacuation or water loss or both?
- What brand of laxatives do you use, and why?
- Are you aware of the different actions of each kind of laxatives?
- Do you ever change brands, and why?
- Do they work well for you?
- Do the laxatives work as expected at first but then become less effective?
- How much laxative do you use (pills, pieces, or teaspoons), and why?
- Do you keep having to increase the quantity in order to have the same desired effect?
- Do some kinds of laxatives work better than others?
- How often do you use them?
- Are there extended periods of time when you do not use them, and why?
- Do you use other eating disorder behaviors when not using laxatives, and why?
- Does laxative use ever interfere with daily events due to unexpected diarrhea?
- Do you time the use of laxatives to coincide with events so as to avoid the embarrassment of having to use the restroom?
- Have you ever had an "accident," and where were you?
- Do you avoid social situations for fear of having to use the restroom unexpectedly?
- Do you ever experience blood in your stool coinciding with laxative use?

Eating Disorder Behaviors 125

- Have you ever felt dizzy or faint or collapsed, likely as a result of laxative use?
- Have you seen a doctor about these symptoms?
- Are you being monitored by a physician to determine metabolic, cardiac, or renal status?
- Are you aware laxative use can be dangerous and even fatal?
- Do you spend a lot of money on laxatives?
- Where do you get laxatives? Do you purchase or steal them from pharmacies? Do you steal them from parents or grandparents, or do friends supply them to you?
- Where do you have bowel movements when toilets are not available?
- Do you weigh yourself after bowel movements?

Suppositories

> *"Now I am at the point where I have to use excessive amounts of laxatives, enemas, and suppositories just to relieve the discomfort of constipation."*

Rectal suppositories, which are solid, were designed to relieve symptoms of constipation. Different kinds come in various strengths of action. They are used by those with eating disorders for relief of constipation and are sometimes used with the hope of losing weight. They are used because they work in minutes, whereas laxatives can take several hours. Where laxatives may cause diarrhea and trigger bowel movements at unpredictable times, suppositories do not cause diarrhea and may be used precisely when desired. They are portable, making them available anytime, anyplace. Also, laxatives may be vomited before they have emptied from the stomach and therefore will be ineffective. Suppositories become a more reliable and predictable form of purging. Though not dangerous, individuals may become dependent on them. It is good to advise that they do not cause weight loss by removing fat or preventing calorie absorption and are costly.

Enemas

An enema is a procedure where a liquid is injected through the anus into the rectum. It is usually performed to relieve constipation. The fluids used are themselves call enemas. Typical liquids may be just tap water or chemical solutions.

Commercial enema solutions purchased over the counter in pharmacies are liquids in containers that have an elongated tip and are inserted through the anus into the rectum. They cause distention of the rectum or chemical irritation to stimulate a bowel movement. They are used for

126   Eating Disorder Behaviors

the same purposes as suppositories. There are different kinds with different strengths. They are not dangerous when used as directed and infrequently but are costly, and some individuals become dependent on their use as well. If enemas are used daily, chemicals such as phosphates can be absorbed into the blood at toxic levels. Enemas requiring large volumes of fluid, even water, can be dangerous and cause tears in the bowel.

What makes some enemas dangerous is that toxic or caustic substances are used in place of water or commercial enema solutions. Any liquid may serve to perform an enema. Harsh cleaning solutions and especially those containing caustic chemicals can be harmful and even lethal. Detergents, sulfuric acid, formalin, ammonia, sodium hydroxide, hydrogen peroxide, and others have been attempted. They can cause toxicity or severe bowel damage and may result in surgery or cause death.

Questions

- Do you use enemas or suppositories, and why?
- Do you use them for weight loss purposes?
- Do you use them to deal with constipation?
- How many do you use in a given day?
- How often do you use them?
- Do they serve the purpose you use them for?
- Do you spend much money purchasing them?
- Are there times you chose not to use them, and why?
- Do you use other eating disorder behaviors deliberately when not using enemas or suppositories?
- If you use enemas, do you use pharmaceutical ones recommended for constipation, or do you use other liquids including water or drain cleaning products, and why?
- Do enemas ever cause pain or bleeding?

Diuretics

Diuretics are medications used to cause a loss of water by stimulating the release of water by the kidneys. Health reasons for their use are to help lower blood pressure as well as to relieve water retention and resulting premenstrual symptoms. Diuretics are also taken to help lose weight. Diuretics can initially work well to cause weight loss, but the body will learn to compensate for the water loss and then learn to counter this phenomenon. Weight retention may occur after diuretics have been discontinued, and individuals need to expect this. The body will then normalize body water needs over days or weeks, leading to some water loss and possibly weight loss. The bottom line is that diuretics, like laxatives, do not result in reliable weight loss. They too may be costly. Diuretics can also lead to metabolic abnormalities (Finsterer & Stollberger, 2014).

Questions

- Do you or have you ever used diuretics, and why?
- What kinds or brands do you use?
- Are you being followed by your doctor for medical monitoring of your electrolytes as well as cardiac and renal status?

Breastfeeding

Breastfeeding serves to provide nourishment to infants. For those with eating disorders it may serve as a mechanism to lose weight after the inevitable weight gain of pregnancy. It is estimated that a woman will lose between 500 and 800 calories daily with breastfeeding. After delivery, women are expected to increase their daily nutrition to compensate for calorie loss due to nursing. Some will breast feed as well as restrict, vomit, or exercise to expedite weight loss.

Questions

- Do you use breastfeeding to lose weight?
- How many calories have you heard you can lose with breastfeeding?
- Are you eating enough extra to make up for the calorie loss of breastfeeding?
- Are you hoping to lose weight further as your uterus shrinks and your blood volume normalizes after delivery?
- Have you begun to introduce eating disorder behaviors that were put on hold while you were pregnant, and what are these?

Withholding Insulin: Insulin-Dependent Diabetes Mellitus

Diabetes is a health condition where the body cannot process blood sugar adequately or at all. Type 2 diabetes can usually be controlled with diet and exercise, while type 1 diabetes or insulin-dependent diabetes mellitus (IDDM) requires injecting insulin as well. Those with IDDM are required to monitor their blood sugar levels by poking a finger with a lancet and placing blood onto a chemstrip that is then inserted into an electronic glucose monitoring machine. The monitor displays an accurate blood sugar value. There are insulin pumps that read blood sugars and dose an appropriate amount of insulin automatically.

Those who have an eating disorder and have IDDM may choose to withhold taking insulin (Moosavi, Kreisman & Hall, 2015). What this does is to raise the blood glucose level, after which glucose is excreted in high concentrations. This prevents glucose from being taken up into various body organs needed for valuable energy. Those who withhold insulin are reluctant to monitor their blood sugars regularly. They also may take doses of insulin blindly while not knowing how much insulin they really need to take. These behaviors can induce a diabetic coma where someone's blood sugars are so high, individuals become unconscious and may die. Taking too much insulin can lead to insulin-induced coma and have the same catastrophic result. Those with IDDM need to be followed very closely to ensure regular daily monitoring and they are taking accurate insulin doses. If controlling blood sugar is difficult, they may need to be hospitalized for close medical observations and professional management of their diabetes. Acquiring regular HbA1c blood levels will help to assess the average blood glucose concentration over several months.

Anyone with poorly controlled diabetes may be considered impaired because of the risk of dizziness or losing consciousness while driving a vehicle. It may be necessary to have their driver's license suspended until they are deemed medically stable. The medical risks of uncontrolled blood glucose such as kidney failure, gangrene of extremities, and blindness need to be discussed.

General questions for those with insulin dependent or non-insulin dependent diabetes include:

- Are you using insulin, pills, diet, or exercise to control diabetes?
- How long have you had diabetes?
- Is there anyone else in your family with diabetes?
- Who are your medical caregivers—family physician, endocrinologist, diabetic clinic?
- Are you currently being followed by these professionals?
- Do you have a nutritionist?
- Do you have adequate diabetic control, and if not, why?

Questions for those with *insulin-dependent diabetes*:

- How long have you been using insulin?
- How old were you when you started to use insulin?
- What kinds and doses of insulin do you use?
- Have there been any recent changes in your insulin regime, and why?
- How does diabetes affect your eating disorder, and why?
- Do you alter your diet, exercise, or insulin use for body image or weight issues?
- Are you currently doing this, and for how long?

Eating Disorder Behaviors | 129

- Are there times when you do not withhold your insulin, and why?
- What triggers you to alter insulin use, diet, or exercise?
- Do your health care workers know, and which ones?
- Do you ever get any symptoms?
- Have you ever fallen or lost consciousness?
- Have you ever had to go to the emergency room as a result, and why?
- Do others warn you about the dangers of playing with your insulin and diet?
- Do you know the possible risks?
- Do you know that it can be fatal or cause premature organ damage such as blindness, kidney damage, or gangrene of the fingers and toes and even limbs.
- Did you know that you would not be a candidate for a kidney transplant if you have been known to deliberately cause kidney damage due to the eating disorder?
- Where did you learn to withhold insulin?
- Do you know anyone else who withholds insulin?
- Do you have a suicide wish because you withhold insulin and do not monitor blood sugars?
- Who monitors your diabetes with you?
- Who gives you insulin if you do not do it yourself?
- Is withholding insulin connected with other eating disorder behaviors?
- Is it used in place of another eating disorder behavior?
- Has there been any organ damage to date that your doctors are monitoring?
- Do you use other eating disorder behaviors while withholding insulin or instead of doing this? If so, why and when?

Phlebotomy

Phlebotomy is the act of removing blood by inserting a needle into a vein then draining a quantity. Self-phlebotomy would usually be done by health care professionals who are trained in this such as nurses, lab technicians, or physicians. The removal of blood will cause some degree of temporary weight loss (Grewal & Birmingham, 2003). Frequent users of this method will become anemic and may require blood transfusions. Ask how often, why, and where phlebotomy is performed as well as how much blood is taken. Is it done for weight loss, superstitious reasons, spiritual cleansing, or punishment reasons?

Rumination

Rumination is a behavior in which someone eats then regurgitates the food back into the mouth, where it is chewed then swallowed again.

130　Eating Disorder Behaviors

Questions

- Why do you ruminate?
- Do you ruminate in specific situations or locations or anytime?

Calorie Burning and Metabolism Altering Behaviors

Exercise

Exercise is commonly engaged in in many societies. It may be used for physical, mental, and spiritual well-being. It may also be used for competition or for social interaction. For those with eating disorders, it may be used for these reasons but also specifically for body image and weight control. Exercise may be used for several purposes at the same time or vary depending on what it is required for. Some may engage in competitive sport, healthy objectives, and weight loss at the same time. At other times exercise may only focus on weight loss.

Engaging in exercise for body image or weight control may be a minor or major commitment. Exercise may be the primary eating disorder behavior valued above restricting, vomiting, laxative abuse, or any other eating disorder behavior. The importance of exercise for those with eating disorders may be greatly underestimated and therefore contribute to an ineffective treatment.

When someone with an eating disorder relies on exercise but is unable to engage in it, they may then depend on other eating disorder behaviors to cope. As an example, when a runner sprains an ankle or grows a wart on the bottom side of the foot that prevents them from running, extreme restricting, vomiting behaviors, or any other eating disorder behaviors may arise in compensation. Some of the severest forms of anorexia nervosa evolve from those with major exercise compulsions.

For some, the eating disorder will not have been in place before experiencing an injury that has prevented someone from exercising. There may or may not have been a body image concern prior to an injury, but an eating disorder may evolve in response for some.

A consequence for those who depend on exercise for weight control can be significant weight gain when they decrease or stop exercising. This is often seen in teenagers who have been active in sports during their school years then become sedentary when they go to college or get into the work world and have dropped athletic activities.

The dependence on exercise can be compared to a shark that must keep swimming or it will drown. Any letting up on exercise demands can make individuals feel they are at risk of weight gain and are failures for giving in. Some who are exercise committed cannot imagine they will ever be able to decrease exercising. They may be devastated by this prospect.

Exercise may have a regular predictable pattern or be intermittent and unpredictable. Regularity depends on the opportunity to exercise and triggers to engage in it. Any other eating disorder behavior may be substituted for exercising.

Exercise, as an eating disorder behavior, can be performed in plain sight of others without suspicion. How often do we see people running, jogging, biking, hiking, or training for competition such as for a triathlon, marathon run, or rowing? Vomiting in public is socially unacceptable but going to the gym is not. Those who exercise are seen as having it together or disciplined and are envied for their diligence and success with being able to stick to such healthy and weight controlling endeavors. Exercising is something that has multiple venues available to it. Some venues are public while others will be private, such as in someone's home.

The end point for exercising may be for the purpose of being healthy, toned, buff, in shape, firm, or not flabby or to become trim, thin, or even emaciated. Determine the goals of exercising. If a goal is identified for one specific reason, be sure to ask if there are other reasons as well. For those who feel they are exercising for health reasons, inquire further to determine if there could be an underlying weight control component to their motives. When querying about exercise or physical activity, it is necessary to ask what they mean by exercise, as they may not feel that walking a dog, shopping, or doing housework are important physical activities or kinds of exercise.

Those who use exercise to control weight or body image will give reasons such as:

- To burn calories.
- To burn fat.
- To prevent weight gain.
- To lose weight.
- To maintain weigh.
- To look emaciated.
- To look bony.

We need to ask the end point for each kind of exercise session. Why do they stop after a given exercise period?

Exercise may be a family affair. A parent or sibling may be involved with exercise as well. There may be competition between family members involving the amount someone exercises or between those who are trying to lose weight deliberately. The one with an eating disorder may be triggered by a thinner sibling or parent who may not be body image conscious. Family members may exercise together. A mother or father and daughter may run together and even share the same diet. They may both be in competition for weight loss.

132   Eating Disorder Behaviors

Competitive sport brings many sources of body image pressures. There does not seem to be a sport that is devoid of the risk of these pressures. There are competitive sports for which there are defined weight categories. Rowing and wresting are examples.

Competitive swimming, including university, national and Olympic levels, are rife with body image and weight control problems. For swimming there are no weight-qualifying criteria. However, weight can be an issue for coaches. Swimmers tell stories of having to be weighed in front of other swimmers where their weight is announced to all in a weight-shaming way. Swimmers may be told they have to lose weight in order to stay on the team. Teams may be told that they have to lose weight so they look good on TV. Team members who have never been body image conscious or been on a diet will take up eating disorder behaviors to meet weight expectations. Restricting as well as laxative, diuretic, or diet pill consumption may be starter weight loss behaviors, but with limiting calories leading to starvation the drive to binge will likely come to the forefront. In order to counter bingeing and the risk of weight gain, swimmers may indulge in vomiting behaviors. Whole swim teams are reported to be engaged in bulimia. Once invested in bulimia, there then may come significant medical risks including electrolyte, cardiac, or renal compromise. Further risk comes with athletes underperforming due to weakness, and lethargy as well as depression. Dehydration due to restricting fluids, vomiting, and the use of laxatives and diuretics leads to weakness and medical risks.

Competitive *horseback riding* brings similar weight and body image pressures, as do other sports. Why would a rider need to control body image? They report that they need to look as good as the horse. It is believed that if a rider is seen as trim that this will be registered by the judges and be factored into their rating of the rider. Also, the added confidence one gains with feeling good about their weight will possibly intimidate other riders who are not as self-assured or feel bad about their own weight. Those that participate in the ice sport curling may feel they, too, will have the competitive edge over rival teams if they feel comfortable with their own body image and radiate self-confidence.

Non-sport or athletic physical activities may be used. *Fidgeting* is seen as a calorie burning activity. Some people are naturally fidgety, while some will deliberately fidget by keeping feet and legs in motion while sitting or standing. *Sitting straight* is believed to also burn calories, as sitting in a straight position requires active engagement of back muscles. Standing instead of sitting in the workplace or other situations is used to burn calories, as standing, too, requires active engagement of groups of muscles. The current trend in standing at work stations is an excellent example of someone burning calories for body image control in full view of coworkers without giving away eating disorder intent. The amount of time someone can invest in *house cleaning* in a day can rival a full day of paid employment. The actions of being on their feet and moving around the whole time provides dedicated physical activity without leaving the home or even being noticed. *Walking the dog* becomes a legitimate reason to exercise and can take up hours daily.

Injuries are an inevitability for many. Some injuries are minor and may be only be seen as a nuisance or minor setback, while others may be deemed as major or even life threatening. Runners run the risk of being hit by traffic when crossing roads. This can lead to significant injury or even death. Minor injuries to the rest of us may be interpreted as catastrophic to someone using exercise to control weight. Injuries can lead to terrible anxiety and even severe depression. An individual may become suicidal or deal with the stress of an injury by using drugs and alcohol or self-mutilation to cope.

When asking individuals about physical activity, we need to determine how they clothe themselves during exercise. As mentioned in the section on "Clothing," some will dress in excess to help them burn calories by sweating more or by underdressing to become cold, with the idea of burning calories while the body reheats itself. Those who attend gyms may have a set regime they follow. There may be a number of exercise activities that they engage in. Each may have a specific calorie-burning goal attributed to it.

Weights are typically used to build muscle tone and to build muscle mass. This leads to weight gain in muscle. Muscle-induced weight gain may be tolerated because it is not weight gain due to fat tissue and will increase the muscle-to-fat ratio of the body. It may be seen as a healthier cause of weight increase compared to fat tissue. Exercise is not a very good way to lose weight. It requires an immense amount of time and effort to lead to modest weight control.

Exercise or other activities can be extremely habit forming. The drive to exercise may be regardless of body image purposes. It can be a full-on obsession. It may be associated with obsessive-compulsive disorder and not necessarily be an eating disorder-founded obsession. The kinds of exercises and combinations of their use along with other exercise practices is near endless.

Although there are countless inexpensive ways to exercise, there can be financial costs to others. Money for gym memberships can be costly. Funds escalate when activity coaches are hired. The financial costs can be prohibitive. Those in competitive sports will incur additional costs with hiring professional athletic coaches. As well, they have to purchase expensive bicycles and associated equipment such as GPS devices. Bicycles alone can exceed $10,000 each. Swimmers may have to purchase pool time. Exorbitant costs can prohibit some from having money to purchase food. The obsession with exercise and competition as well as the need to pay for coaches and equipment plays heavily into the eating disorder mentality.

134 Eating Disorder Behaviors

Gyms provide an added set of eating disorder pressures. Gyms often have ceiling-high mirrors where no one can look around without seeing themselves as well as others. These mirror images are triggering and can make individuals feel bad or even good about their body image. Regardless, they can be motivating and deflating at the same time. As well, there will be others in the gym who are deemed as trim or slimmer or more fit driving eating disorder attitudes further. Gyms always have scales for members to weight themselves. For those trying to recover, it is best to avoid most gyms.

Questions

- Do you exercise?
- What kinds of exercise do you use?
- Why do you exercise?
- Where do you exercise and why?
- Do you exercise to control body image and weight?
- Do you exercise for enjoyment, because you are in a competitive sport, or for health reasons?
- Are you in competition with others involved with exercise or sport such as family, friends, others with eating disorders, or teammates?
- Are you in a competitive sport with formal weight categories or weight expectations set by coaches?
- Are you worried about being kicked off of a team if you do not control your weight?
- If you exercise in a gym, are you affected negatively regarding your body image by mirrors or the trim bodies of others?
- Do you engage in other eating disorder behaviors along with sport activities in order to control weight such as vomiting or laxative or diuretic use?
- Does exercise put you at any serious health risks, including being hit by traffic or cardiac arrest?
- How many days of the week do you exercise, and how much time do you spend with each exercise?
- How do you motivate yourself to exercise?
- Are there periods of time when you do not exercise, and why?
- Do you exercise with others, and who are they?
- Do others admire your dedication to exercise?
- Does the exercise dedication of others cause you to feel inadequate with regard to your own exercise?
- Have you ever been criticized for being physically lazy or out of shape?
- What is your goal for exercising with regard to weight or body image control?

Eating Disorder Behaviors 135

- Do you have a set exercise calorie burning count that you have set, and how much is this?
- How do you determine the degree of calorie-burning potential for any given exercise, and where do you get your information for establishing this?
- Do you experience exhaustion, a faint feeling, dizziness, or chest pain or notice your heart race during or after exercise?
- Have you experienced an injury from exercising, and how did this affect your attitude toward not being able to control weight through exercise?
- Do you use other eating disorder behaviors to compensate for being able to exercise, and which ones?
- Do you underdress, then run or power walk in cold weather?
- If you have not been exercising as you hoped for, how does this make you feel, including having feelings of self-loathing, guilt, shame, or being a failure?
- Do you think exercise is a compulsion?
- If you run, jog, or power walk, do you add weights to your arms or legs?
- Is exercise linked to other eating disorder behaviors, or are some put on hold during periods of exercise focus?
- Do you use exercise to punish yourself?
- Are you afraid to decrease or stop exercising for fear of gaining weight?
- Are you following the advice of an athletic coach?
- Do you hide exercise from others and how do you do this?
- Do you think exercise or sport activities allow you to engage in your weight loss agenda without others suspecting?
- Do you use your pet to aid with exercising, such as walking your dog?
- Are you involved with other activities that are not specifically exercise or sport activities to aid in burning calories, such as doing housework, walking the dog, or commuting to work and school by walking or cycling?
- Do you stand for prolonged periods of time while at work or studying or fidget deliberately to burn calories?
- Does engaging in physical activity cost much money?

Heating Blankets

Heating blankets may be used to increase body temperature with the hope more calories will be burned. Some may wear multiple articles of clothing to bed as well as add multiple layers of blankets including a heating blanket. Under all of these blankets and extra clothing, some may exercise in bed as well. Heating blankets may be used just for warming, as those with

136 Eating Disorder Behaviors

eating disorders often feel cold and may actually have a lower core body temperature. Heating blankets are used to aid with refeeding.

Metabolism Boosters

Metabolism boosters come in many forms. Caffeine, nicotine, and a number of over-the-counter diet pills stimulate metabolism. Prescription medications including those to treat attention deficit hyperactivity disorder (ADHD) including dexedrine are sought-after drugs to raise metabolic rate for weight loss purposes. Illicit drugs including amphetamines and narcotics serve the same purposes. Stimulants can raise metabolism and possibly suppress appetite temporarily, but they can present serious medical risks that can result in cardiac dysrhythmias and death.

Questions

- Do you or have you ever taken metabolism boosters?
- What kinds or brands do you use?
- Do you use those that are over-the-counter, prescription, or illicit drugs?
- Are you aware that some of these medications are dangerous and can even result in death?
- Have you ever noticed your heart race, experienced chest pain, or developed shortness of breath with use of these medications?
- Do you think they really work, or are you just hopeful?

Nonchemical Methods of Altering Metabolism

Paying attention to the natural metabolic functions of the body or trying to actually control metabolism may be key focuses for those with eating disorders. There are beliefs based on hard scientific data and others that have not been proven or are just myths. Regardless of the validity of the beliefs, the power they inject into directing the course of the eating disorder can be profound.

Some perceived ways of increasing metabolism are:

- Taking vitamins B6 and 12.
- Eat before 7 p.m., as metabolism drops at night.
- Consuming apple cider vinegar, spices including black pepper, chili, and garlic, sea weed as well as green tea, cayenne pepper, and citrus water.
- Eating four 100 calorie meals will burn more calories than one 400 calorie meal.

Eating Disorder Behaviors 137

- Eat high calorie foods earlier in the day.
- Any exercise.
- Maintaining body posture, which involves the active use of several muscles, burns calories.
- Consuming protein increases metabolism.
- As with maintaining good posture, eating while standing.
- Changing exercise patterns and nutrition will help to increase metabolism.
- Binge after you eat a normal meal, as your metabolism will be up.
- Eat cold foods and drinks.
- Exercising in cold or hot environments.

Questions

- Do you believe you can alter your metabolism?
- What methods have you used?
- Have these methods to alter metabolism worked to your satisfaction?
- Have you experiences weight loss and then rebound weight gain, resulting in an increase in your weight above what it was before you lost weight?
- Have you heard of the set-point theory of weight?

Body Gauging Behaviors

Scale

Some believe that the term eating disorder is a misnomer and that it is really a *weight phobia disorder*, where control of eating is really just a means to control weight. It then is not much of a surprise that the use of the scale is ubiquitous in the eating disorder world.

The reasons for using the scale are varied, and the weight displayed will have different meanings to different individuals. When someone gets on a scale, the hoped-for weight value displayed can vary between individuals. Most will hope the number will drop or be lower, with weight loss being the desired result. Some will be fine if there is no increase in weight, and some will hope for weight increases. The emotional responses can vary. If someone wishes to lose weight but this has not occurred, then this can be devastating. However, another may be grateful or relieved if there is at least no weight increase.

Scales can be found in the family home, one's own dwelling, the gym, doctor's offices, or in the homes of friends and family. Some may transport them if they are on the move and away from home. Variations in how different scales read creates problems with trusting scale readings.

138 Eating Disorder Behaviors

This variation can cause anxiety with not knowing which scale to trust or indeed not being able to trust any scale.

To achieve the lowest weight at a given time, individuals weigh themselves after they wake up and have used the restroom and will weigh either naked or with minimal clothing. The first morning weight is thought to be the lowest weight of the day by many.

Some will weigh once in the morning and possibly once in the evening. Others do not weight themselves ever, and others may weigh themselves "all day," reporting over 20 times a day.

Some will weigh themselves at different times of the day. The reasons may vary. Reasons for weighing at different times of the day may be:

- To see how much weight has increased with eating
- To see how much weight may have been burned off with exercising
- To see how much weight will be lost with going to the restroom
- To determine normal fluctuations in daily weight
- To punish themselves
- To motivate themselves to work harder at losing weight
- To decrease anxiety by determining that they have not gained a weight they would fear
- To determine if they have vomited all of the food they eat

Questions

- Do you use a scale?
- Why do you weigh yourself?
- What readings are you expecting to see on the scale?
- What weight do you fear?
- Where do you weigh yourself?
- Do you have a scale in your home or have access to one in the home of your parents, friends, or partner?
- Do you believe the scales to be accurate, or do you not trust them?
- Do you have access to one scale that you feel is the most accurate and the gold standard for precision, such as in your doctor's office? Do you adjust the readings of other less trusted scales with this one?
- Have your parents or partner ever hidden the scale?
- How often do you weigh yourself in a given day?
- How many days a week or month do you weigh yourself?
- Do you weigh yourself in gyms?
- Have you ever considered throwing the scale away to rid yourself of this body image trigger?
- How does it make you feel if the weight value is more than you were hoping for?

Mirrors

The use of mirrors is a cornerstone tool for gauging body image and similar to use of the scale and clothing.

Mirrors and other reflective surfaces are everywhere in society including our homes, friends and family's dwellings, schools, gyms, and stores, and in pretty much any restroom in the community. It is nearly impossible to not come across a mirror deliberately or accidentally. There are often several mirrors in homes, including in all of the bedrooms, restrooms, hallway closet doors, living rooms, and basements. Because there will be several mirrors in someone's home, it may be difficult if not impossible to avoid seeing one's self in a mirror. Aside from mirrors, there are other reflective surfaces including windows, especially store windows.

Attempts to avoid mirror exposure in a dwelling may include turning mirrors around so the reflective surface faces the wall, taking them off the wall, and hiding them in a closet. Covering full length mirrors with posters so only the face in visible may be of help. For mirrors that cannot be covered or taken down, such as those in the restroom, it is advised to view the mirrors for as short a time as possible and try to only look at areas of the body that are not a particular focus of scrutiny, such as with cleaning teeth or grooming hair. If there are others who share a home, then it becomes more difficult to decrease mirror availability. Whether at home or in the community, it is advised to follow the *one second rule*, where if someone catches themselves looking at any reflective surface, they turn away immediately and move on. Practice makes perfect.

Different individuals may scrutinize different parts of their body for different reasons. Some look in the mirror to get a general opinion of their body shape. They may want to see an overall thinness, fit, or firm look to their body. They may see what they do not want to see, which is an oversized or overweight body. Others may want to scrutinize very specific parts of their body.

Some will want to observe prominent collarbones, ribs, or hip bones as a visual measure of weight loss success. Some focus on their stomach or abdomen and wish to see a scaphoid or hollow abdomen. Others are fussy about how their upper arms and thighs look. Some do not want to see their thighs touch, as this makes them feel they are too big. The face may be a major source of dissatisfaction, where a thinner face is desired. Those who vomit and as a result experience swollen parotid glands just in front of the ears or swollen submandibular glands located under the jaw deplore these changes. The fear of seeing swollen glands may discourage some from vomiting temporarily.

Other concerns may be that individuals want to see a firm or toned body. Any area deemed loose or flabby is undesirable. The upper arms, thighs, and abdomen are particularly seen as problematic this way.

140 Eating Disorder Behaviors

Questions

- Do you use mirrors to gauge body size or shape?
- What mirrors do you have access to?
- Are there any mirrors you can remove or cover up?
- What parts of your body are you scrutinizing with the mirror?
- Are you triggered by reflections in store windows or mirrors?
- What are you hoping to see in the mirror?
- What are you not hoping to see?
- What do you do in response to not liking what you see?
- Do you want to punish or harm yourself?
- Do you have plans to remove or cover mirrors?
- Can you set a goal to give yourself a one second limit on viewing yourself in mirrors?

Clothing

The use of clothing plays an important role serving many different functions for those with eating disorders. Clothing can be used to hide how an individual looks. Sometimes they are trying to hide how "fat" or "gross" they feel. Regardless of whether someone is severely underweight, normal weight, or a higher weight, these feelings can prevail. For others they may wish to hide how "thin" or starved looking they may be. Some will feel grossly overweight while knowing they are emaciated, and yet try to hide both images from others. There is a tendency to wear loose and bulky clothing. Clothing may be layered to give the appearance of having a larger body. Clothing may be layered for warmth, as well. Wearing extra clothing may help to increase perspiration, thought to increase calorie burning.

Clothing may be used to gauge body size or shape, similar to how mirrors and scales are used. Typically, there will be one or more pieces of tight clothing. Tight jeans are commonly used. The idea is that if someone fits loosely in a particular piece of clothing, they will feel comfortable with their body size, as the clothing has been chosen to create a line in the sand as to when the body is oversized, just right, or under an acceptable size. When clothing is deemed tight, this will motivate an individual to lose more weight.

Another way clothing is used to evaluate body shape is by choosing a desired *clothing size* for which one feels is acceptable. Clothing sizes vary amongst clothing manufacturers and the countries they are made in. Some chose to *underdress* in cold weather with the notion that a cold environment will help to burn more calories.

Questions

- Do you use clothing to gauge body size, shape, or weight?
- What pieces of clothing do you use that act as "tight clothing"?

Eating Disorder Behaviors 141

- Do you use a belt to gauge body size?
- Do you choose clothing by their sizes?
- Currently, what clothing size do you fit into?
- What clothing size would you like to be, and are you trying to lose weight to match this size?
- Do you use clothing to hide your body?
- Do you cover your body to hide how underweight you are or because you feel you are too large? Do you hide your body for both reasons?
- Do you wear heavier clothing or layer clothing in order to cause sweating?
- Do you wear heavier clothing or layer clothing because you are cold?
- Do you underdress in order to cause your body to become cold?
- If you cannot fit comfortably into your clothes, how does this make you feel?
- Do you use loose clothing such as sweat pants or yoga clothing to decrease the sensation of tightness with wearing clothes?

Other Body Size Gauging Methods

Aside from use of the scale, mirror or clothes there are other methods some chose to gauge body size and shape. *Grabbing* thighs, arms, abdomen, buttocks, or hips provides a way to assess body size and shape. A *measuring tape* to measure parts of the body may be used. *Body calipers* used by professional health caregivers to determine percent body fat can be employed. There are commercial electronic devices used that allegedly help to assess body fat.

Binge Eating and Related Behaviors

Binge Eating

> *"When I was at work, I'd be thinking of the pizza or Chinese food*
> *I would order for dinner. Sometimes I would order both on top of the*
> *bag of chips and 2 liter bottle of pop."*

> *"The family I stayed with never mentioned anything, but I'm sure*
> *they saw the empty food cans pile up and the cupboards being*
> *emptied on a regular basis."*

Binge eating or bingeing has been difficult to define with much clarity. Loosely, binge eating occurs when someone eats an inordinate amount of food for what would be expected for any given person in the context of their social norms. Added to this is that there must be a sense of a lack of control with eating. What is hard to do is to describe how much food in terms of quantity or calories constitutes a binge. Also defining a binge

142 Eating Disorder Behaviors

is that it occurs in a discrete period of time. Cultural attitudes toward food need to be calculated in when trying to determine whether someone is bingeing or not. Meal quantities and food kinds vary greatly among ethnic and religious groups.

> *"I could never imagine going out for dinner with family and not be stressed out before, during, and after the meal. I could never imagine sitting down to Thanksgiving or Christmas dinner with my family and enjoying the special time."*

Celebratory or festive occasions such as birthdays, weddings, Thanksgiving, and religious holidays encourage hearty eating. Eating rich foods including desserts and going back for second or even third helpings are the norm. This would not be described as bingeing unless a person does have an eating disorder and is eating for binge purposes. Ordering large quantities of food including pizza Friday nights in a university dorm where individuals may customarily eat whole pizzas would not be described as binge eating in university culture.

> *"But my habits of coming home late from the dance bar that I worked with, ordering two large pizzas and purging them immediately in the downstairs bathroom proved to be a greater issue for my friends than they expected. I was asked to leave. I have never been more ashamed."*

Although people will state that they are binge eating, it is important to ask what they mean by a binge. If they say a binge is eating an apple or two crackers then they are not truly bingeing. This would be described as a *subjective binge.* There is a gray zone as to what a real binge is when it comes to quantities. When is a large meal just a large meal, or when is it a binge? We need to determine when eating is *"binge-like,"* meaning eating out of control or eating foods that one would typically eat during a binge, but the quantity is in question to describe a binge.

When someone eats 3,000–4,000 calories during a single eating period but does not feel out of control, it may just be moot point as to whether it is a proper binge or not. If individuals vomit after this large meal due to fear of weight gain, does it really matter if they have eaten out of control or not?

Emotionally, it can matter little whether someone is truly binge eating or engaging in subjective binges. Self -loathing, self-hatred, guilt, and shame with eating any quantity of food can be the same. It is important to be aware of this so we give clients the support they need.

Binge foods tend to be sweet, salty, or rich in butter, oil, or cream. They come under the umbrella of *snack* or *junk food.* Such foods may include ice cream, potatoes chips, cookies, candies, including chocolate, and any baking, including bread. Pizza, hamburgers, and fries and Chinese food are often binge foods.

Less typically, some binge on what they deem healthier meals, including meat and potato type meals. Some binge on culturally familiar foods. A girl growing up in a Ukrainian family might prefer to binge on perogies rather than doughnuts.

Individuals can binge virtually anywhere in society and in front of others, often without being detected. Binge eating can occur by itself but may be associated with other eating disorders. Commonly, bingeing is associated with vomiting.

Binges may happen in patterns or may not. They may be predictable or unpredictable.

Questions

- What do you describe as a binge for you?
- What foods do you binge on?
- Where do you get binge food from?
- Do you hoard food or acquire food from garbage cans or dumpsters?
- Do you purchase or steal food?
- How much money do you spend on food in a day, week, or month?
- Do you steal money from family, friends, or a partner?
- Why do you binge?
- What triggers you to binge?
- Where are all the places you binge?
- What interferes with you being able to carry out a binge?
- Do you think you binge because you are undernourished?
- Where do you get money for binge food, including stealing money?

Grazing

Grazing is not an officially defined eating term but a common way to describe how one eats. It is often used in the context of "I eat all day" or "I snack all day" or "I eat on and off all day." The quantity of food for any given session of eating will not be of binge quantity. The total daily intake could easily match binge quantities in terms of volume or calories. There are no criteria that include eating out of control, as there is for binge eating or in a discrete time period. Total daily intake may match normal eating limits or even less.

Trap Lines

A trap line is a term to describe the act of going from one source of food to another. There are different food trap lines. One is a sit-down restaurant

144 Eating Disorder Behaviors

trap line where individuals go from one restaurant then to others, one after the other. They may binge in each restaurant as well as vomit in that restaurant's toilet. Some will wait to get home before vomiting. The trap line may only involve two or three restaurants or as many as a dozen or more in a single day. People may start a trap line at a food court where there will be several restaurants. Food may be purchased from any combination of restaurants as well, as they will have easy access to toilets. After this, they may travel to the next food court in a different mall, again feasting from several restaurants. They then may travel downtown, where there will be a cornucopia of more restaurants.

Other kinds of trap lines involve takeout, order-in, or food delivery restaurants. Some may chose not to eat inside restaurants but to order takeout food from one restaurant after another that they will consume elsewhere. Some will phone one delivery restaurant, order enough food for several people, then eat it in their own home. Added to this will be a call to yet another delivery restaurant, after which they consume and vomit this food. Some may engage in sit-down, takeout and delivery restaurant trap lines as well as binge and vomit food already available in the home all in a single day. The financial cost of these practices can be enormous.

Hoarding

Hoarding food is a common practice for those with eating disorders. People hoard food in several ways. They will buy food, then store it in cupboards in their homes. Any type of food, including binge foods, may be hoarded this way. Hoarded food is often stored but not eaten. Some may hoard food in bedroom drawers and cupboards. Some will carry food in plastic containers without ever eating it. Food may be hoarded in cars and in the work place as well.

The reasons for hoarding are varied. For some, it guarantees a food source to be used for bingeing should they need it. It provides a kind of fascination or enticement having food near that is felt to be forbidden.

Some will hoard food then predictably throw it away once it is past its expiration date. Others may just let the food rot. Family, partners, or roommates may need to have to throw food out for them. Hoarding is an expensive and wasteful practice. It helps to deplete individuals of funds.

Questions

- Do you hoard food?
- What food do you hoard?
- Why do you hoard food?

- Where do you hoard food?
- Do you eat the hoarded food or do you let it spoil?
- Do you or others get rid of spoiled food?

Stealing Food

One way of acquiring food is by stealing it. Food may be stolen from grocery stores, convenience stores, subway food stands, or any other venders of food. Food can be put in pockets, under clothing, in hand bags and so forth. Food may even be eaten in the store before leaving. Those who work in restaurants may steal food from work to eat on the job or take home. Some steal food from parents, partners, or roommates, which in return creates strained relationships and mistrust. Parents and partners may lock food storage cupboards to prevent this from happening. Some will replace stolen food. In hospitals, food may be stolen from other patients' trays or from the cafeteria. Patients may go into the doctors' sleeping quarters and take food available there.

Stealing food can create serious legal problems. Stores are very aggressive with prosecuting those that steal. The days of promising not to do it again and not being charged are long gone. Legal charges lead to having to hire a lawyer, appear in court, and face prosecution. The lucky ones will be expected to perform some community service and possibly report to a court-assigned official. Certainly, with repeated offenses, criminal charges will ensue, and this could affect the ability to be hired by business or government agencies. Crossing borders can be denied. A criminal record might remain for life.

Individuals steal food for different reasons. A lack of funds will be a prime reason. It is sometimes due to wanting to experience the thrill of stealing and getting away with it. It also may be in hopes of actually being caught so this behavior will stop or to get attention so they will be directed to resources for dealing with the eating disorder. Stealing food may be impulsive even if there are funds available.

Stealing food, cash, or funds from credit card and debit accounts may be an extension of an already existing theft pattern. Kleptomania is not uncommon in those with eating disorders. Stealing of clothing, jewelry, cosmetics, and anything else available in stores is possible. Some steal purses, wallets, and cars, which will lead to more serious legal entanglements, including jail time.

Questions

- Do you or have you ever stolen food?
- Do you currently steal food?

146 Eating Disorder Behaviors

- What food do you steal, and why?
- Do you steal food because you do not have funds, because it is convenient, or because it provides excitement?
- Where do you steal food?
- Do you steal food from family, your partner, or roommates?
- Have you ever been caught stealing food?
- Have you ever been charged for stealing food?
- Do you steal other items besides food?
- Do you think you are a kleptomaniac?

Dumpster Diving

Dumpster diving is just as it sounds. People will go into dumpsters and rummage for food. This will usually happen after stores close. Grocery stores, big and small, will be prime targets. Because stealing from dumpsters is becoming more recognized, stores will lock the dumpsters. This significantly narrows the options for this practice. It also leads others who dumpster dive to meet at dumpsters serendipitously. Dumpster divers, therefore, may form a kind of social network.

The quantities of food and kinds of food are practically endless. Thousands of dollars of food are thrown out daily where there is often unopened packaged food. Whole hams and desserts exist fully packaged. Hygiene, of course, becomes an issue. For those with eating disorders, dumpster diving provides large quantities of free food to binge on. Some eat out of dumpsters because they do not have enough money for food whether they have an eating disorder or not. Those who owe large amounts of money, including for student loans in the tens of thousands of dollars, engage in this practice.

Questions

- Have you ever taken food from dumpsters?
- Do you still do this?
- Why do you do this if there are other sources of food?
- Do you do this because you do not have funds to purchase food to binge with?
- Do you eat in the dumpster or eat it elsewhere?
- Does this bring feelings of shame and guilt, or not?
- Do you meet other dumpster divers at dumpsters?
- Do others have eating disorders, or are they just poor students or people on the street?
- Which stores have unlocked dumpsters that you access?

Restricting Eating Behaviors

> *"It was not a choice to restrict myself, it was not my choice to hurt my body, it was not my choice."*

Restrictive eating or *restricting* may currently be or have been the core eating disorder behavior for most with eating disorders. It is basically the act of consuming less food than the body requires. This could be within a single day or over weeks, months, or even years. Virtually all other eating disorder behaviors aside from bingeing are ancillary to restrictive eating. These other behaviors are utilized to aid or support restricting or when restricting is not working well enough. They also come into play when people cannot maintain restricting or are in an environment where they are not able to restrict.

> *"The only content in my fridge was water and cream for my tea."*

There are multiple methods of restricting that can come into play and are discussed here.

Definitions and Meanings

Restricting, restrictive eating, or food restriction are the same thing. In a colloquial sense, restricting, dieting, fasting, and cleansing may be used interchangeably as meaning the same thing. We do need, however, to enquire as to what these words mean to the individuals with the eating disorder. They may use each of them to indicate they intend to lose weight through reducing calorie intake. However, they may use them in their literal sense, which may indicate different motivations for eating less or just differently.

A *diet*, from a nutrition perspective, just means the sum of food consumed over a given time period. It also may mean to restrict intake for health reasons by reducing harmful substances such as simple carbohydrates, including sugars for those with diabetes, gluten for those with celiac disease, or lactose for those with dairy intolerances and food allergies. It may also mean to increase nutrients when they are lacking in someone's nutrition. Diets may be part of religious or cultural practices or be part of a fad. Diets may be used for weight loss in those with health problems such as diabetes, hypertension, or hip, knee, or foot pain. Diet, in the general public consciousness, however, tends to imply weight loss for body image satisfaction.

148   Eating Disorder Behaviors

Fasting, often used interchangeable with dieting or restricting, may involve not just reducing but abstaining from eating or drinking. It usually implies total abstinence of any food or liquids or of select foods. This is often a part of religious practices—Islam, Christianity, Judaism, and multiple other religious practices. It may be used as a form of healthy eating. Fasting is usually implemented in discrete time frames and not used over the long term.

Cleanses are eating and drinking practices implemented to *detoxify* the body. Cleanses may also be in the form of enemas used to detox the colon. They may be connected to social fads.

Knowing the definitions for these terms will help to sort out what the individuals are really using their restricting practices for. While fasting or cleansing may be used for religious or health reasons, they can certainly be used for body image control.

For individuals who are restricting, ask about all of the other terms they use to define restricting and ask the reason for utilizing them. There may be a number of motivating factors driving restrictive eating.

The essential reason those with eating disorders restrict is to decrease caloric intake. There are many ways to achieve this. The following are examples of this.

Skipping Meals and Snacks

Skipping whole meals is one way to decrease a significant number of calories. Some will skip only one meal a day, while others will skip two or three in a day. The same may be done for snacks as well. This does not eliminate any particular nutrient such as protein, fat, or carbohydrates. It eliminates quantity and calories only. Skipping of meals may be a regular activity or random depending on opportunity or motivating factors.

Meal and Snack Reduction

People may reduce the size of meals or snacks. This is also a way to decrease the quantity or calorie count generally. This may be done instead of skipping whole meals in an attempt not to create as strong a hunger drive, because others are watching them eat or the drive to lose weight is being dealt with by other eating disorder behaviors such as vomiting or exercising. Reducing intake more may lead to binge eating or cause medical symptoms such as palpitations or falling.

Reducing the Available Volume of Food

Skipping and reducing the size of meals are ways to reduce the volume of nutrition intake. Food volume reduction may be accomplished by purchasing smaller sizes of packaged foods. Purchasing smaller potato chip bags or ice-cream containers serves as an example.

Putting food into containers of a specific volume can guarantee an upper limit of food available. Some use plastic containers or bowls or plates of a smaller size to limit food volumes and, therefore, calorie content. Using measuring cups or spoons puts discrete limits on the volume of food.

Reducing the Weight of Food

Some chose to reduce food intake by limiting the weight of food. Weights may be determined by reading the labels of packaged foods or using food weigh scales.

Reducing the Percentage of Food

Some chose to limit food intake by thinking in terms of percentages. They may want to reduce their intake by 75%, 50%, or altogether at times. Most of the time this will be a subjective evaluation of food intake but could certainly be determined accurately by measuring or weighing food or reading package labels.

Calorie Burning Foods—Negative Calorie Foods

There are foods that some feel burn calories after being ingested, called *negative calorie foods*. These foods are believed to require more energy to metabolize them than other foods do. Some foods are thought to burn more calories than they actually deliver to the body; therefore, eating these foods are believed to cause weight loss though not actually proven to do so. For example, eating 200 calories of red cabbage would burn 300 calories with being metabolized. Calorie-burning foods may be used to augment existing restricting patters. Some of these foods are cabbage, lemons, beets, garlic, turnips, and cayenne. There are a few dozen others that are considered negative calorie foods.

Fat Calorie Reducing Diets

Some selectively reduce the fat content of their diet. Fats come in several forms from plant products, dairy, and meat products. Though some attempt to eliminate all fats from their diet, they may be selective and only be focused on eliminating animal fats or fats in salad dressings. Oils in nuts may not be targeted, as they may be deemed as healthy.

There are multiple ways of reducing fat intake.

- Soaking up fat on bacon, pizza, or other foods covered in oils or fats using tissue.
- Observing the fat content listed on food labels.
- Choosing foods with little or no fat content.
- Cutting fatty parts from food.
- Avoiding foods that typically have fat content such as dairy, dressings, sauces, meats, and nuts.

Some fats may be seen as desirable in weight loss. Nuts and nut butters may be eaten in small quantities as they can successfully satiate hunger for periods of times, thus eliminating the drive to binge. Oils in salad dressings, in limited calculated quantities, may serve the same purpose and be tolerated in small amounts.

Carbohydrate Reducing Diets

Carbohydrates are less calorie dense than fats or proteins. However, they have become avoided nutrients like fats and proteins have. Some commercial diets make carbohydrates the most avoided food, as they are blamed as being the number one food type that causes obesity, and if eliminated from diets will cause the quickest weight loss. Research is ongoing to determine the validity of science based and commercial diets. There are a lot of myths out there. Diets that cause the fastest weight loss tend to have the strongest rebound weight gain.

Carbohydrate containing foods include:

- Sugar
- Starches used in breads, pastries, and other baking
- Starches used in pasta
- Grains
- Cereals
- Potatoes
- Beans

Carbohydrates are found as part of other foods including dairy, fruits, and many other vegetables not mentioned. Some carbohydrates are not readily absorbed as a nutrient, such as cellulose. Dietary fibers are carbohydrates but not absorbed and therefore not much of a threat to the dieter. They actually may be seen as a laxative that helps to increase the frequency of bowel movements. Carbohydrate-reducing diets have been known to be lethal.

Protein Reducing Diets

Protein diets have long been a part of fad dieting. Proteins are avoided mainly because they are calorie dense, as fats are. Reducing their intake is, therefore, deemed an effective way of eliminate calories. Red meats, which are rich in protein and fats, are usually the most targeted food to be eliminated. Poultry and even fish may be eliminated for the same reasons. Cheeses, which are rich in dairy fats and protein, tend to be at the top of the list of restricted foods.

Safe Food Choices

The selection of *safe foods* is a commonly mentioned form of restricting. Safe foods are foods felt to be safe to eat in order to prevent weight gain. Typical safe foods will be any food low on fat, protein, or carbohydrates, thus leaving a very thin food selection, likely made up of safe fruits and vegetables. Fruits high in sugar such as tropical fruits will be avoided as well. The choice of safe foods will vary according to the individual. One person's safe food may be another's fear food.

Fear Foods

The term *fear foods* is self-explanatory. *Unsafe foods* may be another term used. These include any food or nutrient that individuals feel put them at risk of weight gain or becoming fat. As mentioned earlier, fats, proteins, and carbohydrates are at the top of the list.

Other typically feared foods are *snack foods* that contain high amounts of sugar or salt or are rich with fats or oils. They are commonly called *junk food*. These include:

- Potato chips
- Ice cream
- Baked foods
- Candies, including chocolate
- Sugary drinks
- Hamburgers, French fries, and pizza

Popcorn is on the fence of being a safe or feared food. Because popcorn, without butter, is usually considered a low-calorie food, it is often eaten to fill-up on so as to avoid eating other foods richer in calories. Because it is effectively a pure carbohydrate, it may be avoided. Popcorn is seen as a food full of air and, therefore, more of a space-occupying food or filler. It is effectively a nutritional Styrofoam.

Vegetarian Diets

Vegetarianism is the practice of limiting or eliminating meat products from the diet. Meats include red meat, poultry, and seafood. Ovovegetarian diets allow consumption of eggs but not dairy products. Ovolacto vegetarianism includes eggs and dairy products. Lacto-vegetarian diets include dairy but not eggs. Vegan diets exclude all animal products including dairy, honey, and eggs. Veganism can include avoidance of all animal products including leather, silk, beeswax, and any products coming from animal sources.

When enquiring about vegetarian beliefs, we need to sort out what beliefs are for weight control purposes or for personal dislikes for animal foods or ethical and religious reasons. There are often eating disorder reasons coexisting with non-eating disorder reasons. These latter reasons play nicely into the eating disorder weight control mentality.

We can attempt to sort out the motivations for incorporating vegetarian diets by asking when the diet started. We can ask "Did it start before the eating disorder, and why?" This may help to determine the legitimacy of individuals' involvement with vegetarian dieting. Also, some will be vegetarian on and off. They will be meat eaters sometimes then not others. We need to ask "Why do you chose to be a vegetarian from time to time, and is this because you are using it for eating disorder purposes?" Vegetarian eating may be an alternate eating disorder behavior and pinch hit for one they have put on hold temporarily. It may be linked to another eating disorder behavior such as exercising when they reengage with exercising.

I hospitalized a 15-year-old girl who would not eat or drink *anything* day after day. She was a self-proclaimed vegetarian. Her health was sustained with intravenous fluids at this time. One day I came in and said, "If you had to choose just *one* food out of a selection of hundreds available on the planet, and you do have to unless you want to stay here forever, what food would you want? Choose just one!" She thought about this carefully and said, "Chocolate milk!" She started to drink chocolate milk, then introduce other foods, and quite quickly we were able to discharge her. Her choice of starting with chocolate milk loosened the lid, as it were, on greatly improved eating.

Selective Eating

Some restrict by eliminating all foods that are deemed unsafe, except for a very few. They have very selective eating patterns. Any food may be selected for various reasons. Usually selected foods will be a limited number of safe foods, eliminating all feared foods.

Eating Disorder Behaviors   153

A typical selective eater would be someone who only eats carrot sticks and celery and drinks water as the only liquid. A selected food may be a favorite food, such as ichiban noodles, that has some caloric content but if eaten exclusively and in limited amounts serves to help prevent weight gain.

Children who may have selective eating patterns may or may not be weight or body image driven. It is important to determine if selective eating is body image driven or not. Individuals may limit food choices due to undesired symptoms caused by diseases. Gut symptoms such as dyspepsia, abdominal pain, nausea, vomiting, or diarrhea can significantly limit one's choice of tolerated foods.

Cotton Ball Diet

Cotton balls are used by those with eating disorders for a few purposes. Some will soak cotton balls with juice, smoothie, or slushy liquid, suck on them to experience the flavor, then spit the cotton balls out. Others may take the soaked cotton balls and swallow them. Cotton in the stomach can suppress appetite and provide a temporary full feeling without the associated calories that food would provide.

Most cotton balls are made of polyester. They may contain bleach and other toxins that potentially could poison various body organs. Dioxins from the polyester can stay in the body for years. Cotton balls also can cause an intestinal obstruction due to the cotton balls forming a bezoar, much like cats that swallow fur create a "fur ball." Obstructions typically end up requiring surgery to remove the obstruction and any dead piece of bowel. As well, the balls can result in choking and could be fatal.

Any substance that is not believed to be absorbed by the gut may be used for the same reason as cotton balls in dieting. Paper and clay are other substances. This is not true pica. Those experiencing pica will crave these non-nutritive substances and not desire them for weight loss purposes.

Questions

- Are you or have you ever been on a diet?
- What kind of diets have you used?
- Have you ever been on a cleanse or fasted, and why?
- What kind of diet are you using now, and why?
- Have you ever used a commercial diet?
- Do you limit calories by skipping meals or snacks or decreasing meal size?

154 Eating Disorder Behaviors

- Do you restrict calories by specifically reducing protein, fats, or carbohydrates?
- How well do diets work to lose weight for you?
- Aside from dieting, are you using any other eating disorder behaviors to aid in weight loss?
- Do you have a daily calorie limit, and what is that?
- How much weight do you want to lose?
- How much have you lost so far?
- What is the lowest weight you wish to achieve?
- How many days, weeks or months are you able to continue with your diet?
- Do you ever take breaks for prolonged periods of time away from your diet, and why?
- Do you have any feared foods, and what are they and why?
- Are you or have you ever been vegetarian?
- What kind of vegetarianism have you been involved with?
- Do you take supplements?
- What foods do you eat with very low calories to curb hunger?
- Have you ever eaten calorie-burning foods?
- Are you being followed by a physician to monitor health risk?
- Have you seen a dietitian for accurate, up-to-date nutrition information?
- Do you have a very selective nutrition regime, and why?
- Is your limited food selection for weight loss or body image control or for other reasons?

Weighing Food

Weighing food is a practical practice when baking or cooking. It also serves as an eating disorder behavior by being a tool to accurately gauge quantities of food and, therefore, help determine the suspected caloric content in food. It provides a guarantee that the individual will not exceed a hoped-for single meal or daily caloric intake. It may act as an aid in limiting food quantity, thus preventing eating a larger quantity that would otherwise trigger bingeing. Weighing food may help to guarantee a quantity of food that meets a minimum hoped-for intake when trying to prevent restricting. In this situation it becomes a tool in recovery.

Measuring Food

Measuring food may serve the same purpose weighing food does. There are different ways of measuring food. Measuring cups, measuring spoons, and scoops can give a precise valuation of food quantity. Bowls and drinking mugs are used to measure food in a subjective attempt to quantify food intake.

Reading Labels on Food Containers

A common practice for those with eating disorders is to read labels on food packages. Labels provide accurate information such as the caloric value of a given volume of food as well as fat, protein, and carbohydrate content. Quantities of sugar are a much-feared carbohydrate that is heavily scrutinized. Though the label may provide scientifically accurate information about nutrients, it cannot account for individuals' exaggerated belief in their fat-causing potential.

Protein, while being deemed a high-calorie nutrient, may be sought after in food if associated with very low or absent carbohydrate values. High protein and low carbohydrate diets are believed to aid in weight loss by some.

Labels also serve to provide information regarding "healthy nutrients" such as vitamins, minerals, or fiber content. Ingredients from animal sources are often heavily scrutinized.

Those with insulin-dependent diabetes may read labels in order to find very high sugar containing foods. Therefore, by withholding insulin, they can lose more weight by raising blood glucose levels, causing them to void carbohydrates in the form of unmetabolized sugar.

Calorie Counting

"Eating out was awful. I had so much anxiety about what was in the food and the calories it contained."

Calorie counting is a near ubiquitous method of evaluating food caloric content. Most with eating disorders will likely have attempted this or are currently engaged in the practice (Koff & Rierdan, 1991). There are different methods of calorie counting. Some will be accurate and others will be guestimates. Calorie counting may be used to help prevent weight gain, to lose weight, or in some cases to gain weight. Individuals may calorie count to determine the caloric content of a single portion of food (a piece of fruit or small yogurt serving), a meal, or total daily food consumption.

The calorie content of packaged foods is printed on the container. A certain caloric content will be given for a serving. What is considered a serving varies greatly from the type of food and between brands. There will be international variations for what a serving is as well. Serving sizes will also be listed with different units such as British units, which are ounces and cups, and metric units such as grams, kilograms, liters, milliliters, or cubic centimeters (cc's). Depending on whether the food is a liquid or solid will determine the measuring units as well. If someone uses a food measuring scale or volume measuring devices, then the caloric determination will likely be fairly accurate. Those who guess at what a serving is will not have a dependable estimate. It is important to ask when and why they calorie count. The practice may be a daily one or only come into play during different situations. The calorie content as well as ingredients contained in medications are readily available online and may be tallied into the daily acceptable calorie limit.

Counting Servings

Some will count servings for the same reasons they will measure or weight food or count calories. The latter may be used to help determine what a serving is.

A serving of food is a loosey-goosey unit of food measurement. It applies to individual pieces of food or serving size. As an example, a serving of fruit may be considered a *medium sized* apple, orange or banana. A serving of bread will be a single medium sized piece of bread. Gauging what a medium size piece of any food would likely vary from individual to individual.

Depending on the various professional and commercially created food guides the amount of recommended daily servings and kinds of foods suggested be eaten will vary. Food guides may provide suggestions for food choices and daily quantities for given age groups and genders but will not include recommendations based on physical activity, basal metabolic rate or ethnic food considerations.

Questions

- Do you count calories?
- Do you count calories for weight control, health purposes or both?
- What method do you use to count calories?
- Do you read food package labels, measure or weigh food to help determine the caloric content of food?
- Do you think your estimate of calories is accurate and why do you think so?
- Where do you get your information for determining the caloric content of foods?
- Do you use scientifically based food guides or nutrition advise obtained from the internet?
- Do you use pro-ana websites to obtain information about the caloric content of food and other consumed substances?
- Do you count the calories of medications, vitamins, chewing gum or sugarless candies?
- What calorie limits do you aim for and why?
- Do you count calories for individual food items, servings or portions, snacks and meals or total daily food intake?
- What is your end point for controlling calorie intake?

Eating Disorder Behaviors 157

- Do you count calories specifically for food protein, fat or carbohydrate content?

Cigarettes

Smoking cigarettes may be for eating disorder purposes or not. Some smoke because it is a habit or an addiction. It can be used to relieve boredom or loneliness temporarily. It may help someone to fit in socially where smoking is encouraged. It also fills time and gives the mouth and hands something to do. Smoking cigarettes fits in well with body image and weight loss goals. Tobacco is believed to increase metabolism by 10%, thus leading to an increased rate of calorie burning. Smoking aids in suppressing appetite, therefore helping to prevent unwanted eating (Morean & Wedel, 2017).

For those quitting smoking, there may be a real risk of weight gain. This weight gain can be because metabolism slows down, as well as eating may increase to compensate for not smoking. Increased eating may be a distraction from not smoking, to replace the need for oral stimulation and to cope with stress that smoking may have been used for. It can be difficult to encourage individuals to quit smoking for body image control reasons.

It may be helpful to point out the high financial cost of smoking. Spending funds on cigarettes may deliberately help to decrease the availability of money used to purchase food and therefore aid in restricting behavior. Being self-conscious, some do not wish to stink of smoke, and this may be an additional incentive to quit.

Questions

- Do you or have you ever smoked cigarettes?
- Have you ever used cigarette smoking as a weight loss tool?
- Do you purchase your own, or do you borrow them from others?
- How many do you smoke in a day on average?
- What is the least and maximum number of cigarettes you smoke in a day?
- Do you smoke daily, or do ever take a break from it, and why?
- Do you smoke to curb hunger or to increase metabolism?
- Do you smoke just because it is a habit, you are addicted, it is how you socialize with others, or it is how you deal with boredom and loneliness?

Gum Chewing

Chewing gum is ubiquitous as an eating disorder behavior. It helps to curb appetite and give the mouth something to do instead of eating. Gum chewing is thought to burn calories. Though gum chewing doesn't sound

Eating Disorder Behaviors

like a high-risk behavior, some are able to lose significant amounts of weight and keep it off by chewing gum. It is important to ask the degree of importance chewing gum may have in weight loss control. Sometimes gum is just used for pleasure and nothing more.

Being Busy

Those with eating disorders often say they need to be constantly busy. The reasons for this are multifold. Being busy distracts individuals from thinking about food. Busyness often takes them away from sources of food, such as the kitchen. Being busy with going to the gym, studying at school or volunteering may aid this end. Busyness involving being constantly physically active is also perceived as a way to burn calories.

Other reasons for wanting to be busy is that some believe they are being lazy or not serving a useful purpose if they are not engaged in some activity. Individuals may be accomplishment focused and feel they are not accomplishing anything during down time. This all leads to a feeling of worthlessness and lacking an identity. Being busy may be a way to avoid engaging in negative feelings and thoughts that ramp up with time on their hands.

Motivating Behaviors

Engaging in restrictive eating behaviors requires a significant dedication to task and much motivation to maintain a weight loss regime. Because there is such a high failure rate with weight loss diets generally, individuals have to keep finding motivating methods to keep returning to a dedicated weight loss program. Following are a few motivating behaviors. Several motivational 'Tips" or "Advice" are available on pro-ana and pro-mia websites.

Mantras

Mantras, sayings, or eating disorder focused *affirmations* become part of the motivational arsenal. Some are of a positive or encouraging flavor ("Ana girls are strong"), while others are derogatory in theme.

Write Your Weight on One Hand and Goal Weight on the Other

This suggestion keeps the reality of someone's current weight and her goal weight up front and center. It serves to reward the person when the current weight decreases toward the goal weight and is also a form of punishment if she does not succeed in adequate weight loss.

Eating Disorder Behaviors 159

Sleep Over 6 Hours a Night Will Increase Metabolism

Some believe that sleeping longer increases metabolism. Sleeping longer also decreases the number of waking hours one could engage in eating, including bingeing. It also decreases the time individuals feel bad about their body. Sometimes drugs or alcohol are used to increase the number of hours one sleeps. Some will try to sleep longer than 12 hours daily if they can.

Find an Eating Disorder Buddy

There is much camaraderie amongst those with eating disorders. There are often strong bonds between individuals with eating disorders. They can support each other by motivating one another to continue weight loss practices. They also share eating disorder tricks to help escalate successes. Some will find a buddy in treatment programs and follow their relationship out of treatment centers. Efforts need to be made to keep those with eating disorders away from each other on hospital wards or community group treatment programs. Just because individuals are in a treatment program does not mean they are motivated to change. Treatment programs are great places to enable eating disorder behaviors and provide a meeting place or club for those who do not wish to recover. With so many electronic social media platforms available, communicating with each other becomes easy. Many others can join these sites in order to create like-minded groups.

Those with eating disorders also find allies in others who do not have an eating disorder but help them to collude in maintaining the eating disorder. Acquaintances may provide drugs, laxatives, and diuretics for those being treated in hospital.

Eat in Front of the Mirror

This becomes an instant reminder of what they look like while eating. If eating generally is deemed a disgusting act for anyone, eating in front of a mirror will reinforce this attitude for themselves.

Wear a Rubber Band

Snapping a rubber band on the wrist can distract one from eating unwantedly.

Stack Magazines and Remove Them

Some will stack a number of magazines that weigh the same weight one wishes to loss. As weight drops, then the same weight in magazines can be removed from the pile. providing a visual record of weight loss success.

160 Eating Disorder Behaviors

Questions

- How do you motivate yourself to stay engaged in weight loss or body image control?
- What eating disorder behaviors do you particularly motivate yourself to stick with, and why?
- How well are the motivating mechanisms working?
- Do they actually help you to stay motivated, or do they tend not to work well, and why do you think that is true?
- Are your motivating behaviors punitive in nature, leading to self-harm, or dangerous?

Aversion Behaviors

Another method to discourage eating is by doing something or observing something perceived to be disgusting, repulsive, or overwhelming. *Cleaning something disgusting* like a litter box or a dirty toilet may turn someone off of the prospects of eating. Changing diapers or changing the clothes of those who have soiled themselves, as would be the case for personal caregivers, may be an option. Cleaning up one's pile of vomit around a toilet or spray from explosive diarrhea as a result of laxative use serves the same purpose. Cleaning plates of rotting uneaten food that have been sitting around the home for days provides another incentive.

Inhaling any strong and overwhelming odor could discourage eating. Cleaning solvents, turpentine, gasoline, and many other noxious substances are included. Observing and listening to others eat can be disgusting to some. Watching "fat people" eat may be discouraging as well.

Spoiling Food

There are a number of ways of spoiling food to discourage eating.

Microwave Food Too Hot to Eat

Very hot food may be impossible to eat due to its ability to burn the lips, mouth, and esophagus. For some, they will eat it anyway and experience mouth blisters and esophageal pain. They may do this as part of a ritual or as a form of punishment for allowing themselves to eat. It may be a way to prevent them from eating as much as they would if the food did not burn them.

Put "Tons" of Strong-Tasting Substances on Food to Spoil the Food

Putting excessive quantities of spices on food such as garlic, pepper, or salt may create an intolerable taste. Substances not designed to be eaten such as dish soap, vomit, or dirt may ruin the experience of eating. If someone ends up eating these spoiled foods anyway, the process will act as a form of punishment for not being able to resist.

Another way to sabotage food is by adding water or any other liquid to foods, making them inedible. Dipping muffins in water or dousing spaghetti or toast with water are examples of this. Baking what should be a sweet food but not putting sugar in the mix may discourage eating.

Food Associations

Placing pictures of food that make individuals feel ill or are unpleasant beside food that one hopes not to eat may discourage some from eating. Thinspirational pictures of emaciated or grossly overweight individuals placed beside food will have a similar effect.

Questions

- Do you use aversive methods to avoid contact with food, and what are they?
- Do you spoil food, and how do you do this?

Avoiding Behaviors

> *"I felt weird and out of place and didn't want to be around anyone when I ate."*

There are many avoiding behaviors those with eating disorder engage in. Many have been discussed elsewhere. Some avoid restaurants, grocery stores, or other sources of food including the workplace or university. Avoidance of family, friends, and professional caregivers that encourage recovery is a common practice.

Questions

- Do you deliberately avoid situations to help distance yourself from eating or engaging in social situations?
- What situations do you avoid, and why?
- Are these avoiding strategies working?

Delaying

There are multiple ways of delaying eating, with the goal being to provide enough time for strong urges to eat, including hunger, to pass and to allow time to implement distractions from eating. Fullness or feeling satiated is

162 Eating Disorder Behaviors

a process involving stomach stretching signals and hormonal signals triggered from food and the eating process itself. Eating a small amount of food may satiate hunger if given some time. Any delaying behavior allows this time period to pass. Hunger may subside without eating if given time.

Chew Several Times

Chewing food many times—10, 20 or 30 times per mouthful—serves several purposes. It allows the taste of the food to be enjoyed without consuming larger portions. Some will chew until the food totally dissolves or becomes liquefied. It also provides time for individuals to feel guilty for eating at all and allows them time to stop eating before more is consumed. Chewing may be seen as a calorie burning exercise in itself, such as fidgeting.

Set Utensils Down Between Bites

Putting utensils down between bites allows the individual to focus on chewing and to take time eating. It serves to disengage the feeding process from the eating process mentally as well as physically.

Paint Nails or Whiten Teeth

The drying of fingernail polish and teeth whitening takes time to complete, allowing time to further avoid eating. They not only take time, but the result of both would be ruined if the process were to be interrupted too soon. Who wants to be seen with a bad nail polish job or dull teeth?

Eat With the Opposite Hand

Eating with the opposite hand requires more concentration as well as delays eating time due to poorer eating coordination capacity.

Other delaying methods include:

- Eating frozen fruit and other frozen food takes longer to eat.
- Count to 100 before eating.
- Wait at least one hour before bingeing.
- Take a deep breath or count to 10 before bingeing.

Questions

- Do you have specific delaying techniques to help prevent engaging in eating, including binge eating?
- What are these techniques, and when are they used?

Eating Disorder Behaviors   163

- Are there other eating disorder behaviors you use to delay or prevent using?

Dehydration

Some deliberately restrict fluids. One major reason is to prevent weight gain. Water is known to be surprisingly heavy. One cubic foot of water weighs 62.43 pounds. A 16-ounce bottle of water weighs about one pound—1.04 lbs. Minor water shifts in the body may result in noticeable and even significant weight changes.

Dehydration may ensue for individuals unwittingly. This comes from being unaware that fluid intake is inadequate. Some may not be aware that when they restrict water-containing solid foods, their water intake is inadvertently decreased. Many foods have a high proportion of water content, including fruits and vegetables. Salt restriction may decrease the amount of water retained. Restricting protein may lower blood levels of protein in extreme cases. Protein is essential for blood to hold water in the circulation. Sweating, due to hot environments or exercise, results in water loss. Water is also lost from the lungs through breathing. Any activity that accelerates breathing rates, such as exercise, will increase water loss.

Medical conditions such as renal failure can prevent the body from retaining water (Stheneur et al., 2017). High levels of blood sugar, such as those with uncontrolled diabetes, will cause profuse water loss through frequent high-volume urination. Anyone with rapid weight loss must be investigated for diabetes even if they have a known eating disorder. Another way to develop dehydration without restricting fluids is the use of diuretics or laxatives. See "Diuretics" and "Laxatives" earlier in this chapter. Even though weight loss is through dehydration and not due to reduction of fat stores, dehydration becomes a reliable weight control method for some.

> *"It wasn't the surgery or the IV needle that scared me but all the fluid they were going to pump into me. I hate IVs! How was I going to purge that from my body? I left against medical advice after pulling the IV needle out of my arm myself."*

There is a point where fluid restriction results in the body holding on to any water, preventing water loss by decreasing urine flow. It then, due to hyperaldosteronism, attempts to hoard water even if the body is receiving enough. Fluid replacement orally, through IVs, or other fluid lines may result in edema, which is swelling of the hands, feet, lower legs, and possibly the face. Water weight gain can be rapid, approaching five or more pounds in a single day. Rapid water retention may lead to congestive heart failure and heart attack. Symptoms of dehydration may include dizziness, fainting, palpitations, cramps, anxiety, depression, and weakness.

164 Eating Disorder Behaviors

For pregnant women, dehydration can present risks to the fetus. Pregnant women with eating disorders will need to be monitored closely for dehydration. Hyperemesis gravidarum, is a condition during pregnancy where the woman experiences uncontrollable vomiting, resulting in a rapid rate of dehydration.

Rehydration requires the expertise of medical specialists to coordinate a graduated, controlled rate of fluid replacement. Electrolytes must be added in addition to fluids to prevent catastrophic outcomes.

Questions

- Have you lost weight because you were dehydrated?
- How did you become dehydrated?
- Was becoming dehydrated deliberate on your part?
- Have you experienced swelling of your hands, legs, and feet or face with refeeding or rehydrating?
- Are you aware that the body will hoard water, resulting in weight gain, after being dehydrated?
- Did you know that rebound water retention can result in congestive heart failure and death?

Throwing Food Away

Throwing food away can be an effective and reliable aid to restricting. Success depends on the availability of disposal sources and the ability to not be noticed. If food is not available, then it can't be eaten. Depending on the situation, getting rid of food can be easy or difficult. This can be a costly eating disorder behavior.

Fluid Loading

Filling up with water is a non-caloric way to curb hunger for some. Aside from pure water, there are several sources of water for fluid loading in the form of coffee, tea, and diet drinks. Fluids distend the stomach and give a temporary sensation of some fullness and possibly hunger decline. Some believe that cold water or other cold liquids further help to curb appetite. Thirst can be confused with hunger signals. For those who vomit, water and other fluids aid to liquefy food in the stomach to make it easier to vomit.

Water may be added daily in various patterns. Some will drink a glass of water every hour or so. Some will drink water before every meal or snack to help decrease hunger and hopefully eat less. Others may have a drink of water with every bite. Fluid loading happens before some get weighed with their doctor, creating an artificially increased weight on the scale.

Some have a goal to become dehydrated, as water is quite heavy. Rehydration can add significantly to one's weight. This is one of the problems with refeeding and rehydrating in the hospital, as water retention can add large amounts of water-induced weight. It can cause edema, including puffiness of the face. This can create intolerable fears in those being treated. Drinking excessive amounts of water can be lethal. It creates dangerous metabolic abnormalities.

Medication Avoidance

Medications may be avoided for many reasons. One reason is fear of weight gain with taking certain drugs. Medication contraceptives such as oral contraceptive pills, Depo-Provera, and the NuvaRing as well as psychotropic medications are a few. People look on the internet to find out weight gain risks for any medication. Withholding the use of some medications may present with risks.

Those sexually active who require protection from becoming pregnant will be at risk of an unexpected pregnancy. They need to be educated regarding this as well that the birth control pill and NuvaRing do not statistically cause weight gain. A small percentage of women actually lose weight, and some gain weight temporarily due to fluid shifts in the body. Depo-Provera, an injectable hormonal contraceptive utilizing a synthetic progesterone or progestin, may be associated with some weight gain. Individuals need to be asked if they wish to face an unwanted pregnancy and face gaining 25–30 pounds during pregnancy or experience a termination.

Psychotropic medications including antidepressants, benzodiazepines, mood stabilizers, and antipsychotic medications have a varying degree of weight gain potential. Antiseizure drugs may not be taken because of the same fears. Weight increase is usually dose dependent. It is important to mention the risk versus benefit of taking these medications. It should be stated that individuals make the ultimate decision as to whether they continue a medication or not.

Questions

- Are there medications you avoid due to fearing you may gain weight by taking them?
- Are there medications you know you should be taking but have not been that can result in harm to yourself?
- Where have you acquired the information that instructs you that these medications do indeed cause weight increases?

Some do not necessarily fear weight gain from medications themselves. They fear weight gain from medications that decrease bingeing will, in turn, result in decreasing vomiting. Decreasing vomiting frequency may lead to weight gain. The prospect of recovery from an eating disorder is a major trigger to ramping up feared body image awareness, including body shape changes or weight gain. Some avoid taking medications of any kind as well as vitamins and mineral supplements because of the caloric content of pills or liquids themselves.

Dark Plates

Eating off of dark plates is believed by some to psychologically cause individuals to eat less.

Peppermint to Decrease Hunger

Peppermint is an herb that is believed to decrease hunger. It is used in teas to settle stomach ailments as well.

Licking Chopsticks or a Fork

Some will want to taste food but not consume appreciable calories. Dipping chopsticks or a fork into soups, dressings, powdered food, or any other food that leaves a taste residue will suffice. This can bring a form of satisfaction when flirting with food. Sometimes, though, the smell of food or the smallest taste of food leads to uncontrollable eating.

Chopsticks

Chopsticks are used for eating disorder purposes. Eating with chopsticks, especially for those of us who are not very adept at eating with them, become an aid to eat slower and in smaller portions than using a fork or spoon. This allows a delay in eating time when the individual believes she will feel fuller or satiate hunger on less food than if she had eaten quickly. The delay may provide time to gather motivation to just stop eating sooner than later.

For those brought up in a culture of chopstick use, food can enter the mouth faster than using other utensils. With the traditional use of chopsticks as used in Chinese, Korean, Thai and other oriental cultures, individuals eat food from a bowl placed right at mouth level, and this assists in bringing food into the mouth at a surprising rate. Chopstick use may just be a cultural thing and not in use for eating disorder purposes.

Eating Various Foods With Different Flavors

Some prefer to sample various foods with varying flavors in order to at least enjoy this one aspect of eating but not acquire calories.

Offering Food to Others

One way of disposing of food without throwing it away is to offer food to others. Because some feel guilty throwing away food, this is a no-guilt way of eliminating food from one's diet. It also provides a feel-good moment, as a person will feel she is doing someone a favor. It acts as an "in your face" but inconspicuous way of restricting. Food may be given to friends, family, classmates, or coworkers, but also food from restaurants may be packaged up and then given to someone on the street.

Ordering Sauces on the Side

Another subtle way of restricting calories is to have sauces presented on the side rather than coming already mixed in with food. This helps to control the amount of sauces consumed, whether they are sweet or rich with butter and oils. Salad dressing may be ordered the same way. It is a way to restrict while eating with others and may be missed as a restricting behavior. Hundreds of calories can be eliminated this way without significantly reducing the volume of food.

Asking for Lunch or Child-Sized Portions

Eating in restaurants creates a real challenge for some. The ingredients and quantities of food are largely out of the control of individuals even if they order safe foods. Ordering lunch or child-sized portions, if offered, is a way of limiting caloric content. Again, this can be done in plain sight of others and not be noticed as a weight loss method.

Saying "No Thanks" for Dessert

Declining food, including desserts, is a socially acceptable way to limit intake eating. Other foods aside from desserts may be declined as well. Side orders such as French fries, onion rings, or potato salad may be declined without others caring. Individuals' excuses for declining food may be that the doctor said they have to avoid certain foods, that they have food allergies or intolerances, or that they have an upset stomach. Claims of having eaten earlier may work as well. Refusing food due to humanitarian reasons such as being a vegetarian is a common practice. A history of family health problems – "My father has high cholesterol and high blood pressure, so I have to avoid rich foods" – is an option as well.

Sugar Substitutes

Stevia, a natural sweetener, is believed to be 23 or more times sweeter than sugar. Sugar substitutes including artificial sweeteners are a way of providing sweetness to food without significant caloric intake. Some use these sweeteners because they may cause nausea, thus discouraging some from wanting to eat more. Sugar-free products including soda drinks do not successfully help individuals from gaining weight. They are not successful in tricking the body into thinking it has had real nutrition.

Although sugar-free gum and candies have little calories, they do have some. Those who restrict will even add up the calorie content of sugar-free products and add them to their daily calorie count (Klein, Boudreau, Devlin & Walsh, 2006). Most sugar-free gum has 5 calories in one or two sticks. The calorie content of sugar-free candies varies but is often reported as around 5 to 10 calories each. The calorie content of these products can be found online. Accepting the calories from sugar-free products as opposed to potentially taking in more if not using them to curb hunger may be seen as the lesser of two evils. The estimated caloric content from pills used as medications may also be calculated. Some avoid all sugar-free products to avoid consuming any extra calories.

Don't Eat in Patterns—Eat Normally

Many with eating disorders eat in very precise patterns and can be easily recognized as being eating disorder related, especially by those who know the individual. Mixing up eating patterns may dissuade others from catching on. Eating the occasional food that is normally avoided may send recovery signals. Eating at times of the day or with others when one typically would not may give similar impressions of recovery efforts.

Eating disorder behaviors well known to others such as eating then going to the restroom afterward to vomit could be disrupted at times by not going to the restroom during or immediately after eating. Not attending the gym or going for runs may also give recovery signals to others. A smoke-and-mirrors or shell game kind of deception comes into play where others see one thing—recovery efforts—while the eating disorder progresses largely unnoticed.

Mustard and Other Strong Condiments

Mustard or other strong-tasting condiments in small amounts can provide a powerful taste sensation yet deliver little in the way of calories. Some may like the taste of mustard, but others may find it offensive and eat it as a way to spoil the taste of food. Horseradish is another condiment with a very powerful taste and smell that some will love while others will be repulsed by it.

Picking Apart Food

Picking apart food, especially sandwiches, is a way to examine the content of food and remove ingredients that are unwanted. It's a way of deselecting

Eating Disorder Behaviors 169

food as opposed to selecting food. The same could be done for other prepared foods such as sushi and pizza as well as salads.

Reducing the Amount of a Single Food in a Day Only

One whole portion of food that is usually eaten a few times daily may be reduced to only having one portion of it in a day, but it is eaten in pieces throughout the day. Each piece is eaten as a meal in itself or as snacks. As an example, if someone usually eats three servings of fruit a day, one serving may be divided up into three pieces to be eaten three different times in the day.

Foods With Fiber

Fiber is sometimes considered a calorie-free filler. Foods with fiber or even artificial sweeteners with fiber may be chosen. Food high in fiber include many fruits, vegetables and grains. Bran, a form of natural fiber, may have much sugar added in order to make it palatable. This surprises those who wish to use it as a diet aid.

Chewing and Spitting

Chewing and spitting is a frequently utilized eating disorder behavior. It is used in order for the individual to taste coveted food without acquiring much of the calories. It is effectively one step removed from vomiting, which is designed to decrease caloric absorption as well. Some will chew and spit in the presence of others unnoticed as they can spit food into tissues or napkins without suspicion.

Questions

- Do you chew and spit?
- When is chewing and spitting relied upon, and why?
- Does it replace another eating disorder behavior, or is it an add-on to the already established eating disorder arsenal?

Rules Aiding Restricting

Although many eating disorder rules can be made for any eating disorder or motivational behavior, here are just a few.

- Don't eat any food with over 3 grams of fat.
- Don't sample food while cooking. Sampling food while cooking can add to the total calorie count. It may be thought that sampling food

170 Eating Disorder Behaviors

may decrease the urge to eat more later. The attitude toward this depends on the individual.

- Leave at least one bite behind.
- Have available "stand-by foods" that are low in calories. Use them when really hungry. Restricting can be attempted in extreme or miniscule efforts. The slower rate of weight loss is deemed to help reduce the drive to binge. Leaving at least one bite behind for any given meal is a slow way to edge into restricting behaviors.
- Use sugar-free gum or candies all the time. Sucking on sugar-free candies and chewing sugar-free gum throughout the day is done to help decrease the urge to eat. It provides flavor plus gives the mouth "something to do" instead of eating.

Eat Nothing White

Many forbidden foods are white, including many carbohydrates such as sugar, breads, rice, and potatoes. White foods of dairy origin include ice cream, cream, milk, whipped cream, and white cheeses.

Never Eat Out

Eating out may bring the temptation to binge. Restaurant foods are prepared by others; therefore, the nutritional content and size of servings will not be in the control of those individuals wanting absolute control of their own food intake. There will be some latitude with regard to food selections in restaurants that provide buffet options or a salad bar. All you can eat smorgasbord restaurants provide a treasure trove of food selections and quantities for those who binge. Those who binge eat regularly in all-you-can-eat restaurants may be identified by staff as binge eaters and denied dining there in the future.

Glass of Water Every Hour

As mentioned elsewhere, water consumption on a regular basis is a way to curb hunger temporarily.

Weigh Yourself Twice a day or More

This rule insures a reliable, frequent check on weight, thus not allowing for unwanted weight increases to go unnoticed. It also provides a frequent guarantee that individuals are maintaining a weight they desire or are meeting weight loss goals. Daily weighing may be an adjunct to meeting recovery weight goals.

Stop Eating in Your Bedroom or Car

Some locations are triggers to bingeing. These locations will want to be avoided by those who do not wish to binge.

Only Eat in Front of Others

Eating with others may give family, partners, or friends the impression that the eating disorder is not particularly active or provide an environment where one is not likely to binge eat or that discourages vomiting behaviors.

Never Eat in Secret

Secret eating allows the opportunity to binge eat and possibly to vomit for some. Secret eating is also isolating.

Never Eat Out of Food Containers

Eating out of food containers, such as boxes or jars, provides the opportunity to eat an overabundance of unportioned food. Unless food containers are designed for single portion use such as small yogurt containers or snack packages, the rest are typically created for multiple serving use and provide binge quantities. Food containers are portable and can be taken to any location; someone may be alone to binge such as in a bedroom, bathroom or car.

Questions

- Do you have any firm eating disorder rules?
- If you are unable to stick to a given rule, does this have a negative effect on how you feel?

Time Rules

> "I planned my whole day around when I was going to eat and didn't want anyone to interrupt that."

> "The first thing I thought about in the morning was food, and I fall asleep planning the next day's intake."

Time considerations are important in the eating disorder world. Meeting time goals can have profound consequences if achieved or not achieved. It depends on what the time parameter means to the individual. To some, meeting time obligations is the biggest determinant of the course of the eating disorder. Time rules may be eating disorder focused, while others are not. They may be entrenched in the long term or be applied on and off. They also may be applied to all eating events of the day or only one or two.

Knowing the reason for setting time goals may be essential to determine treatment options. There are a few basic determinants that help establish time rules.

- They help to meet eating disorder weight and body image control goals.
- They maintain a general sense of control in one's life.
- They help to assuage feelings of guilt, anxiety, shame, and depression whether created by body image issues or otherwise.
- They are part of obsessive-compulsive traits.
- They are a part of superstitious beliefs.
- They are part of established family or cultural time expectations.
- They meet any number of these needs at the same time or at different times.

Eating Disorder Focused Time Rules

Time rules often apply specifically to routine eating behaviors as well as to eating disorder behaviors. Body image control reasons for rules may include needing to eat at specific times of the day, as it is believed this will affect metabolism, control hunger, and of course control total nutrition intake.

Eat by a Certain Time

Eating by a certain time or up to a certain time is what is important. There will be a given period of time for which someone has to complete a predetermined meal or snack. An example of this is that during a given day, breakfast must be eaten by 8 a.m., lunch by 1 p.m. and dinner by 6 p.m. The evening snack must be eaten no later than 8 p.m.

Eat at Certain Times

Eating at a certain time dictates someone must eat at precise times of the day. There will be a small window of time to achieve this. Similar to the example given in "Eating by a Certain Time," individuals will set goals to eat *at* 8 a.m., 1 p.m., and 6 p.m. for breakfast, lunch, and dinner, respectively.

Eat in a Given Time Period

Similar to eating by a certain time, the rule explicitly requires food be eaten between one time until another time of the day. An example would be that breakfast must be eaten between 8 and 8:30 a.m., lunch between 1 and 1:30 p.m., and dinner between 6 and 6:30 p.m.

The Consequences of Meeting or Not Meeting Time Rules

If time goals are met, then this establishes a certain assuredness within the eating disorder momentum. This may establish a good feeling or avoid a bad feeling or achieve both at the same time.

If these rules are not met, various potential consequences result. There can be a sense that things are all ruined. If individuals haven't met their goal, this may make them feel like a failure and bring guilt. Negative feelings will be an immediate consequence triggering corrective or compensating actions.

Individuals may experience bad feelings such as guilt or of being a failure until they successfully meet their next time goal. For any of the eating time goals not met, some may choose to not eat at all. They wait for the next time goal to determine when they eat next. They may try to make up for failed time expectations by escalating other eating disorders such as restricting, exercising, or vomiting more. Bad feelings may lead to other destructive behaviors such as drug and alcohol use or not taking exams, which may put them at risk of failing or having to drop out of university.

Time rules may apply to other eating disorder behaviors beside restricting. Some will have time rules for exercising, vomiting, or laxative use as examples. Time rules may usually be easy to implement but are vulnerable to events that can disrupt them. Any unforeseen distractions apply. If someone becomes ill or has unplanned visits or social expectations, food is not available, or the opportunity to purge is disrupted, time goals cannot be met.

Time rules may be applied to any life situations. If someone is late for a class or others are late to arrive, cancel, or don't show for an engagement, this can bring great disappointment and a sense of lack of control or worth in her life. It can shatter expectations for the rest of the day or longer. Control of time events can be at the core of self-worth, perfectionism, and people pleasing. Time rules may also be applied to others, as well. Others disappoint by not honoring her time expectations. Some do not seem to accept normal human laxness with regard to time.

Questions

- Do you have any particular fixed time rules, and what are they?
- Does trying to adhere to these time rules interfere with meeting personal, social, work, or school expectations?
- How do you feel if you are not able to meet your time regime, and what do you do about it?

174 Eating Disorder Behaviors

- Are you critical of others who do not meet your expectations of being on time with regard to returning text messages or arriving on time for activities?
- Do you ever take extended periods of time from not engaging in time rules, and why?

Rituals

Cutting food into specific sizes, shapes, or numbers creates smaller food pieces, which aids the individual with eating slower. This helps prevent the feeling of being rushed when eating and develops a sense of control over eating. It allows time for a full feeling to develop while eating smaller amounts of food.

Specific *cutlery* may be desired. Some will choose to eat only with select eating utensils. Cutlery may be smaller than average with the belief that smaller utensils allows them to eat slower. Doll's cutlery may be used specifically for this purpose.

Some will choose to eat from only one particular *bowl, plate, glass,* or *cup*. The bowls and plates they chose will typically be small, therefore allowing for only relatively small portions of food that can be eaten. They effectively serve as food measuring devices. They provide a guarantee that they will not unknowingly eat more than hoped for. It must be remembered that some will chose specific cutlery or serving dishes as they will have purchased them just because they like them or are possibly a gift from their grandmother.

Some chose to eat either *clockwise* or *counterclockwise* on a plate as a ritual, possibly related to superstition. This may just be a pattern they have developed and not necessarily be related to superstition, an obsessive-compulsive disorder, or an eating disorder.

Individuals will choose to *not allow one food to touch each other* on a plate. This may be due to a fear of one food "contaminating" adjacent food with calories and specifically with fat. Some do not want one food flavor being mixed with another.

Sometimes *food is eaten in a specific order*. Typically, the "healthiest" or lowest calorie foods are consumed first. This is to help decrease the drive to eat higher calorie or fear foods in order not to eat as much as if they had begun with them.

Patterns of eating may have *superstitious* or even *religious* meaning. If they are not successful at meeting an eating disorder goal, some may think "I'm a bad person" or "God will hate me." There may be a belief that something bad will happen to family or friends. These negative beliefs may lead to a feeling of having to be punished, and then they may actually punish themselves in some manner.

Some find it an issue to eat *mixed foods*. This may include soups, stews, chili con carne, casseroles, sandwiches, and wraps as well as other food. This stems from a fear of not knowing what might be in food. The fear is typically of high-calorie nutrients, especially fats. Some will not eat any food prepared by others, including packaged foods purchased from grocery stores, for fear of not knowing what might be in them. It sometimes becomes a significant issue for family or partners to be able to cook for their loved ones with an eating disorder. Being able to eat at restaurants becomes an impossible task.

Questions

- Do you have any rituals relating to your eating disorder or anything else, and why?
- What are your rituals?
- How important is completing rituals to you?
- Do you believe that harm will come to you or others if you do not stick to rules, and why?
- Do you punish yourself for not adhering to specific rituals?
- Does having to engage in rituals interfere with your emotions or functioning at different levels of your life?

False Information

> *"I think one of the greatest difficulties I faced that I would like professionals in the field to be aware of was the ability to be honest. I was so scared of being forced back into treatment that I couldn't express when I was struggling."*

A mainstay for being able to perpetuate eating disorder behaviors is being skilled at disseminating *false information*. An adage in the eating disorder world is "Be a good liar!" Multiple other words have been used to describe relaying false information such as telling fibs, making excuses, and being manipulative and deceitful.

Probably one of the most difficult situations clinicians face is being lied to. They feel manipulated or used. Unfortunately, these ruses can be taken personally. Staff may say, "I'm trying to help her, and look how she repays me!" It must be understood that lying is a part of the eating disorder to be expected, and clinicians should not interpret deceptions as not cooperating. The reason for deceptions is individuals wish to protect themselves from being discovered engaging in eating disorder behaviors or other destructive behaviors, including drug and alcohol use. Staff in a coronary

176 Eating Disorder Behaviors

intensive care unit would not take it personally if a patient experiences a cardiac arrest under their care. Nor would they make comments that the patient is not cooperating.

Manipulative behaviors create a kind of sleight of hand, smoke and mirrors, shell game, or "pulling the wool over our eyes" scenario. A form of deception gymnastics evolves. It is a way for individuals to keep their cards close to their chest. While family, partners, and clinicians are trying to track the course of the eating disorder, they can be distracted by talk and behaviors that are used to reroute attention. An illusion manifests that presents a picture of things being okay, not so bad, or not happening at all. Whether this illusion is successful or not depends in large part on what the individual has been able to get away with before. One ruse may work for one person and not another, so there may be selective patterns of deceit depending on who needs to be fooled. It all depends on the naievite of and previous experiences with the individual and the level of denial of those being targeted. Parents who really don't want to know what's going on will fall hook, line, and sinker when given false information. The phrase by Sir Walter Scott, "Oh, what a tangled web we weave . . . when first we practice to deceive" comes to mind. Deceptive practices may become so ingrained that they become second nature and essentially are on autopilot.

A problem for the one with the eating disorder is that when they do eventually attempt to recover and relay their recovery efforts, others who know them may say, "Oh, we've heard that one before." This lack of being believed when actually telling the truth may bring a "Why should I even try" attitude. Reversing mistrust to regain trust needs special attention.

> *"Even as an adult in my twenties, I was afraid that if I admitted that I purged that week, following months of restraining, my parents would be called to pick me up and bring me back to treatment."*

False information may be created by leaving out facts and only divulging on an as-needed basis. Others may fill in the blanks as to what may or may not be happening. Some deceptive practices are mentioned here.

Tell Others They Are Sick so They Have an Excuse to Not Eat

Feigning illness, especially of a gastrointestinal nature such as having stomach flu, food poisoning, indigestion, heartburn, or celiac disease, provides an immediately plausible understanding why someone would not want to eat. Stating one has symptoms such as pelvic pains due to having menstrual cramps, migraine, or morning sickness during pregnancy seem viable reasons as well.

Act as if Efforts Are Being Made to Eat

Actions such as going to the kitchen and opening the fridge door help to create the illusion of having contact with food. Microwaving food elicits the typical microwave oven sound and creates the smell of cooking food, which also gives the impression someone is engaged in eating activities. Food handled in the kitchen can be taken to the bedroom and then thrown out. Others may assume that food is going to be eaten in the bedroom. Remnants of food preparation such as leaving the residue of food on a dirty plate or leaving food wrappers and boxes out on the counter provide false evidence of meal preparation and expected consumption. Throwing food away at night when others are asleep gives the illusion of food having been eaten. If someone notices food missing, then a comment such as "I had a snack last night" provides a good reason for the missing food. Making eating-related comments after pretending to eat such as "I think I ate too much" help propagate the myth one has eaten.

Other ways of giving the appearance of eating may include:

- Leaving food containers in the car.
- Pretending to chew and swallow food.
- Eating just a few bites of food from a bowl, then going back to the kitchen and putting the remainder back in the pot.
- If being watched, one can pretend to be eating and swallowing but instead spit the food into an opaque cup while pretending to drink. Food in the cup can then be thrown out.

Purchase Tampons to Hide Not Having Periods

Amenorrhea, which is the loss of one's menstrual period for three cycles or more, used to be part of the diagnostic criteria for anorexia nervosa. Because so many women are on hormonal contraceptive methods such as the combined oral contraceptive pill, contraceptive ring, and patch—all which contain both a synthetic estrogen and progesterone—periods are artificially triggered, therefore disguising that one could be amenorrheic otherwise. Hormonal intrauterine devices and Depo-Provera tend to eliminate periods, resulting in amenorrhea, or they may cause erratic bleeding; thus, diminishing periods or amenorrhea resulting from significant weight loss cannot be determined. Men with eating disorders do not experience this phenomenon, and therefore amenorrhea can't be a criterion for determining the extent of eating disorder health risks.

Regardless of the fact that amenorrhea is no longer a clinical criterion for diagnosing anorexia nervosa, it is still a benchmark for significant weight loss in some. To fool family members and convince them that the individual has not lost enough weight to lose her periods, purchasing tampons gives the illusion she is menstruating. To compound the myth, she can also say she is having her period and possibly fake being unwell due to having menstrual cramps. Fake blood or red nail polish painted on tampons or pads then left in trash bins may aid in giving an impression she is having her period.

Check Fridge When Others Are Around, Then Remove Food as if One Has Eaten It

Food removed from the fridge or cupboards can be thrown away to give the illusion food is going to be eaten.

Buying Food

Others will logically think that purchased food will be eaten.

Eating Food With Strong Odors That Can Be Smelled on One's Breath

Strong food odors may give others the impression an individual has been eating. Eating any food that can leave a strong food smell on one's breath gives the illusion someone has eaten. Onions or spices such as garlic or chili are examples.

Ways to Look Healthier

The healthier individuals look, the less others believe they are ill. Those with anorexia nervosa tend to have pale or sallow-looking skin. Spending time in a tanning booth can create a tan that gives others the impression they are healthier than they may actually be. Keeping hair in good condition and using makeup on the face may give a healthier look.

Increasing Weight Artificially

Wearing hidden objects before being weighed can increase scale readings. Cutlery taped to the body or placing a shampoo bottle in underpants serves this purpose. Weights may be inserted into the vagina or rectum as well. Some will drink fluids before being weighed by their dietitian or physician. Withholding bowel movements and urinating until after being weighed can help.

Recalibrating the Scale

Scales can be recalibrated. Scales in the home, physician, or nurse's offices or on hospital wards can be altered successfully if one is not caught doing so. A pound or two increase in calibration may be subtle enough to go

Eating Disorder Behaviors 179

unnoticed. Lower readings may be desired instead to give the impression the individual is not well enough to be released from the hospital or an eating disorder program. Some fear weight gain may indicate to caregivers and family that one has recovered enough to be able to get on with life and therefore be expected to return to work, attend school, or face other feared life tasks.

Play Music or Run Water in the Bathroom to Hide Vomiting Sounds

Because vomiting can be heard beyond the bathroom or bedroom, distracting or covering sounds help to prevent others from hearing. Turning up the TV or playing music in the living room may serve much the same function.

Red Eyes

Eye redness can occur on the eyeball itself or as broken blood vessels around the eye called petechiae. The redness evolves from head pressure caused by vomiting or strenuous physical activity, including push-ups. One could tell others that they have seasonal allergies, have something in their eyes, or have an eye infection. Also, individuals could say their eyes are irritated from their contact lenses or they have been rubbing their eyes.

Eat a Portion of Food in a Restaurant, Then Have the Rest Packed Up to Go

Many feel trapped by having to eat in restaurants with others watching. It can be hard if not impossible to not eat at all, throw food away, or leave the table to vomit in the restroom without suspicion. Eating a portion of food then having it packed up shows that some food has been eaten, therefore illustrating signs of recovery while being able to successfully take uneaten food away that later can be thrown out. Taking away a portion of uneaten food may also be used later to binge on. It may also be used to feed pets as well, therefore eliminating the risk of feeling guilty for wasting food. One could also forget the doggy bag in the restaurant, providing a plausible reason the remainder of the food had been left behind.

Citing Doctor or Nutritionists' Recommendations

Because there are so many foods that have been recommended that one should or should not eat due to health or pop culture beliefs, expressing to others that certain foods must be avoided or have been recommended to eat will be deemed as legit reasons to pick and choose. Claiming to have a gluten allergy or that one is prediabetic allows the person to eliminate large varieties of carbohydrates. Stating one has a lactose intolerance provides reason to not eat a variety of dairy products. One could claim to

180 Eating Disorder Behaviors

have familial hypercholesterolemia and should not eat anything with fats, including meat products.

Genetically Modified Food Restricted Diet

Many foods have been genetically modified. Some will eliminate these from their diet for perceived health or ethical reasons or as a reason to restrict.

If One Can't Avoid Eating With Others, Don't Eat Before

To help prevent one from eating what will be felt to be too much, not eating before being expected to eat with others may prevent unwanted caloric intake. This gives others the impression eating is not a problem. Missing meals and snacks normally consumed earlier in the day can aid in this. Avoiding eating after eating with others also works to control daily intake.

Excuses With Wearing Braces

Dental pain as a result of wearing braces may be seen as a reason to not wish to eat.

Delete Browsing History on the Computer

Virtually everyone with an eating disorder will use a computer. There may be traceable evidence of having cruised the internet for eating disorder information. Pro-ana and pro-mia websites will remain in the browse history unless deleted. Others who have access to one's computer may be able to have a peek at computer activities. Emails to acquaintances with eating disorders may create a track record of these contacts as well. Similar to a computer, smart phones catalog many transactions from various apps used in social media. Cell phone histories can be deleted as well.

Only Eat When People Notice

Eating in front of others gives an impression at least some food is being consumed in a day. What can't be seen are times when food is not being eaten.

Talking as if Individuals Do Not Have Weight Control Issues

Complaining to others how skinny celebrities and others are relays a false impression that one does not understand or support excessive weight loss.

This may possibly deflect concerns by others regarding suspect weight loss efforts.

Other examples of relaying false information:

- Tell parents you are going out with friends and will eat with them.
- If parents always want you to eat with them, join a club or get involved with a sport so you have an excuse not to eat with them.
- Don't get angry if confronted by others about the eating disorder. Tell little lies to hide bigger ones.
- Wear nail polish to hide blue nail beds.

Questions

- Do you do or say anything to prevent others from being aware of your eating disorder?
- Do you relay false information to others?
- How do you do this?
- Do you fib, fabricate, or tell lies?
- Has anyone said that you are manipulative or are a liar, and who would this be?
- Who do you do this for, and why? Do they include family, friends, partner, coworkers, doctors, nutritionists, or counselors?
- Have your deceptions gotten you into trouble, and how?
- Have you lost the trust of others, and why?
- Have you lost friendships?
- Do people not believe you anymore even when you are telling the truth?
- Do you do or say anything that could result in causing harm or death to yourself, and what is it?
- Does creating the illusion that you are doing better than you really are lead to isolation in order to prevent confrontation from others?
- Do you wish you could just fess up in order to relieve the pressure of keeping secrets?
- What do you think would be the consequences of being truthful?
- Who do you think would be the most understanding of your honesty?
- Who are you worried would not understand or be supportive, and why?

Organizing Behaviors

Executing eating disorder behaviors can require meticulous organization. Planning, including making lists and putting failsafe strategies into place, comes into play.

182 Eating Disorder Behaviors

Specific Plans

Concrete plans are a hallmark of organization for those with eating disorders. There may be short-term to long-term plans. Plans can be made for a single eating disorder behavior such as what to eat or not to eat meal to meal or how to arrange a single exercise event in a day. Plans can be created for a given day, week, or month as well as for years.

Minute to minute or *short-term plans* deal with the here-and-now management of eating disorder activities that require micromanaging in the short term. Engaging in a single evening binge session may require purchasing of food and finding a place to binge while making sure others are not around to witness the event. Short-term plans may be made for any eating disorder behavior including exercising, laxative use, and vomiting as well as others.

Daily planning may include putting into place a full day of eating disorder activities. It may also include putting in order all daily events so that they happen as hoped for, such as attending classes, meeting friends, or texting family. Since there can be dozens of daily events to navigate, daily planning is not necessarily an easy thing to do. Unpredictable interruptions can seriously disrupt one's plans and bring great disappointment along with a sense of failure and being out of control.

Weekly planning may or may not require detailed day-to-day planning. For those with eating disorders, a week of planning may be all they can manage.

Due to repeated failed attempts at meeting short-term goals, long-term goals may be out of the question. Short-term goals may aid in providing a bite-sized, hoped-for manageable goal to reach.

Plans may be developed not because they work but because they are being aimed for. Repeated unmet plans can be demoralizing. Plans may be seen as eventually doable or impossible resulting in a self-fulfilled prophecy that one is a failure. Failed plans can be a form of punishment or self-flagellation.

Specific planning may not be utilized, either, because the eating disorder and other life tasks are on autopilot and fall into place as expected. It may be plans have never really worked, so why bother now? Planning may be intermittent depending on the need.

Questions

- Do you have specific plans in your life?
- What goals are you trying to achieve as a result of your plans?
- Do you have plans for implementing eating disorder focused goals?
- What are these plans and goals?
- Do you prepare meal plans or food diaries?

Eating Disorder Behaviors 183

- Do you have non-eating disorder goals, and what are they?
- How do you feel if you meet your goals?
- How do you feel when you do not meet goals?
- Do you ever feel like harming yourself or become suicidal if goals are not met?
- How do you cope with an unmet goal?
- Do you make lists of daily, weekly, or monthly plans, and what are they?
- Do you have plans to stop drinking or using drugs?
- Do you have plans to socialize more, go back to school, or look for work?
- Do you have any recovery focused plans?
- Do you have support from others around recovery plans?
- Do you have plans to harm yourself?

Documenting

Journaling eating disorder activities and associated feelings may help to motivate eating disorder actions. It is a task to document successes as well as failures. These successes and failures may be with regard to any life events and not just the eating disorder. Successes or failures with regard to academic achievements, work, peer, and family interaction can be recorded. Writing can be a form of punishment by reporting what a loser or failure individuals feel they are.

Pro-ana scrapbooks are journals created largely for tracking specific eating disorder interests. Thinspirational photos and writings, journal writing, lists of eating disorder goals, or self-deprecating comments may be included. As self-harm suggestions including suicide tips are part of the pro-ana world, photos and writings supporting self-harm and suicidal urges, printed material along these lines may be included.

Questions

- Do you document thoughts, feelings, or events in your life?
- Do you document eating disorder attitudes or activities?
- How do you do this?
- Do you document by journaling, making scrapbooks, or using social media?
- How do you document? Do you write, speak into a voice recorder, or take photos?
- Why do you document?
- Do you document as a motivating factor for eating disorder purposes?
- Do you document as a form of catharsis or to punish yourself?
- Do you document as an aid to recovery?

184 Eating Disorder Behaviors

Lists

A cornerstone of organization is list making. Lists may be eating disorder focused or in regard to many other aspects of life. Some eating disorder focused lists are as follows.

- List of restaurants that make low fat dishes
- List of current binge foods that may be eliminated one at a time with the goal of never eating them again
- List of forbidden foods
- List of safe foods or bad foods
- List of pro-ana sayings, tips, derogatory comments, and mantras
- List of rewards or punishments for meeting or not meeting eating disorder goals respectively
- List of weight loss goals
- List of recovery related goals such as improved nutrition and weight expectations
- List of significant others one can rely on for support such as emergency mental health help lines, counselors, caseworkers, friends, and family

Questions

- Do you make lists?
- Do you make lists that are eating disorder specific?
- What items are on your lists?
- Do list items address weight loss, restricting, or exercise goals?
- How important is it to you to complete the items on your list?
- Are any items on your list dangerous?
- Are there any pro-ana tips or hints on your list?
- Do you have a list of recovery goals?

Eating Disorder Action Tools or Packages

As carpenters have tool kits filled with a variety of tools to approach construction tasks, some with eating disorders have their bag of tricks, as it were, to motivate or execute their eating disorder directives. They are part of their eating disorder arsenal.

Pro-ana kits are made up of various items placed into an inconspicuous box. Lists of foods to avoid, exercise schedules, distractions from eating, weight targets, thinspirational photos and tips, and possibly a piece of undersized clothing may be included. Individuals may include fashion and diet magazines, a pro-ana scrapbook, journal, and photos of themselves when either overweight or underweight. It acts as a sort of eating disorder survival kit that can be brought out at will when needing motivation.

Alternate Plans

When original plans do not work due to unexpected or unavoidable events, alternate plans need to be put in place. Alternate plans or plan Bs help to cope when events do not unfold as hoped for. These are a way of running interference or juggling unpredictable life events. They create checks and balances. They help to avert the perceived devastating consequences of not meeting goals.

Questions

- How well can you stick to plans?
- Which plans are most useful, and which tend not to be useful, and why?
- Do some plans work sometimes and not others, and why?

Organizing for Recovery

As there can be great attention given to support eating disorder goals, there can be organizational directives to aid in recovery. Many of the organizational steps used for maintaining eating disorder behaviors may be implemented for recovery purposes, the difference being that recovery efforts will have pretty much the opposite goals and planning.

Lists can be made to assist better eating including weekly and daily planning. Lists of food with real nutrition value and of goals to eat adequate amounts can come into play. Plans made to lessen or eliminate binge eating, vomiting, over-exercising, taking laxatives, or virtually any other eating disorder behavior or to reverse weight lose are possible. Journaling positive thoughts about recovery or any other life challenge may be useful.

The organizational tasks and dedicated efforts for recovery may require as much as and more than perpetuating the eating disorder itself. Support surrounding recovery efforts by significant others is paramount.

The recovery process may bring serious or even life-threatening risks, especially when individuals who have been severely restricting then attempt to introduce nutrition quickly. They may develop the *refeeding syndrome*, where acute metabolic disturbances can result in critical medical instability. Those in recovery need to be followed closely by their physicians until potential risks have been reduced.

Questions

- Do you have any plans for recovery?
- What plans have you made?
- Do you make journal entries focused on recovery, and what do you write?

186 Eating Disorder Behaviors

- Do you make lists of plans for recovery?
- Have you set any time limits for recovery, and what are they?
- Do you think your goals are realistic given the time you have allowed to achieve them?
- Have you set one or two goals or several?
- Do you think you have set too many goals to work on at the same time?
- Do you think you should triage or prioritize recovery goals to make the recovery process more doable?
- Do you have a physician following you closely during the recovery process?

Symptom Management Behaviors

Because many with eating disorders experience physical or medical symptoms, attempts are made to prevent them in the first place or to alleviate them when they do occur. As symptoms may originate from several causes, details of what may cause a given symptom have been elucidated here. How symptoms may be dealt with will vary depending on the etiology. The methods individuals may use to deal with the symptoms listed here are what some believe to be of help but may not be based in evidence. There are several medical causes for these symptoms, and all clinicians should be familiar with them whether they are medically trained or not. The management of these health issues, though, will be the responsibility of medical folk.

Relieving Hunger

Hunger can be an uncomfortable feeling, plus it can be a precursor for binge eating or even eating anything at all when not wanted. There are several ways to curb hunger in the short term.

- Drink fluids. Sparkling water or fizzy pops are believed to give a full feeling more than flat fluids. Hot water or cold water are believed by some to be more filling. Thirst can be confused with feelings of hunger.
- Smoke a cigarette.
- Chew gum.
- Eat a small amount of food that has little caloric content such as carrots, celery, or lettuce.
- Eat food with high fiber content.
- Drink alcohol instead of eating. Alcohol may have an appetite suppressing effect.

Eating Disorder Behaviors   187

- Use cocaine, ecstasy (E) or methylenedioxymethamphetamine (MDMA), heroin or other street drugs.
- Suck on sugarless candies.
- Eat a spoonful of honey or other food that can satiate sweetness or other cravings.
- Eat foods with high water volume.
- Take a shower or a bath.

Questions

- Do you experience hunger, and why?
- Do you hope to feel hungry or want to avoid it?
- What does it mean to you when you become hungry? Does it make you feel you have been successful with restricting or will put you at risk if it triggers eating, including bingeing?
- What do you do to curb hunger?
- What happens when you cannot control hunger?
- Is managing hunger a core control issue for you?

Some with eating disorders say that they do not experience hunger regardless of how little they eat or vomit.

> *"I lost all ability to eat based on my hunger and fullness. Instead I relied on counting calories or making eating schedules and plans."*

> *"I had no idea what comfortably full was and only a vague idea of what hunger was. I felt that if I ate until I was full, I would never stop eating."*

Questions

- If you do not experience hunger, is this a desired thing, and why?
- If trying to improve your nutrition, does not being hungry make it more difficult to eat?
- Is not feeling hungry a goal of yours?
- Is lacking hunger due to drug or alcohol causes?

In the eating disorder world, hunger will often and likely be a result of restricting or not keeping in an adequate amount of food as well as from burning calories with exercise. If for any reason individuals do not meet their daily nutrition requirements, they will likely become hungry. It may be necessary to inquire as to other sources of hunger. High blood sugars with diabetes will cause an insatiable hunger. Malabsorption syndromes prevent nutrients from being absorbed, leading to hunger.

Indigestion

The term indigestion is a loose term to describe a variety of abdominal symptoms from different causes. Heartburn, sick stomach, and upset stomach are a few other terms that might be used as well. Because the word stomach if often used to describe anywhere in the abdomen, there needs to be clarity as to what is meant by stomach. Gut symptoms are often vague and sometimes difficult to describe; therefore, it is important to differentiate amongst different plausible diagnoses. A complaint of upset stomach may be due to having eaten too much greasy food or subtle early symptoms of pancreatitis. While having eaten greasy food is not serious, pancreatitis can be fatal. Some malignancies and metabolic abnormalities may initially present similarly.

Indigestion may be the result of:

- Gallbladder disease
- Acid reflux caused by a hiatal hernia, hyperacidic stomach, and repeated vomiting that makes the lower esophageal sphincter lax and less competent
- Gastritis
- Intestinal motility disorder
- Food intolerances including gluten and dairy intolerances
- Celiac disease
- Excessively spicy or acidic foods
- Stomach or duodenal ulcers
- Esophagitis
- Pancreatitis
- Irritable bowel syndrome
- Crohn's disease
- Ulcerative colitis
- Gut infections including parasites and Helicobacter pylori (H. pylori)
- Food poisoning
- Cardiac problems such as an irregular heart, angina, or pericarditis
- Vomiting
- Laxative use
- Excessive alcohol use
- Street drug or OTC medications
- Medications including antidepressants, antibiotics, and hormonal contraceptives taken orally, vaginally, or in patch form

Antacids, Pepto-Bismol and Gaviscon may help relieve an upset stomach and a growling stomach. Audible stomach sounds may indicate to others that one is hungry and has not eaten for a while. Family members may have a heightened awareness of this concern. Eating ginger or peppermint

Eating Disorder Behaviors 189

is used to sooth the stomach. Eating yogurt and probiotics are used to normalize gut flora and relieve symptoms. Stopping bingeing, vomiting, or laxative use temporarily may help to alleviate symptoms. Not eating foods or taking medications associated with indigestion may bring some relief.

Questions

- Do you experience indigestion?
- How do you describe indigestion?
- What do you think causes it?
- How often does it occur, and how long does it last?
- Does it present the same way every time or differently?
- What makes the symptoms worse or better?
- Have you seen your doctor about this?
- Have there been any medical tests performed, and if so, what was found?
- How do you cope with indigestion?
- Do you take any medication for this?
- Do you think anything you do as part of the eating disorder such as vomiting, eating including bingeing, food choices, or laxative use contribute to indigestion?
- When did these symptoms start for the first time, and why?
- Is there a family history of bowel disease such as Crohn's disease, ulcerative colitis, or gallbladder disease?
- Have you seen a physician with regard to these symptoms?
- Are you sure you really know what is causing your indigestion?

Abdominal Cramps

Abdominal cramps possibly caused from not eating, eating, or constipation may be relieved by using a hot water bottle placed on the abdomen and curling up in the fetal position. Cramps caused from not eating may subside with eating a small amount of food. Cramping caused by refeeding may be treated with prescription gut dysmotility modifiers. If cramps are the result of binge eating, then eating less or not at all may be a solution. Eating small amounts of food frequently throughout the day can decrease cramping. Avoiding foods such as salads that require larger volumes to deliver the same nutrition value as higher calorie-dense foods may be of use. Drinking liquids with good nutrition value is sometimes better tolerated than solids. Commercial liquid meal replacements and homemade shakes are examples. Since select foods may result in cramping in some individuals and not others, some will avoid specific foods on an individual basis. If cold foods or hot foods increase cramping these can be avoided. See "Indigestion" to identify other causes of abdominal cramps.

190   Eating Disorder Behaviors

Questions

- Do you experience stomach cramps?
- Point to the part of your abdomen where they occur.
- Do they present the same way every time, or do they occur in different places in the abdomen?
- Do they come due to specific triggers or spontaneously, or both?
- What will make cramps better or worse?
- Are abdominal cramps related to eating—eating certain foods, eating anything, eating a given quantity?
- Are they related to bingeing, vomiting, or the use of laxatives?
- Does not eating over a period of time result in cramps?
- How do you deal with them?
- Do they prevent you from being able to do anything—going to classes or working or socializing?
- Are cramps associated with vomiting or diarrhea?
- Are these cramps possibly related to having your period or a urinary tract infection?
- Have you seen a doctor regarding your cramps?
- Have you had any investigations performed, such as an abdominal or pelvic ultrasound, X-rays, urinalysis, stool samples, or scoping of the stomach or colon?
- Have you been prescribed medications to relieve cramps, and if so, do they work?
- Do you use an intrauterine device?
- Do you have a history of ovarian cysts or endometriosis?

Diarrhea

Diarrhea may result from many sources. For those with eating disorders, laxative use comes to mind. Enema use can also create a brief diarrheal episode. Erratic eating may also be a cause. Constipation may be a source of diarrhea, as liquid stool can build up behind constipated stool and pass around it. Medical conditions such as Crohn's disease, ulcerative colitis, food poisoning, malabsorption syndromes, food intolerances, and gut infections, including parasites, should be considered. After gallbladder removal, a state of chronic diarrhea may result. If diarrhea is associated with indigestion or abdominal cramps, then ask questions related to these symptoms.

There are several ways diarrhea may present. Each may indicate a specific etiology, some of which will suggest higher risk concerns.

Questions

- How often do you have diarrhea?
- When did you first notice diarrhea?

Eating Disorder Behaviors 191

- Do you know what causes it?
- Is the cause of diarrhea deliberate?
- Is there any pattern to when it occurs?
- Is there blood in the stool, or do you see it in the toilet bowl?
- Do you use chemicals such as enemas that could cause bleeding? Caustic drain cleaning fluids could cause bleeding from the colon.
- Did you eat beets prior to having red stool?
- Do you get cramping before, during, or after a bowel movement?
- Have you seen a physician regarding this? If so, what was stated as to the cause and how to deal with it?
- Have you had any diagnostic tests such as stool sample evaluations or X-rays?
- Is there a family history of Crohn's disease or ulcerative colitis?
- Have you been somewhere where you could have picked up a gut infection, including a parasite?
- Are you sure blood is coming from your bowel, or do you think it could be from your bladder or vagina? Some will discover blood on bathroom tissue but will not be sure of its source. Some will say, "When I wipe I see blood on the tissue, but I don't know where it is coming from!"

Damaged Hands

Because stomach acid is so caustic, those that vomit frequently while using their fingers may experience skin irritation or damage of the hands. Damage to fingernails called paronychia may develop. To avoid this, washing hands immediately after vomiting is practiced. Hand lotions may soothe irritated skin.

Teeth and Gum Damage

Dental erosion and gum damage may result from vomiting. Efforts to prevent this may include rinsing the mouth after vomiting. Rinsing with baking soda mixed with water is used to neutralize acid in the mouth. Tooth brushing immediately after vomiting is well known to cause faster destruction of enamel, as enamel is softened by stomach acid. It is believed that low hydration or dehydration increases tooth decay. Keeping well hydrated may help prevent the escalation of dental demise.

Some have had their second or third set of crowns or caps in their early twenties. Costs can exceed $60,000 or more for dental work, and some have spent whole inheritances on dental repair.

Questions

- Do you think there has been any damage to your gums or teeth from vomiting, and why do you think so?

192 Eating Disorder Behaviors

- Have you seen a dentist in regard to this?
- What damage do you think has resulted—cavities, gum recession, infections?
- What kind of dental work have you had to date?
- How much money have you spent on dental work?
- How much money have you been told you will need to spend to repair your teeth?
- Can you afford dental work?
- What do you do to help prevent dental damage?
- Have you been refused dental work because you are too unhealthy to tolerate it? Dentists will not do major dental work, especially requiring a general anesthetic, if their patient is too emaciated or metabolically unstable.

Mouth or Throat Injury

The act of vomiting may result in damage to the throat aside from that caused by stomach acid. Fingernails, spoons, spatulas, or any hard and sharp object may scratch or bruise the throat. In an attempt to prevent this, some will cut their fingernails short and chose not to use hard objects to induce vomiting. Spatulas, spoons, and other cutlery can get caught in the throat, resulting in choking. These same objects may also damage teeth by cracking or breaking them.

Questions

- How do you make yourself vomit?
- Do you ever experience mouth, throat, or dental pain as a result of vomiting?
- What do you do to cope with these symptoms?
- Have you ever had any dental damage from inducing vomiting?
- Do you ever experience bleeding from inducing vomiting?
- Do you think this bleeding is from mouth injury?

Sore Throat From Other Causes

Pain in the throat due to vomiting may be caused by stomach acid or objects that induce vomiting, as already mentioned. Smoking cigarettes or marijuana may also cause throat pain. Drinking very hot liquids or eating hot foods can scald the mouth, including the throat.

There are a few ways of dealing with throat pain. Drinking cold drinks is felt to decrease throat pain. Avoiding any attempt to vomit or drink and eat very hot foods, even temporarily, will also aid in symptom relief. Throat lozenges with some anesthetic action are of some use.

Questions

- Do you experience a sore throat or mouth?
- Why do you think this happens?
- What do you do to cope with the pain?
- If you consume very hot liquids or food, why do you feel you need to do this?
- Is consuming very hot liquids or food a way to discourage yourself from eating more, or is it to deliberately hurt yourself or punish yourself, and why?
- Do you develop mouth blisters or bleeding from taking in hot substances?
- Where did you learn to eat hot food? This behavior may have been learned from someone else who does the same thing.
- Have you seen your physician regarding this?

Weight Gain From Water Retention

Drinking fluids may cause weight gain, along with the possibility of developing puffiness as the result of edema; this is of concern to many with eating disorders. There are various ways of trying to deal with this. The use of diuretics has been mentioned earlier. While some rely on diuretics and even laxatives to lose water weight, others learn that this may eventually lead to the body retaining water in order to counter the dehydrating effect of these medications. Therefore, some will avoid these substances in order to prevent eventual rebound water retention.

Water restriction or any cause of dehydration will lead to the body hoarding water and holding on to it until the effect of dehydration has passed. This is due in part to hyperaldosteronism. It can take weeks for the body to return to its normal hydration state. Rehydrating in the hospital from drinking and intravenous fluids can cause quick water retention that is very upsetting to those experiencing it.

Questions

- Have you ever experienced "water weight" from fluid intake resulting puffiness or edema?
- When has this happened, and why, if you know?
- Have you experienced this during refeeding or rehydrating when in the hospital?

194 Eating Disorder Behaviors

- What part of your body did you notice the swelling—face, arms, hands, legs, feet, or abdomen? Anywhere else?
- Did this happen with IV (intravenous) fluid replacement?
- What were you told by the doctors as to why this happens?
- How did you cope with this?
- Did swelling or weight gain get in the way of your recovery? Has this resulted in you discharging yourself from hospital, pulling IV tubes out, pinching IV tubing, or decreasing the rate of IV flow?
- Have you taken diuretics or restricted fluids or salt intake to compensate?
- What makes the swelling worse, and what makes it better?

Dizziness, Falling, Fainting, and Palpitations

Feeling dizzy, falling, fainting or palpitations can be symptoms of malnutrition, dehydration, drug and alcohol use, metabolic abnormalities, and cardiac or other medical illnesses as well as the use of several prescription, over-the-counter, or illicit drugs. The symptoms may be a result of a combination of these causes. Some will try to prevent these symptoms because they are uncomfortable, fear more serious risks developing, including death, or wish to hide from others how well they actually are. Looking healthy as well as preventing falling or fainting can relay a false impression that the eating disorder is not that bad.

Ways individuals believe they can prevent these symptoms may include:

- Drinking fluids to increase hydration and therefore help to keep blood pressure elevated and regulate the heart rhythm.
- Drinking fluids with electrolytes and minerals, known as "smart waters," to help normalize the metabolic state. Sport drinks such as Gatorade and fluid replacement for children such as Pedialyte are used for this purpose. Cardiac dysrhythmias and renal failure may be corrected to some degree by maintaining normal levels of electrolytes including sodium, potassium, chloride, and bicarbonate. Mineral replacements of iron, zinc, and magnesium serve a similar function.
- Taking a multivitamin daily.
- Normalizing nutrition and hydration generally.
- Discontinuing ipecac, as it causes all of these symptoms and can have lethal consequences.

Questions

- Do you ever feel dizzy, or have you fallen or fainted?
- Have you lost consciousness after falling?
- Do you ever noticed your heart pound or thump in your chest?
- Why do you think these symptoms occur, and when?

Eating Disorder Behaviors   195

- Do you deliberately make them happen or hope they occur, and why?
- Do they upset you or cause you to fear them?
- How do you deal with them when they do occur?
- Have you seen your physician regarding these symptoms?

Shortness of Breath and Chest Pains

Methods that relieve symptoms of dizziness like those mentioned earlier also may aid with relieving shortness of breath and chest pains, depending on the causes.

Blood With Vomiting and Rectal Bleeding

Some will experience blood during vomiting. Blood with vomiting can come from different sources. This may be a desired sign or feared one (see "Vomiting" earlier in this chapter). Causes include:

- Scratches at the back of the throat from fingernails or hard and sharp objects used to induce vomiting
- Tears in the stomach, cardia. or esophagus
- Nosebleeds caused by harsh periods of vomiting

Blood may present as red or black coffee grounds. The coffee-ground appearance is a result of blood in the stomach that has been pooling there for a while. A potentially serious risk is bleeding that is unnoticed. Tears of the esophagus and stomach can cause bleeding that goes undetected if someone is not vomiting. People can bleed to death internally without detection. Black stools are suggestive of intestinal bleeding; however, consuming Pepto-Bismol, a product used to relieve stomach upset, can give the same result. Iron supplements can turn stools black. So as not to mask evidence of bleeding, any food or drink that is red is avoided, as red foods may obscure that bleeding has occurred.

Questions
- Do you notice any blood when you vomit?
- Does this happen every time you vomit or on and off?
- What do you think causes bleeding one time and not another?
- Do you notice chest pain or gut pain when this happens?
- Do you ever vomit black coffee-ground-like matter?
- Do you notice rectal bleeding presenting as a red or black color?
- Do you deliberately try to create bleeding with vomiting, and why?
- What do you do to prevent this from happening, if anything?
- If you see black stool, could it be because you take Pepto-Bismol for stomach ailments or iron supplements for anemia?

196 Eating Disorder Behaviors

- If you see red stools or red in the toilet bowel after a bowel movement, could you have eaten beets in the last few days?
- Have you told your doctor about this?

Bleeding may not be caused from eating disorder behaviors. Other causes of rectal bleeding include stomach ulcers, hemorrhoids, anal sex, the use of caustic enemas, Crohn's disease, ulcerative colitis, polyps in the colon, anal fissures, hemorrhoids, diverticulosis, toxic megacolon, clostridium diffi-cile, opportunistic bowel infections, and malignancies. Sometimes vaginal bleeding and bleeding from the bladder can be confused with rectal bleeding.

Weight Gain Secondary to Metabolic Status

A commonly believed cause of weight gain is a slow metabolism. Attempts to alleviate this feared risk are as follows.

- Eating frequent small meals allows for increased metabolism or burning of calories.
- Never eat late in the evening, as some believe metabolism decreases when we sleep and more calories may be retained.
- Lose weight slowly. Those who experience fast weight loss and then rebound weight gain learn to avoid rapid weight loss.
- Use metabolism boosters.

Anxiety

Anxiety can affect individuals in several ways. It can lead to nervous eating or wanting not to eat. It may increase depression, fears, panic, and obsessive-compulsive traits as well as worsen bipolar symptoms. Sleep may also be affected.

As stimulants may be used to suppress appetite or increase metabolism, they can aggravate anxiety. For those affected by these chemicals, they may be deliberately avoided. Caffeine is likely the most consumed stimulant that aggravates symptoms. Antianxiety medications are, of course, a possible solution to dealing with anxiety.

Questions

- Do you experience anxiety?
- How do you cope with this?
- Does anxiety interfere with socializing, work, or school?
- Does it cause you to isolate?

- Do you use the eating disorder to cope with anxiety, and how do you do this?
- Do you use drugs or alcohol to deal with anxiety?
- Do you currently or have you ever used medications to control anxiety?
- What makes anxiety worse or better?
- Do you take stimulants?

Death

Whether dying is considered a sign or a symptom, it is usually avoided. Normalizing nutrition and metabolic states is helpful. Regardless of the fact that many look as if they have a death wish, they often have a secret fear of dying. Efforts to prevent this may be attempted, even if minimal.

Questions

- Are you afraid of dying from the eating disorder?
- Are you afraid of dying because of suicide or from an accidental drug overdose?
- What do you think you would die from such as a heart attack, stroke, kidney disease, or some other way?
- Do you want to die?
- Do you hope the eating disorder will kill you?
- If you want to die, what is keeping you from doing so, such as not wanting to hurt family or friends?

Some believe they know where the line is between surviving and dying. They will maximize their eating disorder behaviors and medical risks to a point where they feel they are just shy of dying. They learn to eat just enough, as they want to be thin but not dead. It is highly variable as to when one individual will manifest health risks and another will not, including dying.

A significant problem with dealing with those with eating disorders is that they can maintain a virtually identical eating disorder regime and stable medical status for years. Comments by clinicians such as "You're going to die from your eating disorder" often fall on deaf ears, as years of flouting this fear may have not come to being. Because the body has a quite remarkable capacity of compensating for deficient nutrition, there can be a day when it is no longer able to do so, and some do die.

Surgery and Other Cosmetic Altering Methods

> *"I have been through two cosmetic procedures to lose weight. Breast reduction and CoolSculpting on my stomach. I still can't understand*

> *why women want their chest to be bigger. While the plastic surgeon
> did a great job by most people's standards (even the nurses said as
> much post-op), I was upset with her for not taking more tissue off.
> As for the CoolSculpting on my stomach, I was willing to spend
> thousands of dollars to hopefully permanently destroy fat cells. I wish
> I had that money back, as I don't really see much difference."*

Surgery serves different functions for those with an eating disorder. It is sometimes used to cause weight loss by the *removal of body fat*. *Liposuction, tummy tucks* and *breast reductions* are examples. Surgery is also used to reshape the body to a perceived more desirable one. This may include the surgical procedures already mentioned and also may involve *breast augmentation* or buccal fat pad removal of the cheek.

Liposuction

Liposuction is a procedure that involves suctioning fat tissue from various parts of the body. Common targets are the hips, thighs, abdomen, arms, neck, face, and back. It should be performed by trained professionals, but there is poor screening for training credentials. It is relatively safe, less invasive, and less costly than some plastic surgery. The desired result may be achieved, but there can also be devastating outcomes.

Facial Procedures

The face is a prime target for cosmetic alteration. Liposuction under the chin and of the cheeks, jowls, and neck is possible. Surgery of the nose for reshaping is an option. *Botox*, a medication that is injected to paralyze muscle, is used to remove facial creases typically seen at the corners of the mouth, crow's feet, and between the eyebrows. Botox injections usually need to be repeated every so many months. Facelifts are more complicated and expensive procedures likely to be performed on those who are older. *Lip injections* plump up the lips as a desirable facial feature.

Plastic surgery may be used to remove blemishes such as moles, scars, or prominent skin veins.

Labiaplasty

A *labiaplasty* is a surgical procedure that involves trimming the labia of the vulva. It sometimes is required, as some may have large enough labia that cause physical discomfort, including pain or chaffing as a result of physical activities. Friction from a bicycle seat is an example. A labiaplasty is also performed for cosmetic reasons. In an era of easily accessible pornography, some women evaluate their labia based on pornographic images. Redundant labial tissue is sometimes felt to be unfeminine, and some will compare their labia to that of animals. Much assurance needs to be given that their vulva is natural and that the negative body image concerns their discontent evokes are detrimental to their well-being.

Cosmetic altering procedures may lead to regretted consequences. Surgical procedures can result in undesirable results. Liposuction anywhere may cause unexpected puckering and ridges. If individuals hate their body before cosmetic alteration, this feeling is compounded multifold after bad results. Terrible guilt and self-hatred compound an already present loathing of their body. The problem with unwanted results is that they are often difficult and very expensive to repair. Botched procedures may be irreversible, and individuals will have to live with this the rest of their lives.

As clinicians, we need to provide constructive advice. Encourage individuals to not have the procedure or at least postpone it until further thought has gone into it. For those with regretted results, they need emotional support and advice with regard to being careful regarding attempts to reverse poor outcomes. Accepting and living with the unwanted results may be the best or only option.

These procedures can be extremely costly. There are bargain surgical procedures that call into question the skill and competence of the one performing the surgery. Some will not be trained surgeons, or at least not trained in plastic surgery. Surgery may cost someone $20,000 for a nose or labia alteration. Other operations will have similar costs. Botox may cost hundreds of dollars for each set of injections and requires the person to have the procedure every few months.

Questions

- Have you had any cosmetic surgery, and what kind?
- Are you planning to have cosmetic surgery? What kind and why?
- Are surgical operations part of eating disorder drives to lose weight or alter body shape or both?
- Is surgery intended for removal of blemishes such as moles, veins, skin tumors, or scars?
- Is surgery intended to correct previous poor surgical outcomes from cosmetic altering procedures?
- Is surgery intended to correct poor cosmetic surgical outcomes from non-cosmetic procedures such as scarring from gallbladder removal or cesarean sections?
- How much money have you spent on cosmetic surgery?
- How much money do you expect to spend for future cosmetic surgical procedures?
- How important are cosmetic surgical procedures to you?

200　Eating Disorder Behaviors

- Would you consider delaying surgery until you have thought more about it?
- What will you do if you are unhappy with the results?
- Are you afraid that poor surgical outcomes may be impossible to correct, or that it could cost you thousands of dollars more for yet another poor outcome?
- If you have one more operation, will it likely be the last one, or are you likely going to focus on another part of your body that you feel needs alteration?
- Are you trying to look like someone else such as a celebrity, and why?

CoolSculpting or Cryolipolysis

Cryolipolysis is a procedure that selectively freezes fat tissue in order to reshape parts of the body. It is used to treat visible fat from various parts of the body. It is not a treatment for obesity. It is used to decrease fat from submental tissue, abdomen, flanks, thighs, back, under the bra, and upper arms. Reports regarding cryolipolysis are so-so. Concerns are that it works, sort of, but costs a lot of money.

Makeup

Makeup is used for a variety of cosmetic reasons. It may be used to beautify and to create a certain fashion look as well as to cover up acne, acne-created scars, or other blemishes. Makeup is used on any part of the body and is not just for facial use. For those with eating disorders, any kind of perceived flaw may lead to terrible feelings of self-awareness, ugliness, self-loathing, and worthlessness as well as increased anxiety and depression. Suicidal thoughts can come to light.

Makeup may be used to create the appearance of being thinner, especially on the face, as well as other parts of the body, including the legs and knees. Putting makeup on can be an ordeal. To some, if the appearance they are trying to create is not perfect, they may repeat applying the makeup for hours daily. This can create significant problems with social functioning.

Questions

- Do you use makeup to visually reshape parts of your body so they look thinner?
- What parts of your body do you do this to, and why?
- Have you considered surgery for those parts of your body you currently use makeup for, and what parts of your body are you thinking of?
- Do you use makeup to hide blemishes such as acne or surgical scars, hyperpigmentation, or spider veins?

- Do you use makeup on parts of your body that are not exposed just in case you need to be taken to the hospital, where you will likely be examined?

Substance Use

Drugs

Drugs play an intimate role in the eating disorder world. Drugs from pharmacies may come in prescription form or over the counter. Street drugs can be any drug accessed outside of a pharmacy. These may include pharmaceuticals or recreational drugs.

Recreational drugs can be accessed from drug dealers or personal acquaintances. There are a plethora of types of drugs available, and their availability depends on the supply and social circles individuals associate with. A few decades ago, the drug dealer was a shady guy in a trench coat who carried a shotgun in his car and was connected to dangerous crime figures. Today, drugs are easily accessed from close friends and personal social contacts found at school, work, or nightclubs. Family members may be sources of drugs as well.

Non-prescription recreational drugs include marijuana, ecstasy, cocaine, and heroin as well as others. Classic prescription recreational drugs include amphetamines, benzodiazepines, and narcotics such as morphine, Dilaudid, Demerol and fentanyl. Over-the-counter drugs may have recreational uses. Some of these drugs are Gravol and sleeping pills, as well as metabolism boosters that contain stimulants.

Each of these drugs might be used for much the same reasons as others or may serve a unique purpose, depending on the individual. It is important to ask why each drug is used. Some of the uses may be eating disorder driven or not. Each drug may present a different risk as well.

Specific eating disorder reasons for drug use include to:

- Suppress appetite
- Increase metabolism
- Distract from eating
- Induce vomiting
- Create diarrhea, dehydrate, diuresis
- Induce sleeping excessively to avoid eating

Other reasons for drug use include:

- Getting stoned or feeling high
- Numbing out
- Fitting in with peers

202 Eating Disorder Behaviors

- Addiction
- Inducing sleep
- Use as a stimulant
- Decreasing anxiety
- Dealing with depression
- Dealing with loneliness
- Dealing with peer pressure
- Dealing with post-traumatic stress disorder (PTSD)
- Controlling symptoms of attention deficit hyperactivity disorder
- To focus attention during studying
- Pulling all-nighters
- Stabilizing moods in order to feel normal

Drugs may be used for just one purpose or for multiple purposes. The same drug may serve different purposes, or poly-drug use may serve the same or different uses.

Whether a drug is used specifically for eating disorders or not, they all very likely have some direct or indirect effect on the eating disorder. The dynamics of drug use and eating disorder behaviors and attitude are complicated.

Some risks of drug use may include:

- Personal and legal consequences of stealing money from family, friends, or strangers to purchase drugs
- Expectations of sexual favors in exchange for drugs
- Becoming involved in the sex trade
- Becoming connected with the criminal influences of the drug and sex trade community
- Pregnancy or sexually transmitted infections including HIV
- Isolation
- Exacerbation of moods including depression and anxiety
- Escalation of suicidal ideation and subsequent attempts
- Psychosis
- Addiction
- Lack of motivation or mental clarity to attend to life tasks, including eating disorder recovery
- Serious financial costs
- Sabotaging life opportunities including maintaining healthy relationships or education and career aspirations
- Serious and life-threatening health issues

Alcohol

Alcohol is technically a drug. Unless used for medicinal purposes, it is considered a recreational drug. It can be used very much for the same purposes

Eating Disorder Behaviors 203

that many of the prescription drugs, street drugs, and over-the-counter drugs are used. It is undoubtedly one of the most commonly used recreational drugs, along with caffeine and nicotine. Because alcohol is readily available to those of legal age or younger and relatively inexpensive compared to many street and pharmacological drugs, it is the number one drug that creates chemical addiction and the most social, legal, and health problems to those with eating disorders. It will be the major addicting substance for those closest to them, including family and peers. Alcohol consumption is largely socially acceptable, and dependence can be hidden while indulging in front of others.

Alcohol is a multipurpose drug. When used for eating disorder purposes it serves to:

- Suppress appetite
- Distract from eating
- Satiate hunger
- Cause someone to sleep longer so as to not have as much time in a day to eat or think about food, body image or weight
- Induce vomiting
- Create nausea to discourage eating
- Provide less daily calorie intake if one drinks alcohol only and does not eat food

Questions

- Do you use drugs or alcohol in excess?
- Why do you use them?
- Is alcohol or drug use an adjunct to the eating disorder, such as for weight or body image control?
- What drugs do you use, including prescription, over-the-counter, or illicit drugs?
- Where do you get drugs from?
- Do you use drugs or alcohol to suppress appetite, replace eating, or increase sleeping?
- Does drug use get you into trouble regarding financial or legal concerns, relationships with family and friends, or in the work place or school?
- Do you use drugs with others, and who are they?
- Have you exchanged sex for drugs?

References

Elran-Barak, R., Goldschmidt, A. B., Crow, S. J., Peterson, C. B., Hill, L., Crosby, R. D et al. (2017). Is laxative misuse associated with binge eating? Examination of laxative misuse among individuals seeking treatment for eating disorders. *Int Journal Eat Disord,* 50(9): 1114–1118. doi: 10.1002/eat.22745. Epub 2017 Aug 2.

204 Eating Disorder Behaviors

Finsterer, J., & Stöllberger, C. (2014). Recurrent aborted sudden cardiac death with seizures and rhabdomyolysis due to bulimia-induced hypokalemia: Report of one case. *Rev Med Chil*, 142(6): 799–802. doi: 10.4067/S0034–98872014000600016.

Grewal, S., & Birmingham, C. L. (2003). Self-phlebotomy in eating disorders. *Eat Weight Disord*, 8(4): 336–340.

Klein, D. A., Boudreau, G. S., Devlin, M. J., & Walsh, B. T. (2006). Artificial sweetener use among individuals with eating disorders. *Int Journal Eat Disord*, 39(4): 341–345.

Koff, E., & Rierdan, J. (1991). Perceptions of weight and attitudes toward eating in early adolescent girls. *J Adolesc Health*, 12(4): 307–312.

Moosavi, M., Kreisman, S., & Hall, L. (2015). Intentional hypoglycemia to control bingeing in a patient with type 1 diabetes and bulimia nervosa. *Can J Diabetes*, 39(1): 16–17. doi: 10.1016/j.jcjd.2014.04.007. Epub 2014 Oct 1.

Morean, M. E., & Wedel, A. V. (2017). Vaping to lose weight: Predictors of adult e-cigarette use for weight loss or control. *Addict Behav*, 66: 55–59. doi: 10.1016/j.addbeh.2016.10.022. Epub 2016 Oct 24.

Steffen, K. J., Mitchell, J. E., Roerig, J. L., & Lancaster, K. L. (2007). The eating disorders medicine cabinet revisited: A clinician's guide to ipecac and laxatives. *Int Journal Eat Disord*, 40(4): 360–368.

Stheneur, C., Bergeron, S. J., Frappier, J. Y., Jamoulle, O., Taddeo, D., Sznajder, M., & Lapeyraque, A. L. (2017). Renal injury in pediatric anorexia nervosa: A retrospective study. *Eat Weight Disord*. doi: 10.1007/s40519-017-0401-1. [Epub ahead of print].

Chapter 5

Eating Disorder Behavior Parameters

> *"I am turning 42 this year. I began my path into the world of eating disorders when I was about 15, so I have lived and battled with it for more than half my life."*

The parameters in this chapter identify specific attributes for *each* suspected eating disorder behavior. Questions relating to the parameters add various degrees of detail about any given behavior. These provide the basic structure for thoroughness. There may be other attributes that are not covered here and may be queried as well. The parameters are tools to help tease out the finest intricacies of someone's eating disorder. Although these parameters are described to eke out details of eating disorder behaviors, they may be applied to other risky behaviors such as drug and alcohol use as well as self-harm. Examples of parameter-related questions are given in some detail within the fuller descriptions of a few specific eating disorders. The line of questioning used for these may be extrapolated to other behaviors. The parameters, as listed here, are not in any logical order. Depending on answers given, the line of questioning may change the order of the next parameter focused upon. There is no predictable line of questioning.

Risk assessment is improved by use of these parameters. Some risks are touched on here as well as in different sections of the book. Risks from eating disorder behaviors as well as non-eating disorder behaviors need to be evaluated in depth. Medical as well as suicidal risks are of paramount concern.

Eating Disorder and Non-Eating Disorder Uses for Each Suspected Eating Disorder Behavior

When looking for any and all suspected eating disorder behaviors, we need to remember that any given behavior may be used for non-eating disorder purposes. As an example, someone may use laxatives for eating disorder use as a perceived way of losing weight. Laxatives may also be used for a non-eating disorder purpose such as to deal with constipation, a common problem with those with eating disorders. Laxatives may be used for both eating disorder and non-eating disorder use either at the same time or at different times. Some vomit to lose weight for eating disorder purposes or may vomit to relieve abdominal pain and to cope with stress, which are reasons not specific to eating disorders. Vomiting may meet *all* of these purposes. The reason for using any eating disorder behavior may serve an eating disorder purpose one time and a non-eating disorder purpose another or serve both reasons at the same time.

Some genuinely do not have any idea why they use any given behavior. They may say that it is a habit and not be aware of any driving forces or triggers that perpetuate them. Further in-depth questioning may aid in bringing to light reasons for employing these behaviors.

The following behaviors used for eating disorder purposes may also have other uses, as listed here:

- Exercise may serve to aid in dealing with depression and anxiety or be a form of competitive sport.
- Diuretics may be used to deal with premenstrual symptoms such as bloating or depression.
- Wearing multiple layers of clothes may serve to warm an individual.
- Food avoidance may result from a real food phobia developed from exposure to rotting food and a poor hygienic environment.
- Someone may lie to their parents about their eating disorder in order to avoid harsh emotional or physical abuse.
- Many eating disorder behaviors may be used as a form of punishment.
- Cigarette smoking or gum chewing may be a way of dealing with boredom or be due to an addiction, as with smoking, or being an ingrained habit.
- Nicotine, caffeine, over-the-counter metabolism boosters, or even prescription appetite suppressants may be used as forms of self-medicating in order to stabilize moods and impulsive behaviors.
- Restricted eating by avoiding fats and carbohydrates may serve to combat genuine "health" fears such as familial hypercholesterolemia or early heart attacks.
- Thyroid medication, which can increase metabolism, may be being taken due to a hypothyroid condition.
- Refusal to take the oral contraceptive pill may not be just due to fear of weight gain on these meds but to avoid the risk of stroke for those with migraine headache with aura or a family history of a blood clotting disorder.
- Walking the dog, a form of exercise, may be done just because the dog needs its daily walking—"Sometimes a cigar is just a cigar!"
- Some may perseverate over an exact weight on a scale purely because of obsessive-compulsive disorder traits.

Past, Recent, Present, and Future Uses of Eating Disorder Behaviors

Eating disorder behaviors may have origins in the past, may be active currently or recently, and may be utilized in the future. For one individual, vomiting may have begun at the age of 18, have been utilized recently at the age of 25, and be likely to be used in the future. Of course, eating disorder behaviors that began years earlier may not be in current use and may or may not be intended for use in the future. Why identify previous eating disorder behaviors not used for years? Past eating disorder behaviors may be reinstated anytime, and it is helpful to know if someone intends to use them again, as this certainly may be possible.

Examination of the *past* eating disorder history includes the very beginnings of any given eating disorder behavior. "When did it start?" "Why did it start?" and "Where did it start?" are logical questions to begin with. It is important to inquire regarding the course of the behavior after its initiation. What were the perpetuating circumstances after? Were there changes in the frequency of their use, and when did new behaviors arise?

When asking about the *current* use of eating disorder behaviors, we need to also ask about recently used ones as well. Because some individuals answer questions literally, they may give a precise answer about the current use of a given eating disorder behavior. They may not, however, volunteer information regarding recently used but not immediately used ones.

A clinician may ask, "Do you use laxatives?" and the individual may answer no. If the question is rephrased to be "Have you ever used laxatives?" she may say "Yes." If the next question is "When was the last time you used laxatives?" she may answer "Last Sunday." Be aware of the *intermittent* use of eating disorder behaviors. They may be added to those used on a regular basis.

It is important to ask about the intended *future* use of actively and previously used eating disorder behaviors as well as eating disorder behaviors never tried before. When individuals are not getting the results they desire from their eating disorder behaviors, they may consider engaging new ones. Those who typically restrict eating and use excessive exercise and are nutritionally deprived may then begin to binge for the first time. As a result, they may think seriously about incorporating vomiting, laxative use, or any assortment of other eating disorder behaviors never attempted before.

How

How questions may reveal one or multiple methods of executing an eating disorder behavior. There are many ways someone may describe how they induce vomiting. Individuals may use their fingers, a toothbrush, emetics, or bending over and pressing on their abdomen as well as other methods.

208 Eating Disorder Behavior Parameters

When asked how individuals exercise, they may say they run, do push-ups, use the step machine, lift weights, and do housework as well as use other kinds of exercise.

Asking *how* questions with regard to taking laxatives may not translate into a meaningful question. "How do you take laxatives?" There is only one way to take laxatives, and this is orally. Having said this, it is not impossible one might choose to use other routes. One might answer "I take laxatives in a liquid form" as opposed to tablets. There are many substances that are not meant to be taken at all by any route into the human body but may in fact be. Dish soap and floor cleaners may be taken orally for use as laxatives and emetics.

How questions can help reveal relative risks for any one kind of eating disorder behavior. Asking how someone exercises may elicit a response such as going for walks. Walking around a dangerous part of town at night can bring personal harm risk when compared to walking around a safe neighborhood during the day. Asking how someone loses weight can bring an answer such a cutting out junk food. A far more dangerous way to lose weight is to drain blood from veins (phlebotomize).

How questions may be asked with regard to non-eating disorder behaviors. This may also help with risk assessment. When asking how someone deals with stress, an answer such as "I meditate or do yoga" will not bring the same risks as someone who says that they stick darning needles through their chest wall and into their heart. "How do you suppress appetite?" may give a response such as filling up on water, a relatively low risk behavior in small amounts, while sniffing gasoline or glue is not.

What

What questions are largely self-explanatory. They help to deliver the *methods* or *tools* of engagement with the eating disorder. With regard to vomiting, one could ask "What do you vomit?" with answers including food, air, water, blood, bile, or markers. "What toilets do you vomit in?" may elicit answers such as toilets at home, work, and parents or friends' homes. Other *what* questions could be "What laxatives do you use?" or "What diuretics do you use?" or "What gets in the way of you being able to binge and vomit?"

Risk assessment may be enhanced by *What* questions. Asking "What do you use for an enema?" may give a response such as the use of a safe over-the-counter enemas purchased from a pharmacy. The use of caustic cleaning solutions that cause rectal bleeding and scarring is very dangerous.

Non-eating disorder risk assessment questions include "What methods do you use to harm yourself?" "What triggers you to want to kill yourself?"

Why

The *reasons* anyone wishes to engage in body image control or eating disorder behaviors are at the *heart of motivation* for eating disorder drives. *Why* questions may elicit the most essential and pivotal keys to what fuels the eating disorder. Unless we know why someone does or thinks about something, all other history may be of little use.

Having said that we need to know reasons, some may say they do not know the reasons why. This may be a very real situation. Exploring reasons for a given individual may be aided by stating reasons others engage in their eating disorder. Looking back at the origins of eating disorder behaviors and attitudes may jog their memories as well. Some may deny specific reasons why because they do not wish to reveal them yet. Going over the same questions at a later date may help to reveal reasons, with the individual having been provided some time to have thought about questions and come to a new awareness.

Why questions include "Why do you vomit?" with responses given such as to not gain weight or to lose weight, to relieve stress, to punish or reward, to "zone out" or "numb out," or to cleanse oneself due to feelings concerning a history of sexual abuse. Notice that many of the given answers are not specifically for eating disorder purposes. Other *Why* questions may include "Why do you want to lose weight?" "Why do you take diuretics?" or "Why do you feed your dog vomit?" *Why* questions help to expose the crux of non-eating disorder risks such as drug and alcohol and self-harm behaviors.

Finding reasons for behaviors and attitudes may be the *gatekeeper* for successful treatment. Treating someone for any condition without knowing why it exists can only lead to inevitable frustration, failed treatment or even harm, including death. It can lead to unnecessary trial-and-error treatment options and delays in potentially useful treatments and add to financial costs. Treating someone for an eating disorder without knowing why is like a surgeon doing surgery without investigating the cause of symptoms.

When

When questions may not be straightforward and may be somewhat complicated to ask. They help to determine a *time line* for the evolution of the eating disorder from its inception until today. They also establish a *current time frame* including the frequency, length of time (duration), time of initiation, and cessation for each behavior in a day or week. They help identify *patterns* or *lack of patterns*.

The most basic *When* questions would be regarding day, month, and year. Asking "How *old* were you. . . ?" or "What *grade* were you in. . . ?"

210 Eating Disorder Behavior Parameters

may also be appropriate. A typical *when* question would be "*When* did you first start to over-exercise?" These questions would be useful for enquiring about *past* eating disorder history.

Time of day questions will address the more immediate or current behaviors in use. Questions could include "When, in a day, do you vomit, take laxatives, binge, or exercise?" Individuals may have a set routine and a specific time of day for which they begin any eating disorder behavior. Someone may begin to binge at precisely 6 p.m. and continue until 8 p.m. every day. An individual's exercise may begin precisely at 6:30 in the morning at the gym and last for 45 minutes, and she may run 5 kilometers from 4 in the afternoon five days a week. This may be a *set pattern* for her. Others may not have routines or patterns and may implement eating disorder behaviors more *as needed* or *as triggered*. Behaviors may be *random*. Some may have routine patterns mixed with randomly triggered events. An individual may vomit routinely after 7 p.m. every evening. She may also vomit as triggered at other times, such as if she eats a forbidden food when she did not expect to. *When* questions, using bingeing or exercising as examples, also address the time of day a behavior begins and the duration of the behavior as well as when it stops. Questions regarding less than daily uses are equally as important. Weekly and monthly patterns need to be brought forward as well.

It is helpful to ask when one eating disorder behavior is added to the use of another or excluded. Some may state they *add* exercise to their daily restricting behaviors in the evenings. Others might say they *stop* restricting when they begin bingeing at dinnertime. Different parameters may be queried at the same time such as "When and why did you start to throw food away?" Non-eating disorder combined *When* and *Why* questions may include "When and why do you plan to hook up a hose to your car exhaust pipe?"

Where

Where questions help to identify the *locations* where various behaviors occur. This is important in that we need to know where substances (food, vomit) are *disposed of* and behaviors are *acted out*. One could ask "Where do you vomit?" with answers given such as at home in the toilet, the flower bed, garbage cans, or into plastic food containers. Answers could include vomiting at work, the university, in the car, or onto the street when stopped at a traffic light.

Other *Where* questions could be "Where do you get your laxatives?" Answers could include that they are purchased from various pharmacies. Laxatives may be acquired from friends bringing them into the hospital or by stealing them from a grandparent. "Where do you get money to pay for food and cocaine?" may elicit responses such as "I work as an escort" or "I steal money from my partner's bank account" or "I don't need money, as I steal food and cocaine is given to me."

Who

People play a crucial role in the lives of those with eating disorders. Many aspects of the lives of the one with an eating disorder, including emotions, how individuals behave, what is believed, and the utilization of eating disorder behaviors, are influenced by others. Family, friends, classmates, teachers, partners, coworkers, and others can serve as being supportive or an obstacle course to navigate life through including the eating disorder. For each eating disorder behavior, ask about the influences of others on its use. Some may be helpful, while others may be enabling.

Questions may include "Who brings laxatives into the hospital for you to use on the ward?" or "Who do you binge and vomit with?" or "Who prevents you from being able to binge and vomit?" or "Who told you about pro-ana sites?" Non-eating disorder directed *Who* questions may help to determine who is selling them drugs or who is bullying them. Asking who they respect or want to be like may aid in understanding useful life directions they may wish to be supported in.

Increasing, Decreasing, Staying the Same

Eating disorder behaviors may not remain predictable or constant. It is important to ask whether each behavior is changing, including whether it is increasing or decreasing in frequency or amount or is utilized on and off. The *intent* of the use of each behavior is important and could indicate a reason for the worsening or improving of behaviors as well as motivation to recover.

The *escalation* of a given eating disorder behavior could be due to different reasons:

- The behavior could be working quite well to lose or prevent weight gain, and increasing its use will make it work better.
- The behavior is not working well, and with its escalation it is hoped it will work better.
- Another behavior has been discontinued, so the said behavior needs to be increased to compensate.
- The individual is under stress, depressed, or becoming more anxious, leading to worsening of body image perception therefore resulting in her to feel the need to be thinner.

Decreasing the use of any eating disorder behavior could be because:

- Weight control is adequate, and other behaviors are helping to maintain this.
- The weight goals have been met or even exceeded, and further weight loss is not desired.

212   Eating Disorder Behavior Parameters

- The behavior could lead to health issues such as dehydration, metabolic abnormalities, cardiac arrest, renal disease, and others.
- Physical symptoms that scare the person including palpitations, falling, fainting, chest pain, shortness of breath, and vomiting of blood, being a few.
- The fear of having to be hospitalized.
- The behavior is not working as well as hoped.
- Other behaviors have been introduced or escalated.
- Money is short, and behaviors that require money such as binge eating, laxatives or gym memberships need to be decreased or eliminated for now.
- The individual is becoming despondent, feeling hopeless, and becoming depressed. The motivation for body image control is waning.
- The triggers or pressures for the need to lose weight are absent, even if temporarily. For example, a high school rower, where weight targets had to be met, is attending her first-year at university, where she is not on a rowing team.

Always ask why someone is changing the use of a behavior. Some may decrease or discontinue their eating disorder behaviors because they intend to kill themselves.

The use of each eating disorder behavior or all eating disorder behaviors may be *staying the same* or *sustained* for several reasons:

- They are happy with the results.
- They are not happy with the results but don't have the capacity to escalate behaviors for various reasons.
- Escalating them would bring medical risks.
- They are unaware of other weight loss methods.
- They are afraid to use other behaviors.

Absent or on Hold

Eating disorder behaviors may be reported as *absent* because they have never been used or have been discontinued all together or temporarily *on hold*, only being used *on and off*. Because an eating disorder behavior is not in use does not mean it is not waiting in the wings.

Questions

- Why have you stopped using the eating disorder?
- Do you use it on and off?
- What leads you to reactivating an eating disorder behavior?
- Do you intend to start using the behavior again, and why?

Changing in Kind

Eating disorder behaviors may change in *frequency* or *quantity* but may also change in *kind*. For example, laxative use may change from bulk laxatives to stimulant laxatives, such as switching from using bran to taking Dulcolax, a much more powerful laxative with potential for serious consequences if used in excess. Exercise may change from someone doing yoga to running 5 kilometers daily. Here, exercise is escalating in *intensity* as well as in *kind*. Someone may switch from using fingers to induce vomiting to emetics for the same reason. The use of emetics implies that the use of fingers is not working and may be a fatal alternative. However, never assume the reason and always ask.

Linked

Some eating disorder behaviors may occur concurrently with other eating disorder behaviors. Bingeing and vomiting is a classic example of this. For some, if they don't binge, they will not vomit. Others may use laxatives only when they use diuretics. The permutations and combinations are infinite for eating disorder behaviors to be linked. One behavior may be linked with several others at the same time.

Eating disorder behaviors may be linked with other behaviors, emotions, or situations not of an eating disorder nature.

- Binge eating may be linked to alcohol use.
- Getting on a scale may be linked to self-harm.
- Restrictive eating may always be linked to depression.
- Laxative use may be linked to constipation.
- Diuretic use may be linked to ankle swelling and general bloating associated with having a period.

Non-eating disorder behaviors, emotions, and situations may be linked to other non-eating disorder behaviors, emotions, and situations:

- A hypomanic phase in someone with a bipolar spectrum disorder may be associated with excessive spending of money.
- An argument with a parent may be associated with suicidal ideation.
- Exams spike a rise in anxiety.

Mutually Exclusive

Some may use one eating disorder behavior only when they are not using another. It is either or. Some may only exercise when they are not restricting. Others may never use laxatives if they are vomiting.

214   Eating Disorder Behavior Parameters

Questions

- What eating disorder behaviors do you exclude when using others?
- Why do you not use one behavior with another?
- Are they always mutually exclusive or only at various times, and why?
- When an eating disorder behavior is used, do you avoid engaging in non-eating disorder behaviors such as self-harm or cocaine use?

Triggers

Eating disorder behaviors may be triggered without any identifiable cause, when people will say "It just happens for no reason." Often, though, there are obvious and often predictable reasons. Binge eating may be triggered by the sight of food. Vomiting may be triggered by bingeing. Excessive exercise may be triggered by guilt associated with feeling "fat." Laxative use may be triggered by someone standing on a scale and not liking what the scale reads.

Triggers may be caused by *emotions, other eating disorder behaviors,* and *physical symptoms and life situations.* Critical comments by others, media images, or a perceived critical stare by a stranger may be triggers. *Triggers-trigger-triggers!* The presence of food may trigger a binge that triggers guilt that triggers vomiting that triggers shame that triggers binge alcohol drinking.

Questions

- What triggers the eating disorder?
- What aspects of the eating disorder are triggered?
- Who triggers the eating disorder?
- What places or situations trigger your eating disorder?
- What feelings or emotions trigger your eating disorder?
- What do your eating disorder behaviors trigger in the way of other eating disorder behaviors, emotions including feelings of self-loathing, shame or guilt, drug and alcohol use, and self-harm?

Non-Triggers

Knowing what triggers what is important, but it is important to know what does *not trigger* eating disorder behaviors, emotions, and physical symptoms. We expect the thought of food to trigger bingeing, but this may not be the case for some. Bingeing may be only triggered by exam stress or returning home for holidays. We might expect the desire to lose weight to trigger the use of the scale; however, some will use other body

Eating Disorder Behavior Parameters 215

size gauging methods such as the mirror or small clothing sizes instead to subjectively assess weight changes.

After identifying triggers, questioning may lead to inquiring regarding what was not mentioned as triggering. At this point, direct questions will need to be implemented. "You said that hunger triggers binge eating. Why did you not mention the availability of binge foods and time alone as triggers?" The answer could be that they forgot to mention them or these situations do not trigger binges.

Alternative Behaviors

Individuals may use alternative or different eating disorder behaviors for two main reasons. When individuals are prevented from engaging in a given eating disorder behavior, they may resort to a different one that could compensate in the short term. If individuals are prevented from running due to a sprained ankle, they may decide to restrict and possibly induce vomiting until the ankle heals. People may use alternative behaviors that they already are familiar with or utilize new ones never tried before. It is much like the arcade game, Whac- A- Mole, where when one eating disorder disappears another one pops up.

Alternative behaviors may be relatively benign and do not put someone at any increased health risk. Someone who can't afford laxatives may cut out a meal or two, using restrictive eating as an alternative to laxative use, until they can afford them. Some alternative behaviors may be very dangerous. Someone whose gag reflex is unresponsive to being triggered by finger pressure and is unable to vomit may panic and choose to overdose on a lethal amount of medication in order to have their stomach pumped in the emergency room. Some may choose a non-eating disorder behavior as an alternative. An individual may begin to binge on alcohol instead of bingeing on food. Some may shoplift in place of over-exercising.

Patterns

Some eating disorder behaviors may occur in set *routines* and predictable *patterns* either in the same day, from day to day, or possibly month to month. Individual eating disorder behaviors may occur in patterns by themselves or may be associated, that is, *linked* with others.

A typical eating disorder pattern could involve bingeing and vomiting. The pattern may first involve acquiring food. The individual goes to a grocery store, purchases the very same binge foods she does for every binge, then comes home. At home, she prepares for bingeing by unwrapping the ingredients and then mixes the ingredients needed to bake two dozen chocolate chip cookies. She then unwraps Chinese noodles. She takes out a

216 Eating Disorder Behavior Parameters

pot, fills it with water so she may boil the noodles. She then takes a cookie sheet and turns on the oven so that she can bake the cookies. She places the mixed cookie dough on the cookie sheet, then puts this in the hot oven. While she waits for the noodles to cook and the cookies to finish baking, she binges on a large bag of potatoes chips and a bucket of ice cream. Her choices of food never vary. She always eats chips first, then ice cream, then noodles, and finally cookies.

After having eaten each food, she vomits into the toilet with similar frequency. She always induces vomiting by using the second and third fingers of her left hand. She vomits the chips first after drinking a lot of water and finishes vomiting when she sees pure water returning. She vomits ice cream next but does not use water, as she can vomit ice cream easily. She then eats the noodles, drinks water again, then vomits this, continuing to aim for pure water. Finally, she will binge on cookies, eating six cookies at a time, after which she vomits. Water, again, is used.

After bingeing and vomiting, she must clean up all evidence of this. She takes wrappers and puts them into her backpack so that she can dispose of them in a university trashcan. She does this because her partner inspects all garbage bins inside the house as well as outside, as he knows she takes great effort to hide bingeing sessions. She washes the pot and cookie sheet and puts them away exactly where she found them. She then goes to the bathroom and looks for any evidence of having vomited. She scrubs the toilet bowl thoroughly using a non-scented cleaning agent, as her partner will know she has been vomiting if he detects any odor from vomiting or use of cleaning agents. She puts on the fan and opens the bathroom window for a while, then shuts off the fan and closes the window before her partner comes home. She repeats the very same pattern daily and hopes not to be caught.

Other patterns may include *trap lines*, where an individual may walk home from work and binge and vomit at Starbucks, then McDonald's, and finally Subway, repeating this pattern every workday.

Consequences

When someone engages in any eating disorder behavior, there will be *consequences*. These consequences may be *desired* in the eyes of the person, such as preventing weight gain with restricting or vomiting. There may be *regretted* consequences such as feeling guilt or shame or becoming depressed after bingeing. There may be medical consequences such as fainting or cardiac arrest from metabolic abnormalities. There may be consequences with one's relationship with her partner, family, friends, or coworkers. Consequences may lead to more consequences—a chain of consequences.

There may be consequences with engaging in each eating disorder behavior, but as important, there may be consequences with *not engaging*. If someone is not able to vomit because their gag reflex is unresponsive or a family member returns home unexpectedly, the consequences could include experiencing panic, an extreme fear of becoming fat, and feeling the need to severely restrict or over-exercise the next day. She may cut herself as a form of punishment or to relieve stress. Consequences can create a *damned if you do and damned if you don't* scenario.

Not all consequences have to be negative ones. Someone may choose not to binge and vomit as a step toward recovery. This may lead to feelings of empowerment and winning over the eating disorder. Not taking laxatives or not vomiting may decrease or eliminate the medical risks of metabolic demise, which is a healthy desired consequence.

Hiding Behaviors

Those with eating disorders often do not want others to know about their eating disorder, let alone be seen engaging in their eating disorder behaviors. Typically, individuals go to great lengths to hide any evidence of these behaviors. When individuals purchase binge foods they may shop at one grocery store, then go to a different one the next time they are preparing for a binge so that they do not get "made" as someone who is a binge eater. Those who order food by phone to have delivered to their home may phone different takeout restaurants in the same evening—one for Chinese food and the other for pizza—to avoid suspicion. Other examples of hiding behaviors include placing laxatives in cigarette packages so others will not discover them, storing vomit in plastic food containers, and exercising in the bedroom where family members will not be able to see them.

Allowing Situations—Ducks in a Row

For anyone engaging in any eating disorder behavior, there will be necessary conditions that allow it to be carried out. That is, they will need to have their *ducks in a row*. The permutations and combinations of conditions that need to be met are amplified when two or more eating disorder behaviors are linked.

It is surprising how many situations must be in place to allow someone to engage in just one eating disorder behavior, let alone multiple ones. At some level, engaging in eating disorder behaviors is like a house of cards. If one link in the chain of events needed to carry out a particular eating disorder behavior is not in place, then the whole structure falls apart.

218 Eating Disorder Behavior Parameters

To engage in bingeing and vomiting, all of what follows must be in place; that is, individuals must have all their ducks in a row:

- There must be money to purchase food if food is not readily available.
- Individuals must have a source of funds. They must have a debit or credit card, and there must be funds available from these sources.
- To have funds, individuals must have a method of providing the funds such as a job or parents who infuse their bank account with money or provide them with a credit card. Sources of funds may be having a willing partner with money who will share it, or some may sell drugs or sex for money.
- There must be transportation to access the funds in the form of a car, bus, bike, or walking if an ATM is in walking distance.
- Grocery or convenience stores must be open.
- Transportation may be required to obtain food.
- Specific binge foods need to be in the store.
- There must be a place to binge and vomit.
- There must be a place to binge and vomit where no one can notice them. The place where someone binges will likely be different from where they can vomit, but not always.
- There must be time enough to binge and to vomit. A five-minute window of opportunity alone will likely not be enough.
- There must be access to disposal containers to get rid of food packaging without anyone noticing.
- There must be a receptacle to vomit into.
- If not vomiting into a toilet, then there needs to be a place to get rid of the vomit unnoticed.
- There will need to be a way of hiding vomiting behavior if others are in the home.
- There must be a mechanism to hide the smell of vomit.
- Red eyes and a puffy face from vomiting need to be successfully hidden.

If a single situation that allows these things to occur is interfered with, the whole process is stopped in its tracks. If there is no available money, if the person has a broken leg and is in a cast and can't drive to access money and food, or if others are present when not expected, then a session of bingeing and vomiting cannot be realized.

Likely, however, individuals may have built in *alternative ways* to implement these binge and vomit sessions. If they can't drive themselves to access funds or purchase food, they may get others to drive them or may be able to borrow or steal money or food just in case. Planning

Eating Disorder Behavior Parameters 219

ahead is often necessary. This is not unlike those who seek drugs or alcohol.

Questions

- What do you need to have in place for you to exercise, purge, restrict, or engage in any eating disorder behavior?
- How do you ensure that you have all of your ducks in a row?
- What planning is required?
- What are the most difficult situations you have to cope with in order to carry out your eating disorder?

Preventing Situations

When someone wishes to engage in any eating disorder behavior, they hope that there will not be any interfering occurrences. As touched on earlier, however, there may be many conditions that could interrupt or prevent individuals from engaging in their eating disorder rituals.

A typical example of this, for those who binge and vomit, is someone returns home when someone was not expected. The individual with the eating disorder may then choose to binge and vomit in her car instead in order to avoid being noticed. Other preventing factors could be that someone does not have the funds to buy binge foods or laxatives. Someone may be on holidays with family and, therefore, not have the opportunity to be alone or have a space to binge and vomit or restrict unnoticed. A minor injury may prevent an individual from exercising. Unexpected hospitalizations put a serious spanner in the work as well.

Questions

- What things get in the way of you not being able to carry out eating disorder activities?
- How do you cope when your plans are interrupted?
- Do you have alternative plans when opportunities shift?
- Do you use drugs or alcohol as an alternative way of coping?
- Do you think you put yourself at risk, such as planning serious self-harm or suicidal actions, when things go wrong?

Quantifying

For any eating disorder behavior, we need to quantify its use. Statements regarding quantities may be very precise, such as describing how many times daily one attempts jumping jacks, or wild guesses, such as estimating how many calories individuals burn by wrapping themselves in a heating blanket.

Quantifying may be determined by asking about the *volume* of a substance used:

- How much water do you drink in a day?
- How many tablespoons of laxative do you consume in a day?

Or the *number* of a substance used:

- How many diet pills do you use a day?

Or the *duration of time* one takes to engage in a behavior:

- How long does it take you to run a half-marathon?
- How long does a typical binge take?

Or the *number of times* a behavior is repeated:

- How many push-ups do you do in a day?

Or the number of *sessions* dedicated to executing an eating disorder behavior, including how many times the behavior is attempted during each session or how long each session is:

- How many times or sessions a day do you use the stationary bike, as well as for how long?
- How many sessions of vomiting do you do in a day and for every session of vomiting, how many times do you vomit?

Or the *distance* achieved during physical activity:

- How far do you bike in a day?

Or the *number of calories* one eats daily or burns with exercise:

- How many calories do you consume in a day?
- What is your daily calorie limit?
- How many calories do you burn at the gym?

Someone may begin a vomiting session at 8 p.m. We need to know *how often* she vomits during any *individual session*. She may vomit 10 times during a given session of bingeing and vomiting for each of the three sessions she creates in an evening. In other words, she will be vomiting

30 times in an evening. With regard to laxative use, asking about *quantity* is very important, because the risks of someone taking two Ex-Lax tablets a day will be very different from someone who takes 100 tablets daily. We also need to know the *range* of utilization. Someone may vomit 1 to 8 times per session of vomiting. Or she may take from 5 to 50 tablets of diuretics a day. Exercise may increase from half an hour a day to two hours a day.

Questions

- What is the *least* and *maximum* number of laxative pills you use in a day, and why does it change?
- What is the *average* number of laxatives you likely use in a day, and why?

Many have an idea of the *portion* or *fraction* of how much they will vomit. They may state "I vomit half of what I eat" or "I vomit until *all* of my food comes out." They may feel that they know this because they may fluid load to make vomiting easier, and when they see pure water return will feel assured all of the food has been removed. They may depend on a marker to give the same assurance.

Questions

- Do you have a sense of what *portion* or *percentage* of the food you get rid of each time you vomit, and how do you know this?
- What percentage of the day do you think about body image and weight?

Intent

Knowing someone's intent with regard to the use of any or all behaviors is important. This is one way to help assess motivation and risk. If individuals are taking 10 laxative tablets daily, it matters if they intend to increase their use to 100 tabs daily, plan to continue the same usage, or are working to eliminate their use. During an initial assessment, we only capture a snapshot of patterns of eating disorder behaviors. Knowing the intended continuation of the behaviors or *future use* is essential to supporting them in recovery.

Determining intent with regard to *weight goals* is important as well. During an assessment we may have learned that someone is 5'6" and 140 lbs. This weight is in an average weight range—a BMI of 22.6. If individuals had been 150 lbs. originally and lost weight to 140 lbs., this loss does not imply as severe a drive to lose weight as if they said that they had been 260 lbs.

222   Eating Disorder Behavior Parameters

We also want to know what their goal weight is. If it is 130 lb., then we may not worry as much as if they say they are working toward becoming 75 lbs. However, because some individuals' initial weight loss goal may be 10 pounds does not rule out the possibility that their goal weight will not change. Met goal weights seldom bring long-term satisfaction, as "the fat feeling" they are trying to eliminate never really goes away at any weight.

Questions

- What is the maximum weight you want to lose?
- What is the lowest weight you wish to achieve?
- Are you willing to risk dying to meet your eating disorder goals?
- Is your drive to achieve your weight goals increasing, decreasing, or staying the same?
- What is your benchmark for success?
- Where do you draw the line when it comes to achieving the limits of your goals in terms of health risks, including death or relationship, academic, and career losses?

Assessing someone's *realizable* intent or the likelihood of meeting one's goal may be measured by the success or lack of success of previous attempts. As an example, if she says she wants to lose 75 pounds in three months, we want to know if she has been able to achieve this before. If she has achieved extreme goals before, then this provides evidence for a real achievable goal. If she has tried multiple times but has only been able to lose a maximum of 15 pounds, then there may be less reason for concern. Sometimes reaching extreme goals is a try, try again, phenomenon, and the goal may yet become realized. We need to keep a close eye on what we feel are lower risk trends in case they do become dangerous. Serious risks may evolve when we are looking the other way.

Questions

- Have you ever achieved this weight goal before?
- Why do you keep this same goal if you have not been able to achieve it in the past?

Why Stop?

People end a period of use of any eating disorder behavior they engage in. We often *assume* reasons why they stop but very easily could be wrong. Why does someone end a binge or a vomiting session in a given day or even stop for weeks? Never assume and always know!

One would naturally think individuals would end a vomiting session because they feel there is nothing left in their stomach. This is very likely for most. If we ask further, we may find that there are other very specific indicators for ending a session. Seeing blood, bile, or clear water returning may be the end goal. Other times it could be exhaustion, chest pains, or palpitations that behoove someone to stop. Emotions such as fear of tearing the esophagus or stomach as well as guilt or shame may result in cessation. Laxative use or going to the gym may stop temporarily due to not having the funds to continue their use. Discontinuing a behavior may have nothing to do with wanting to recover. Remember, if someone is discontinuing one eating disorder behavior, ask what other behaviors, eating disorder related or not, she may be replacing it with. Any eating disorder behavior may be discontinued because she has met her weight goal or because it does not seem to be working as expected.

Questions

- Why do you stop exercising once you've begun?
- Is there more than one reason why you stop engaging in a session of any eating disorder?
- Why do you discontinue any eating disorder behavior from time to time?
- Do you replace the behavior you have stopped and replace it with another eating disorder behavior or use of drugs and alcohol?
- Are you planning a suicide?

Other Parameters

The parameters already mentioned cover the bulk of different lines of questioning for each eating disorder behavior. Other targeted questioning may be required as needed.

Chapter 6

Medical Symptoms and Complicating Health Concerns

"Nothing but skin and bones, my weak heart was tired of trying to keep me alive."

A detailed medical eating disorder history includes a general medical history as well as an eating disorder directed medical history. The eating disorder directed medical history encapsulates eating disorder behaviors and attitudes as well as possible eating disorder related medical risks. This chapter, "Medical Symptoms and Complicating Health Concerns," identifies physical and emotional symptoms as well as delves into a few health conditions that may complicate eating disorder management. See the section on "General Medical History" in Chapter 3, "General Eating Disorder History." Also see Chapter 4, "Eating Disorder Behaviors."

Symptoms may have their origins in eating disorder behaviors, or they may not. Taking a medical symptom history is needed in order to aid in determining the organ or system each symptom or set of symptoms originates from and whether it could be caused by eating disorder behaviors or other causes. Sometimes symptoms may be the result of eating disorder *and* non-eating disorder origins. There will be times when the precise organ or system creating symptoms cannot be identified, at least in the moment.

Symptoms may not develop as single entities or necessarily be a function of a given organ or system. They may be the expression of a specific disease entity that elicits multiple symptoms, generated from multiple organs from multiple systems. Specific medical diagnoses experienced by those with eating disorders are described in this chapter.

The descriptions of symptoms and the questions that follow suggest possible causes that may be attributed to eating disorder activities as well as from other causes. The reason for this is that there may be a tendency for clinicians to focus on the causes of these symptoms being of eating disorder origin only, risking ignoring other important causes. The opposite is possible as well, where symptoms may be assumed to have developed from non-eating disorder causes but, indeed, are the product of an eating disorder. In short, important medical risk factors, including those that are life threatening, may be attributed to eating disorder or non-eating disorder causes or may be a combination of both.

Determining the source or sources of symptoms can be a very complicated process due to them resulting from any number and combination of etiologies. Although many symptoms have been listed under a given system or body region, symptoms are often a result of multi-system involvement. For example, the symptom of a racing heart, typically attributed to the cardiovascular system, may have its origin in potassium loss from the kidneys that in turn aggravates an autoimmune induced cardiac disease. The awareness of a racing heart is neurologically delivered. Underlying *all* body functioning, *all* of the time is an endocrine or hormonal and immunological influence. Therefore, a simple sounding symptom such as a racing heart, in this scenario, is derived from cardiovascular, renal, neurological, hematological, immune, and endocrine influences. It was mentioned earlier that triggers-trigger-triggers when it comes to emotions and eating disorder behaviors; likewise, physical triggers trigger other physical triggers to create compounding symptoms and illnesses.

As a single symptom may be the result of combined influences from several sources, multiple physical symptoms may result from a single disorder or illness. Multiple sclerosis may present with numbness, weakness, depression, poor hand coordination, and poor gait.

The *Questions* in several sections help to punctuate items from the preceding discussion as well as add additional information. These sets of questions are not necessarily complete but serve as sample or suggested questions. Additional questioning options should be pursued when necessary.

Symptoms have been grouped by *systems* as well as by two *body regions*. The *systems* include:

- Cardiovascular system
- Neurological System
- Gastrointestinal system
- Musculoskeletal system
- Endocrine system
- Respiratory system
- Dermatological system
- Urological system
- Gynecological system

The hematological, lymphatic and immune systems have been touched on in discussion of the other systems.

The two *body regions*, as described here, include

- Head region
- Chest region

226 Medical Symptoms and Complications

The reason for identifying these two regions of the body is that they each possess portions of almost all of the systems. So, if someone says, "My head hurts!" the source could be from organ tissue of the head of neurological, musculoskeletal, dermatological, respiratory, cardiovascular, endocrine, immunological, lymphatic, or gastroenterological origin. Though renal or genitourinary systems are not represented in organ form in the head, these systems can have a profound effect on head symptomatology. Renal failure resulting in severe hypokalemia can result in headache. As well, a headache may be of gynecological origin, resulting from menstrual-induced migraines. In kind, the chest and abdomen may present symptoms potentially from any of several systems represented as well as those that are not. The abdomen possesses tissue from all body systems and may present with a cornucopia of symptomatology. Abdominal symptoms have been described in depth under the topics "Gastrointestinal System," "Urological System," and "Gynecological System." For any symptom, it is important to determine if the individual has been seen by a physician, and if not, encourage her to do so.

Cardiovascular System

Palpitations

Palpitations will likely be reported as a *racing heart* or *thumping in the chest* and are caused by an irregularity in the heartbeat. Palpitations of eating disorder origin will typically develop from metabolic abnormalities resulting from vomiting, restricting, or laxative or diuretic use (Sachs, Harnke, Mehler, & Krantz, 2016). Stimulants that are intended to increase metabolism for weight loss purposes including thyroid medication may trigger palpitations. Stimulant use such as caffeine, nicotine, and narcotics may be used for personal gratification as well as for eating disorder purposes. Preexisting mitral valve prolapse, sometimes associated with dysrhythmias, may be made worse by weight loss. Severe weight loss may cause a normal mitral valve to prolapse due to depletion of heart muscle mass. Shrinking of the heart changes the architecture of the mitral valve unit, resulting in dysfunction, including creating a murmur or poor blood flow during contractions as well as, possibly, heart irregularities. Palpitations may also be of genetic origin expressed by congenital abnormalities of the heart including heart valve disease, septal defects, or aberrant conducting pathways. Viral infections of the heart muscle (myocarditis), pericardium (pericarditis), and fever, as well as hyperthyroidism may also cause cardiac irregularities. Eating disorder behaviors resulting in nutritional and metabolic changes may exacerbate cardiac disorders of any etiology, whether preexisting or acquired.

Ischemia of the heart or a lack of oxygen to the heart during a myocardial infarction or heart attack may trigger palpitations.

Questions

- Do you ever notice your heart race or thump in your chest?
- When did these symptoms start?
- How often do you notice your heart race, and for how long does it last?
- Is chest pain, shortness of breath, falling, or fainting associated with palpitations?
- Could the palpitations be associated with any eating disorder behaviors such as during or after bingeing and vomiting, exercising, or laxative and diuretic use?
- Do palpitations present themselves as a result of weight loss?
- Are they triggered by stimulants including caffeine, nicotine, alcohol, or street drugs?
- Are they triggered by anxiety?
- Do you think they could be triggered by medications including those that treat depression, anxiety, mood changes, psychosis, or ADHD?
- Have you had an ECG, chest X-ray, echocardiogram, or blood and urine testing?
- Have you used a Holter monitor or event monitor to record cardiac rhythm activity?
- What were the results of any of your tests?
- Have you been to the hospital including the ER or intensive care unit for these symptoms?
- Is there a history of heart disease in your family such as heart irregularities, heart valve disease, congenital cardiac disease, or heart attack?
- Has anyone died of a heart attack at a young age in your family?
- Is there a history of thyroid disease in your family or yourself?
- Have you seen your doctor regarding your symptoms?
- Are you deliberately trying to experience palpitations, and why?
- How are you causing palpitations?
- Are you trying to stop your heart?

Syncope

Fainting or *syncope* is a brief loss of consciousness with quick recovery. Individuals may fall or slouch where they have been sitting momentarily. Syncope can be just a nuisance or a life-threatening condition. Fainting while sitting in a couch watching TV may be a relatively safe place to be when this happens. On the other hand, fainting while driving a car,

228 Medical Symptoms and Complications

walking on stairs, or working in a room with stainless steel counters and a cement floor could result in serious injury including death. Fainting must be considered a serious health issue, and the cause needs to be diagnosed and treated quickly.

The reasons for syncope are multifold.

- Dehydration
- Cardiac dysrhythmias
- Metabolic irregularities
- Drug or alcohol intoxication
- Congenital or acquired cardiac abnormalities
- Cardiac arrest
- Starvation
- Loss of blood
- Very low iron stores (anemia)
- Medication sensitivities that cause low blood pressure or dysrhythmias
- Vasovagal event
- Acute anxiety
- Fear
- Pain

The causes of fainting may be due to a series of events or compounding situations. Restricting food and water as well as vomiting may result in dehydration, starvation, and metabolic abnormalities that in turn initiate low blood pressure and dysrhythmias, all of which may aggravate a preexisting cardiac anomaly, a kind of chain of events. Syncope may be the final event in a cascade of compounding medical risks. Many of the causes of syncope, such as dysrhythmias, metabolic abnormalities, or cardiac anomalies, could lead to *sudden cardiac death*. The symptom of fainting may be the precursor to sudden cardiac death or a kind of critical warning signal that needs to be paid attention to.

When I was in general practice, a 31-year old mother came into my office in tears. I asked what she was upset about. She said that her 19-year old babysitter had died but she did not know why. Being curious as to why a 19-year old woman would suddenly die, I called the coroner to find out more, if known. Apparently she and her mother were going to take a holiday in Hawaii in a few weeks, and they made a bet as to how much weight each could lose. The babysitter had been watching TV with her brother. He went to get something to eat, and when he came back she was sitting up in the couch, not moving, and was dead. At autopsy they found that the young woman had tears in the upper part of her stomach, and she had vomit in her lungs. The babysitter's parents would not allow me to visit with them to inquire regarding any suspected eating disorder etiology of her death. With talking to the coroner and internal medicine specialists, a specific cause of death was never ascertained. I suspect that she had been vomiting as a way to lose weight and therefore developed the tears in her stomach. She may have had a dysrhythmia, such as a torsades de pointes or ventricular fibrillation, while sitting, lost consciousness, and inhaled vomit. The dysrhythmia would have ended up being lethal. We will never know for sure.

Questions

- Have you ever fainted?
- When did this happen, and why, if you know?
- Do you think fainting is likely the consequence of your eating disorder such as from weight loss, dehydration, or electrolyte irregularities?
- How often have you fainted, and when was the last time?
- What situations result in you fainting, and are they predictable?
- Is there any forewarning when you are going to faint, and do you have time to prevent it or get yourself in a safe situation in time?
- Do you notice your heart racing or experience shortness of breath or chest pain or pressure before you faint?
- Have you ever had an injury due to falling, and what was the injury?
- Have you ever been taken to the hospital because you have fainted or due to injuring yourself?
- Have you seen a doctor and been told why you faint?
- Have you had a thorough medical assessment including a physical exam, lab work, ECG, or other testing?
- Have you been told you need a pacemaker or require defibrillation?
- What treatment has been tried, and do you follow medical recommendations?
- Does becoming afraid or experiencing pain, such as from migraine headaches, trigger fainting?
- Is there anyone in your family who has a history of fainting, and what is the reason for this?

Shortness of Breath

Shortness of breath may develop for different reasons. With regard to eating disorders, shortness of breath caused by dysrhythmias, metabolic abnormalities, or cardiac arrest are of prime concern. Anxiety and panic are relatively common causes of shortness of breath. Other causes of shortness of breath include exacerbation of asthma or oxygen deprivation from overexertion while exercising. Blood clots that travel from the deep veins of the leg to the lungs (pulmonary embolism) may result in shortness of breath. Pulmonary emboli can be fatal.

Monitoring someone with anorexia nervosa who develops chronic critical electrolyte levels and also has a history of blood clots will need even closer monitoring. Those who are not reliably taking potassium or

230 Medical Symptoms and Complications

magnesium supplements will likely not be reliable taking medications that thin blood such as warfarin to prevent more clot formation. They then will have two potentially life-threatening health conditions. Hospitalizations may be required to stabilize electrolyte levels as well as blood clotting parameters. Excellent contact information by phone, text, email, or any other social media is essential. Reliable contact information for significant others such as family, partner, friends, or other caregivers will aid in being able to relay urgent medical information when you may not.

Questions

- Do you ever experience shortness of breath?
- When, where, and why does this happen, if you know?
- Is it associated with vomiting?
- Is shortness of breath associated with your heart racing, chest pain, or pressure?
- Do you have asthma, or do you smoke?
- Have you ever been taken to the hospital for this?
- Do you ever get short of breath with little physical activity?
- Do you hyperventilate?
- Do you get short of breath when anxious?
- Have you or anyone in your family ever had a blood clot in the legs or lungs?
- Do you smoke or take a hormonal contraceptive method, especially one containing estrogen?

Feeling Generally Cold or Having Cold and Blue Extremities

In those with eating disorders, feeling generally cold may be due to various factors. With starvation, the body is not receiving enough nutrition to provide fuel for proper functioning of cells and organs. To compensate, it makes every attempt to conserve energy by lowering metabolism and thus decreases the rate of energy consumption. The body also constricts blood vessels in the extremities mainly to decrease heat loss from the limbs. Constricted blood vessels result in the extremities feeling cold and the fingers and toes turning blue. Feeling cold may be the result of not wearing adequate clothing in cold environments.

Questions

- Do you experience cold hands or feet?
- Do your fingers or toes turn blue as well?
- Do you generally feel cold when others seem to not feel cold?

Medical Symptoms and Complications 231

- Do you wear extra clothing including gloves or require extra blankets when sleeping to keep warm?
- Do you drink hot drinks to keep warm?
- When did you first notice becoming cold?
- Do you underdress in colder environment to aid in making your body cold?
- Do you feel becoming cold will result in raising your metabolism in order to burn more calories?
- Do you think feeling cold is from restricting or weight loss?
- Do you fear feeling warmer because it might be an indication of gaining weight?
- Is feeling cold and having blue fingers and toes a measure of success with achieving weight loss?

Abnormal Bleeding

Abnormal bleeding may occur from different parts of the body and result from any number of causes. Some causes of abnormal bleeding are benign while others may be serious. A number of examples of abnormal bleeding have been discussed elsewhere, including from the renal, gastrointestinal and reproductive organs. Abnormal bleeding may be caused by genetic blood dyscrasias or medication that "thins" blood.

Questions

- Do you experience abnormal bleeding?
- From what part of your body does this occur?
- Do you cause bleeding deliberately such as by cutting or using emetics or caustic enemas?
- Do you get nosebleeds from vomiting?
- Do you get nosebleeds from using cocaine?

Chest Region

Chest Pain or Pressure

The chest contains physiological structures from the cardiovascular, respiratory, gastrointestinal, musculoskeletal, dermatological, neurological, lymphatic, and endocrine systems. Breasts may be a source of chest pain as well. The chest, however, does not possess renal or reproductive organ tissues, although chest symptoms may be influenced from these systems.

Chest pain or *pressure* can have many etiologies. Many of the causes or precursors of chest pain and pressure are the same as has been described in the sections on "Palpitations" and "Syncope" and are of cardiac origin.

232 Medical Symptoms and Complications

The most critical cause of chest pain or pressure is due to ischemia or lack of oxygen to the heart leading to cardiac arrest and death. A squeezing or pressure in the chest as a result of ischemia is called *angina*. Other causes, however, may be serious in themselves (Sundararaghavan, Pitts, Suarez, & Johnstone, 2005)

Respiratory causes of chest pain can be bronchitis, pneumonia, pleurisy, and a collapsed lung. Chest wall pain may develop from physical stress of the ribs and intercostal muscles created by exercise, periods of harsh coughing, or direct trauma. Costochondritis is inflammation of rib and cartilage joints. Pain of breast origin may be caused from trauma, infection, or hormonal shifts. Lymphatic reasons for chest pain may be due to chest cancers including Hodgkin's lymphoma. Skin manifested chest pain of neurological origin could be shingles or nerve root compression. Spontaneous neuralgias of unknown cause may cause chest pains as well as pains anywhere else in the body. Infections and trauma of skin may be sources of chest pain.

Eating disorder generated chest pain may result from vomiting. Vomiting may cause stomach acid induced esophagitis or heartburn. It may also result in tears in the stomach and esophagus. Vomiting leads to repeated contraction of intercostal muscles and rib movement, resulting in intercostal joint strain. The diaphragm also contracts harshly during vomiting and can cause chest or abdominal pain.

Questions

- Do you ever experience chest pain or pressure, and if so, when and why, if you know?
- Do you notice your heart race before or during chest pains?
- Do you experience shortness of breath while having chest pain or pressure?
- Is the pain or pressure related to vomiting?
- If the pain is related to vomiting, do you think the pain is coming from your chest wall or diaphragm or esophagus (heartburn), or are you worried about your heart?
- Is chest pain due to coughing, and if so, is the coughing the result of a cold or allergies or from inhaling vomit or food during episodes of bingeing and vomiting?
- Is it the result of drinking very hot liquids?
- Is it due to eating very spicy foods?
- Does chest pain occur while smoking?
- Could it be due to drinking caustic substances that induce vomiting such as drain or floor cleaners?
- Have you ever had a collapsed lung?

Medical Symptoms and Complications   233

- Since experiencing chest pain or pressure, have you noticed fever or sweats?
- Have you seen a doctor and had a thorough medical workup, and if so, what is the diagnosis and recommended treatment?
- Have you been to the emergency room for these symptoms?
- Could you have Crohn's disease?
- Have you been screened for eosinophilic esophagitis?

Neurological System

Numbness, Tingling, and Sensory Loss

Causes of numbness, tingling or sensory loss have multiple origins. For those with eating disorders, the cause may be from nerve damage caused by starvation. As muscle and bone tissue wastes or degenerates secondary to malnutrition, so does nerve tissue. Radiographic images of the brain, a part of the central nervous system, may cause profound wasting of brain tissue in those with severe weight loss due to anorexia nervosa. Peripheral nerve tissue also can be affected.

Non-eating disorder causes of nerve dysfunction need to be identified as well. Degenerative neurological disorders such as multiple sclerosis. amyotrophic lateral sclerosis (ALS), Huntington's chorea, Parkinson's disease, Charcot-Marie-Tooth syndrome, and others may result in neurological compromise. Spontaneous neuropathies and nerve root compression due to arthritis of the vertebrae are possibilities, though pain may be the primary symptom.

Those with eating disorders may experience neurological symptoms both from eating disorder origins and others. Numbness and weakness triggered by multiple sclerosis, a non-eating disorder etiology, may be exacerbated by starvation resulting from the eating disorder.

Numbness or a burning sensation of the feet may be a product of vitamin B_{12} deficiency. This vitamin deficiency may be caused by a lack of food containing vitamin B_{12} or pernicious anemia, an autoimmune disease that prevents the absorption of vitamin B_{12}. Vitamin B_{12} is essential for nerve health. Because vitamin B_{12} is naturally produced only in animals, vegetarians may develop this vitamin deficiency. Vitamin B_{12} oral supplements or injections may be required.

Questions

- Do you experience numbness, and if so, in what part of your body?
- When did this first occur?
- Does it come and go, or has it been persistent?

234 Medical Symptoms and Complications

- Do you hyperventilate?
- Does tingling lead to numbness?
- Could you have a degenerative neurological disorder such as multiple sclerosis, ALS, Parkinson's disease or Charcot-Marie-Tooth syndrome?
- Is your strength or coordination affected as well?
- Do you experience pain in place of numbness at times?
- Could numbness be due to street drug use?
- Could numbness be attributed to medications including antidepressants or antipsychotic drugs?
- Is numbness associated with migraine headaches?
- If numbness is associated with migraine, are you on a hormonal contraceptive method containing estrogen?
- Is numbness always in the same spot, or does it spread or originate from different locations?
- Are there any degenerative neurological conditions in your family?
- Have you been tested for vitamin B_{12} deficiency?

Coordination Concerns

Coordination of the body is a very intricate process. It involves multiple brain centers and spinal cord pathways as well as hundreds of peripheral nerve branches and hundreds of muscles. While motor neurons activate the muscles used in coordination tasks, the sensory nerves provide feedback to the brain and spinal cord, informing them where any limb or body part is in use. This includes physical tasks such as walking and moving hands and arms, along with all head muscle movement. Motor and sensory nerves are required for all other muscle coordination functions including those of the back, chest, and abdomen. Coordination is a product of the sympathetic and parasympathetic nervous systems. As a result, coordination has both a controllable aspect as well as an autonomic or subconscious component. Added to this is that virtually all other systems, aside from the neurological system, play a part in healthy coordination function.

With regard to those with eating disorders, starvation can result in a profound loss of several nutrients that have a direct influence on nerve cell integrity. Mineral and electrolyte blood levels need to be determined. Overt hand or leg coordination problems need to be investigated for neurological conditions including multiple sclerosis, Guillain-Barre syndrome, Huntington's chorea, and Charcot-Marie-Tooth syndrome. Vitamin B_{12} deficiency should be considered as well. Of note is that multiple sclerosis and Guillain-Barre syndrome originate as autoimmune disorders. Huntington's chorea has its origin as a genetic disorder. Guillain-Barre does not affect coordination specifically but causes weakness. Weakness itself affects coordinated functioning, too, sometimes making it difficult to walk. Brain shrinkage in those with severe anorexia nervosa could present with any number of neurological symptoms, including coordination difficulties and cognitive dysfunction.

Coordination concerns may result from central nervous system infections of viral or bacterial origin. Meningitis and encephalitis can cause sweeping, irreversible neurological damage. Devastating consequences may occur in hours; therefore, there needs to be a high index of suspicion and very quick response to determine diagnosis and treatment. Meningitis and encephalitis caused by tuberculosis should always be considered along with other infectious causes right from the beginning of investigation. If tuberculosis is only considered after all other infectious etiologies have been ruled out, it will be too late. Certainly, cerebral palsy or spinal cord damage affect coordination.

Questions

- Do you have any coordination problems?
- Do you have any problems with being able to walk or reach for or hold onto objects?
- Do you have a hard time holding onto a pen or being able to write easily?
- Do you have any difficulties with being able to maintain posture?
- Do you have disability status at university so you are allowed to take extra time writing exams?
- Do you trip or fall over?
- Do you shake involuntarily?
- Do you find it is hard to feel objects, or do you drop things?
- Do you have double vision?
- Have you been having difficulties controlling your bowels or bladder?
- Have you been diagnosed with a neurological disease?
- Is there any history of neurological diseases in your family?
- Did your symptoms start before or after you developed an eating disorder?
- Have you had a head injury or nerve damage to a limb?
- Have you had blood work to determine magnesium, zinc, vitamin B_{12}, folic acid, or other mineral or electrolyte levels?

Poor Balance

Poor balance may result from coordination problems, ear infections, vertigo, hypotension, substance abuse, and neurological disorders of various etiologies. For those with eating disorders, poor balance or unsteadiness on the feet may be due to poor nutrition and dehydration. If balance becomes acutely unstable, this may be due to an intermittent cardiac dysrhythmia. Dysrhythmias may only last seconds, resulting in momentary unsteady balance, or may last longer, resulting in extended periods of unsteadiness

236 Medical Symptoms and Complications

or falling. Positional induced low blood pressure after sitting or standing up may cause poor balance, at least temporarily.

Questions

- Do you ever feel unsteady on your feet?
- When and why does this happen?
- Do you notice ringing in the ears?
- Do you think this is the result of poor nutrition or dehydration?
- Is your balance affected during or after vomiting?
- Does this happen with alcohol, illicit drug, or prescription drug use?
- Does this happen with hangovers or drug withdrawal?
- Are you taking any medications that are sedating?
- Do you notice unstable balance with palpitations?
- Have you had a head injury?

Weakness

Weakness may be described as general weakness affecting much of the body or as local resulting from weakness in an individual limb or the head. As with other symptoms, the cause may originate from any number of sources.

Weakness is a common symptom for those with eating disorders. Weakness may develop due to starvation. Starvation may result in anemia, dehydration, muscle wasting, and a lack of adequate energy stores, all of which can result in general weakness. Metabolic abnormalities as a result of low iron, potassium, magnesium, calcium, or glucose may contribute to general weakness.

Weakness may be a symptom of depression, exhaustion, poor sleep, overuse of muscles from exercising, or substance abuse. Some prescription medications including sedatives cause weakness. Neuromuscular diseases as mentioned earlier and including myasthenia gravis or endocrine disorders such as hypothyroidism should be considered. Unilateral weakness or paralysis may develop but are not necessarily a result of an eating disorder. Bell's palsy, which is paralysis of one side of the face, or single limb weakness due to radiculopathies tend to occur spontaneously.

Questions

- Do you experience weakness?
- Describe your weakness?
- Is weakness general or specific to a part of your body?
- When did this begin, and do you have an idea why it started or still persists?

Medical Symptoms and Complications 237

- Do you think it is related to a lack of adequate nutrition or low weight?
- Could weakness be due to drug or alcohol use?
- Are you using diuretics or laxatives?
- Are you drinking excessive amounts of fluids?
- Could weakness be due to depression?
- Could weakness be due to exhaustion, including not getting enough sleep?
- Is weakness constant, or does it come and go?
- Have you had a physical exam with accompanying lab work including investigations for mineral and electrolyte levels?
- Are you using ipecac as an emetic?
- Have you been screened for anemia or vitamin B_{12} deficiency?

Headaches Including Migraine

Headaches are common in society. Most will not be of important significance or be particularly troublesome, while others can be very debilitating. Most causes of headaches will be benign, while some could be the result of serious or even lethal etiology. The causes of headaches are extensive. A few items of interest will be mentioned here.

Headaches may be the result of stress, anxiety, worry, poor sleep, drug or alcohol misuse, caffeine and nicotine use or withdrawal, second hand smoke, eyestrain, and other etiologies. It is important to determine if headaches are mild and short lived or disabling, resulting in a significant loss of functioning.

Serious causes of headaches include brain tumors, head injuries, and brain swelling as well as infections. In pregnancy, eclampsia may result in a severe rise in blood pressure leading to seizures and coma and may be fatal. Migraine headaches put people at increased risk of stroke (Mustelin, Raevuori, Kaprio & Keski-Rahkonen, 2014). The synthetic estrogen, ethinyl estradiol, found in some hormonal contraceptives is associated with an increased risk of stroke in those with migraine with aura. This view is supported by the World Health Organization. Serious symptoms of migraine headache, described as aura, are loss of vision; severe blurry vision; tunnel vision; seeing flashing lights, black spots or zigzag lines; unilateral numbness; or paralysis of the face or lower body, as well as the inability to speak, need immediate attention. Any aura, even without headache, is just as important to pay attention to. Those taking estrogen products should see their doctor immediately.

Questions

- Do you experience headaches?
- When do these occur?

- Why do they occur, if you know?
- Do you notice any visual disturbances or numbness, paralysis, or difficulty speaking, with or without headaches?
- Are headaches associated with restricting or binge eating and vomiting?
- Are they associated with low weight?
- Do headaches have an effect on your eating disorder?
- Are they associated with low blood sugar or potassium?
- Is your balance or coordination affected?
- Could the headaches be caused by illicit drug, alcohol, caffeine, or nicotine use?
- Could they be caused by chemical withdrawal?
- Is there a history of headaches in your family, especially migraine?
- Do they occur with eyestrain from studying, watching TV, or viewing a computer screen?
- Do you take any medications to control pain, and what are they?
- Are headaches associated with your periods?
- Have you had a head or neck injury?
- Are headaches and other associated symptoms getting worse?
- Is your ability to concentrate or remember things affected?
- Has depression been increasing since your headaches have been getting worse?

Poor Taste (Dysgeusia)

The inability to taste has several origins as well. For anyone, including those with eating disorders, a decrease in the ability to taste, dysgeusia, may result from smoking, zinc deficiency, decreased saliva from dehydration or medication use, diabetes, gastric reflux, and burning mouth syndrome, as well as several other causes. Facial nerve damage due to trauma or surgery is to be considered. Certainly some brain tumors or infections may affect taste.

Although dysgeusia has been associated with anorexia nervosa, there is yet no known cause. Mineral deficiencies including zinc have been considered as the cause but not proven. Improving nutrition may, however, improve the ability to taste for those with anorexia nervosa.

Questions

- Do you have any difficulty tasting?
- When did this start?
- Could it have happened as a result of malnutrition and weight loss due to the eating disorder?
- Did poor taste begin after initiating medications?
- Do you smoke or experience heartburn?

Medical Symptoms and Complications 239

- Are there any other symptoms associated such as headache, visual disturbances, difficulty speaking, numbness, or poor gait or balance?
- Do you have a problem tasting anything, or is it just specific kinds of foods or taste sensations?
- Does this affect what or how you eat and does this also have an effect on the course of the eating disorder?

Inability to Smell (Anosmia)

Anosmia is the inability to smell. Because taste is intimately related to smell, both taste and smell may be lessened together. Common causes of anosmia are colds or flus, nasal infections, seasonal allergies, medications, cocaine use, smoking, and nasal polyps. Head trauma including to the nose as well as head surgery may also be causes. Less common causes would be brain tumors, multiple sclerosis, diabetes, or a brain aneurysm. As with dysgeusia, zinc deficiency has been implicated for those with restrictive eating disorders.

Questions

- Have you had zinc blood levels checked?
- Do you smoke, use cocaine, or have seasonal allergies or asthma?
- When first developing poor smell, had you been taking antidepressants, antibiotics, or anti-inflammatory medications?
- Do you have a deviated nasal septum, or have you ever had a nose or head injury?
- Have you noticed other symptoms since noticing a decline in the ability to smell?
- Has it had any effect on your ability to eat

Involuntary Movements

Involuntary movements would be a rather rare symptom. One needs to consider degenerative neurological conditions as well as brain tumors or aneurysms. Illicit drug use must be ruled out as well.

Questions

- When did involuntary movements begin?
- Could they be due to substance abuse?
- Have you noticed any other neurological symptoms such as visual changes, headaches, coordination problems, difficulty walking or holding onto things, or weakness in any limb?
- Could you be experiencing drug or alcohol withdrawl?

Muscle Spasm

A common complaint of those with eating disorders is that they experience leg cramps or spasms. There are a few causes of this. Electrolyte abnormalities, mineral deficiencies, and excessive exercise are a few. Some antipsychotic, antidepressant, and antiemetic medications may cause severe muscle spasms and jerkiness as a result of extrapyramidal symptoms.

Memory Loss

For those with eating disorders, memory loss may be associated with starvation, drug and alcohol abuse, or electroconvulsive therapy (ECT). ECT can result in profound memory loss that is not retrievable. The risk of memory loss must be clearly explained before ECT is carried out. Persistent and progressive memory loss may be due to dementia. Memory loss may be of recent or past events.

I have seen a patient diagnosed with dissociative identity disorder with anorexia nervosa. When she assumed the personality of a specific alter, she did not possess any signs of the eating disorder. Both body image control concerns and restrictive eating patterns were absent. Another young woman with cerebral palsy and anorexia nervosa had been found unconscious on a sidewalk and was then taken to the hospital. When she became alert, she did not have any memory of myself, her psychiatrist, or her mother. During much of her stay in the hospital, she ate well and did not show any evidence of an eating disorder. As her memory returned, so did the eating disorder. The cause of fainting and unconsciousness was attributed to ipecac use resulting in a near lethal cardiac dysrhythmia. While ipecac can be fatal in a little as two bottles weekly, she had been taking six bottles daily. A *torsades de pointes* cardiac irregularity or other life-threatening dysrhythmia was suspected as the cause of her unconsciousness but could not be proven.

Another patient, with bulimia, was experiencing the return of memories of child sexual assault. Her flashbacks were so vivid that she could not take care of her three children, so I admitted her to the hospital. Here, we observed the unfolding of abuse experiences as memories returned. During the two weeks of monitoring her in the hospital, she ate remarkably well and, again, did not have any body image control issues. She seemed to have forgotten her eating disorder during this somewhat disturbing but revealing episode.

Questions

- When did you first notice losing your memory, if you indeed can remember?
- Could memory loss be due to substance abuse?

Medical Symptoms and Complications 241

- Could memory loss be the result of prescribed medications, including sedatives?
- Have you had ECT treatments, and did memory loss occur after this?
- Do others comment on your poor memory?
- Had you experienced trauma prior to losing memory?
- Is there anyone in your family with early onset dementia?

Forgetfulness

For those with eating disorders, forgetfulness may be due to poor nutrition, substance abuse, psychotropic medications, exhaustion, or depression. Forgetfulness may also be a result of life distractions or preoccupations. Occasional forgetfulness such as forgetting where one parked one's car or put one's wallet or to return a text message will not be of much concern. Of course, dementia or other neurological conditions should be considered if forgetfulness is escalating.

Forgetfulness may be very specific and predictable. I have always been surprised that individuals who are able to attend classes, finish school assignments, and get straight As will phone me an hour after our therapy session was to have taken place and ask, "Did I have an appointment today?"

Questions

- Are you forgetful about many things or very specific things, such as appointments?
- Why do you think you are forgetful?
- Could you be forgetful because you are distracted by tasks, thoughts, or emotions?
- Is forgetting a guilt-free way of avoiding situations?
- Could you be forgetful because of substance abuse, use of sedating medications, exhaustion, or poor sleep?
- Are you preoccupied by a particularly troublesome problem such as parents divorcing, ongoing abusive events, the suicide of a friend, or being fired from your job?
- If you keep forgetting our sessions, should you be seeing another therapist?

Dementia

The progression of dementia is usually insidious and diagnosed late in the day. Once accurately diagnosed, family and friends will have aha moments where, upon looking back in time, they could recognize early signs of dementia. Some forms of dementia progress quickly and are diagnosed sooner rather than later. Periods of momentary forgetfulness or vague memory loss may precede well-established dementia.

242 Medical Symptoms and Complications

In my experience, I have noticed anorexia nervosa develop after early signs of dementia. I have seen dementia in a 70-year-old woman as well as a woman in her early 40s, both who expressed believable body image dissatisfaction. Their negative body image resulted in deliberate weight loss through extreme restricting. When discussing all this with their families, both families denied any awareness of any significant body image or weight dissatisfaction previously. Nor were they aware of any weight loss attempts prior to developing dementia. Regardless of dementia symptoms, both individuals gave a clear picture of their weight issues and dedication to further weight loss.

Questions for family and friends:

- Were there any body image or weight control issues before dementia began?
- Did she have an eating disorder before dementia was noticed?
- What kind of body image or weight dissatisfaction did she express, and what eating disorder behaviors were first and which ones followed, if any?
- Is she safe to take care of herself on her own, or is she at risk of dying from starvation or an accident if not cared for by others?
- If coordination problems or psychosis developed along with dementia, has she been investigated for Creutzfeldt-Jakob disease (mad cow disease)?

Drooping Eyelids

Drooping eyelids may be the result of many factors that create other neurological symptoms, as mentioned earlier. Myasthenia gravis, an autoimmune disease causing progressive neuromuscular dysfunction, may cause drooping eyes, double vision, and facial and general body weakness. Myasthenia gravis has not been associated specifically with eating disorders. Drooping eyelids may just be a product of aging.

Visual Disturbances

Visual disturbances have been discussed earlier with regard to migraine, eyestrain, brain tumors, cerebral aneurysms, and multiple sclerosis. Certainly inebriation from any drug can result in visual changes.

Pain

There are many sources of pain symptoms for those with eating disorders. Though pain is experienced through the nervous system, it could have its

Medical Symptoms and Complications **243**

origins in various organs from various systems, many of which have been discussed elsewhere.

Kinds of pain may include the following.

- Headache
- Joint pain
- Back pain
- Vertebral spinous process pain
- General muscle pain
- Leg and foot cramps
- Buttock pain
- Skin pain
- Abdominal pains
- Bladder pain
- Kidney pain
- Pelvic pain
- Throat pain
- Jaw pain
- Dental pain
- Chest wall pain

Questions

- Do you experience pain?
- Does pain affect how you engage in eating disorder behaviors?
- Does pain make the eating disorder worse or better?
- In what part of your body do you experience pain?
- When did these pains begin?
- Do you know why these pains developed?
- How do you cope with pain?
- Is pain due to self-harm such as hitting, burning, or cutting?

Head Region

The head region has organ tissue from most systems. The systems not represented in the head, however, can have a major impact on functioning there, including the brain. Some head-related symptoms have been discussed elsewhere. See the sections on the "Neurological System" and "Gastrointestinal System."

Facial Swelling

Facial swelling may present in a few ways. General facial swelling may result from water retention or edema, possibly caused by refeeding and rehydration, a result of hyperaldosteronism. General facial swelling may

244 Medical Symptoms and Complications

also result from regular vomiting. Facial swelling may be very distressing, as it is a part of the body that one can't cover and hide easily. The individual will describe this as having a fat face.

Swelling in front of the ears on both sides of the face will be caused by *parotid gland swelling*. Parotid gland swelling is associated with vomiting. It is believed that the act of vomiting can cause acidic fluid to track up the parotid salivary duct resulting in inflammation of the parotid gland. Once the glands have become swollen, it can take weeks or months to recede. Pain is not usually associated. Sometimes the swelling is permanent.

Another reason a parotid gland may swell is that the parotid gland duct has been blocked by a stone or calculus, much like a kidney stone. The swelling will be on one side unless there is a calculus in both ducts. Pain may result, and some complain of a foul-tasting substance in the mouth caused by infected parotid gland fluid escaping around the stone. Calculi may be generated as a result of dehydration, the same reason some kidney stones form in those with anorexia nervosa. Calculus formation may be of genetic origin.

Swelling of the submandibular salivary glands, located underneath the jaw on both sides, is likely a product of vomiting for the same reason as parotid gland swelling. Again, unilateral swelling may be the result of a calculus in the salivary ducts. As well, a foul taste may occur due to infected salivary fluids.

Parotid and submandibular glands may swell for other reasons. Benign and cancerous tumors may be the cause. An ear nose and throat (ENT) specialist needs to be consulted if symptoms do not resolve as expected.

Questions

- Have you noticed any facial swelling?
- Is swelling of your whole face?
- Is swelling on one side or both sides of your face, and is it localized in front of your ears, under your jaw, or both?
- Do you ever notice a foul taste in your mouth?
- Do you think the swelling is due to vomiting?
- Are you chronically dehydrated?
- Does your face swell only with episodes of vomiting or with refeeding?
- How do you deal with facial swelling?

Sore or Sensitive Teeth

As a result of vomiting, dental damage may develop. Stomach acid can cause precipitous enamel erosion and cavities. Dental erosion and decay can destroy several if not all teeth, leading to dental extraction or multiple crowns. The cost of repair can be in the tens of thousands of dollars.

Medical Symptoms and Complications 245

Some who persist vomiting after crowns have been placed may require yet another set due to continued dental destruction. Dental decay, especially of the front teeth, compounds further a person's focus on negative body image and low self-worth. Gum damage including receding gums may evolve due to the same reasons.

Questions

- Are your teeth sensitive?
- Are you developing cavities or receding gums, likely from vomiting?
- Will you be requiring extensive dental work?
- How does dental damage affect how you feel about yourself?
- Are your gums damaged as a result of vomiting?
- How much will it cost?
- Can you afford the cost?

Hearing Loss

Hearing loss needs to be investigated. Any number of neurological conditions may be the cause. Infections of the middle ear, inflamed Eustachian tubes due to infection, allergies, or smoke sensitivity as well as noise-induced hearing loss from listening to loud music with headphones are common reasons. Vomiting, as with salivary duct inflammation, may lead to Eustachian tube inflammation. Wax buildup in the ear canals is worth consideration. Permanent hearing loss may develop from chronic ear infections as a child, head trauma, or very loud noises. Hearing loss may be of genetic origin.

Questions

- When did your hearing loss start, and why, if you know?
- Is the hearing loss in both ears or just on one side?
- Do you have seasonal allergies, get ear infections, or smoke?
- Have you had many ear infections as a child or experienced a head injury or extremely loud noise?
- Do you listen to loud music with headphones?
- Do you experience ringing in the ears or a spinning sensation, or have you been told you have Meniere's disease?
- When were your ears last cleaned?
- Did your hearing loss begin with vomiting?

Tinnitus

Tinnitus is ringing in the ears. It may occur by itself or be associated with hearing loss, buzzing in the ears, or difficulty balancing, which are

Gastrointestinal System

There are numerous symptoms of gastrointestinal (GI) origin. Several have been mentioned earlier. Some gastrointestinal symptoms are mentioned briefly here.

A single symptom does not define a diagnosis. Any gut disorder may have a few to many symptoms that could be attributed to it. There may be more than one gastrointestinal disorder active at a given time. One person with an eating disorder may experience symptoms from intestinal motility disorder, celiac disease, and gallbladder disease concurrently. This is not an unlikely scenario. Alternatively, symptoms may arise from non-gastrointestinal systems but be mistaken to be of gastrointestinal origin. Abdominal pain, bloating, and nausea may result from endometriosis and renal disease.

Some symptoms of the gastrointestinal system are listed here. Because many of these symptoms are associated with several medical disorders of gastrointestinal and other system origins, specific disease entities will be discussed in some depth.

- Pain
- Cramping
- Belching
- Vomiting
- Pain with swallowing
- Pain with vomiting
- Sore throat
- Sore mouth
- Sore tongue
- Blood in vomit
- Bile in vomit
- Heartburn
- Distention
- Loud bowel sounds
- Diarrhea
- Constipation
- Hematochezia
- Mucous in stools
- Floating stools
- Undigested food identified in stool

Superior Mesenteric Artery Syndrome

Superior mesenteric artery syndrome (SMAS) is a rare condition where the duodenum is compressed by the superior mesenteric artery against the aorta. It can cause acute or chronic symptoms of obstruction of the bowel (Mascolo, Dee, Townsend, Brinton & Mehler, 2015). The obstruction may be partial or complete. This condition may develop in those with anorexia nervosa due to diminishing of the fat tissue as a result of starvation that normally protects the bowel from compression by the artery. This can result in increasing dilatation of the stomach resulting in pain, infarction of the bowel, and perforation. All acute or undiagnosed chronic abdominal pains require urgent attention to rule out serious causes of bowel pain, including superior mesenteric artery syndrome.

Intestinal Motility Disorder

Many with eating disorders develop abdominal symptoms from various sources. A cause of gut symptomatology may be due to intestinal motility disorder. This is a condition where peristalsis of the gut is altered. In normal bowel function, one section of the bowel contracts while the adjacent one relaxes in a coordinated fashion to propel digesting food from the stomach to the rectum. In the healthy gut, food typically leaves the stomach and enters the small intestine well within a couple of hours, if not much sooner. Liquids tend to leave the stomach faster, while solid foods will take longer. The composition of the food also affects the rate of gastric emptying.

With intestinal motility disorder, both coordination and the rate of peristaltic activity have been altered, resulting in cramping and bloating. The capacity for food to move from the stomach into the small intestine then further along can come to a standstill. This condition occurs in those with anorexia nervosa and bulimia as well as others with various forms of disordered eating. Symptoms affect those with eating disorders in multiple ways.

For those who vomit, some will report that they bring up food or pills that were consumed several hours earlier, a period of time over which food and medications should have progressed to the small intestine. Patients have reported they have vomited food eaten as long as 12 hours earlier. A number of times I have sent individuals for a barium swallow with follow-through to examine the upper GI tract from the stomach to the end of the small intestine. I would later receive curt reports from the radiologists stating that they had to terminate the procedure because the barium had not left the stomach after three hours.

Intestinal motility disorder may create severe abdominal cramping and bloating. These symptoms may be made worse by eating, therefore greatly

248   Medical Symptoms and Complications

discouraging the need to eat. Restricting and vomiting then become behaviors to cope with these symptoms. Recovery efforts to encourage refeeding or to discontinue vomiting may be halted.

Intestinal motility disorder also may result in constipation. Constipation may be quite severe. Patients report not having a bowel movement for a week or longer. As well, bowel movements may only occur after enemas or suppository use. Constipation further exacerbates bloating and cramping. Laxative use is deemed a way of dealing with constipation but may not work, still aggravate bloating and cramping symptoms. For those engaged in laxative abuse, decreasing or discontinuing laxatives may lead to an increase in constipation, cramping, and bloating. Attempts at weaning off of laxatives can be very frustrating.

Aside from bloating and cramping resulting in significant physical discomfort, they also amplify body dissatisfaction by triggering the fat feeling. Although individuals intellectually know symptoms are not the result of escalating fat tissue growth, emotionally they may not be able to detach from expanding body image loathing.

Here is a perfect example of triggers-triggering-triggers or a domino effect of cascading feared symptoms. Gut dysmotility leads to cramping, bloating, and constipation, which in turn triggers restricting, vomiting, and laxative abuse that further aggravates intestinal motility disorder symptoms and, as well, compounds body image dissatisfaction. The body image dissatisfaction perpetuates more eating disorder behaviors used to control physical symptoms and body image dissatisfaction. All of this triggers increasing depression, anxiety, and self-loathing, possibly fueling substance abuse or suicidal ideation.

Compounding all of this is that many other gastrointestinal and non-gastrointestinal conditions may cause similar or identical symptoms. Abdominal pain and bloating may be symptoms of irritable bowel syndrome, inflammatory bowel disease, celiac disease, gallbladder disease, and appendicitis as well as of non-gastrointestinal conditions such as endometriosis, menstruation, or urinary tract disorders, to list only a few mimicking conditions.

Questions

- Do you experience bloating, abdominal cramps, or constipation?
- What makes these symptoms better or worse, if you know?
- Do they make you want to restrict, vomit, or use laxatives, enemas, or suppositories to relieve symptoms?
- Do these symptoms make you feel worse about your body?
- Do they increase your drive to use eating disorder behaviors further?
- Do they interfere with recovery efforts?
- What do you do to compensate for worsening body image?

Medical Symptoms and Complications 249

- Do they affect your moods, and in what way?
- Do they encourage you to use non-eating disorder behaviors to cope, such as engaging in substance abuse or self-harm?

Crohn's Disease

Crohn's disease is an inflammatory bowel disease causing inflammation of the digestive tract. It typically affects the small bowel but can also affect anywhere from the mouth to the anus. It is an autoimmune disorder that may have a hereditary link (Wotton, James & Goldacre, 2016). Symptoms may be relatively minor but may evolve to be severe. The destruction of the bowel due to inflammation and possible infection can be contained with adequate treatment or become extensive and even life threatening.

Anyone with an eating disorder and Crohn's disease brings added emotional and medical management challenges. An extreme situation of an individual with an eating disorder and Crohn's disease is this. One young woman had had such extensive damage to her gastrointestinal tract that most of her intestine was surgically removed, including her stomach. She was not allowed to eat or drink anything as pockets or diverticuli in her throat would retain food particles and become infected. Her eating disorder included eating anything regardless of the medical consequences. She just wanted to experience the taste and texture of food but would suffer greatly if she did. Her total nutrition was provided giving liquid nutrition through parenteral means or intravenously. She was body image conscious because she was an actor, not because of nutritional weight gain concerns.

Because Crohn's disease is a chronic and often progressive condition, it adds great uncertainty and a degree of dread as to what the course of the disorder may bring in the future. Because those with eating disorders use eating disorder behaviors to cope with feelings and physical symptoms, close attention to the path the eating disorder takes is paramount.

Another inflammatory disease is ulcerative colitis. It causes similar symptoms to Crohn's disease but more often affects the large bowel. It is associated with a high risk of bowel cancer.

Crohn's disease may result in:

- Diarrhea
- Malnutrition
- Abdominal cramps
- Pain anywhere from the mouth to the anus
- Bloody diarrhea
- Mouth, vulvar, and anal ulcers
- Skin lesions
- Bowel obstruction

250 Medical Symptoms and Complications

- Bowel cancer of the colon
- Fistulas
- Anal fissures
- Loss of appetite

Questions

- Do you experience abdominal pain and cramps, chronic diarrhea, or blood in the stools?
- Do certain foods such as raw vegetables make symptoms worse?
- Have you been told by a doctor that you may have inflammatory bowel disease such as Crohn's disease or ulcerative colitis?
- Have you had any treatments, including medications, diet restrictions, or surgery?
- Are you sticking to the recommended treatments?
- Do your eating disorder behaviors aggravate symptoms of Crohn's disease due to bingeing, vomiting, or other eating disorder behaviors?
- How extensive is your Crohn's disease?
- How do your symptoms affect your daily living?
- How do your symptoms affect your body image concerns or eating disorder behaviors?
- Are you optimistic about the future course of the Crohn's disease, or are you fearful that it will progress?

Celiac Disease

Celiac disease, or gluten-sensitive enteropathy, is an immune reaction to the protein gluten found naturally in wheat, barley, rye, and foods with malt or any foods made from these sources. It may present itself as bloating, nausea, diarrhea, abdominal cramps, constipation, flatulence, and malabsorption. Weight loss may result. In children, it may lead to short stature. Symptoms of celiac disease may be so minor that it may not be diagnosed; therefore, symptoms continue unchecked (Marild et al., 2017)

For those with eating disorders, any one of the symptoms may discourage one from wanting or being able to eat. Multiple symptoms further discourage recovery efforts. The clinician must have a high index of suspicious regarding the possibility of celiac disease and encourage medical assessment.

Gluten is not just found in breads or grains but is an additive in many other foods. A few are listed here.

- Soups
- Cold cuts
- Commercial broths and bullion

Medical Symptoms and Complications 251

- Processed cheese
- Salad dressings
- Mayonnaise
- Ice cream
- Soy sauce and teriyaki sauces
- Beer and wine coolers
- Hot dogs and sausages
- Breakfast cereals

With gluten being found naturally in grains and added to dozens of prepared foods, finding gluten-free foods can be difficult. Because gluten is nearly ubiquitous in so many foods, gluten intolerance may be a "good reason" to restrict, playing into eating disorder mentality. For those attempting to improve nutrition for recovery purposes, increased effort needs to be made to select gluten-free foods. Gluten-free foods tend to be expensive; thus, inadequate finances become an issue in the recovery process.

Questions

- Do you have any intolerance to foods?
- Which foods do you not tolerate?
- What symptoms do you experience after consuming these foods?
- Do your symptoms affect how you deal with your eating disorder, and how?
- Are you aware of the plethora of foods that have gluten added?
- Have you been told you may have celiac disease?
- Have you been tested for celiac disease?
- Have you altered your diet to eliminate symptoms, and what specific non-gluten foods are part of this diet?
- Can you afford a gluten-free diet?

Malabsorption Syndrome

There are a number of conditions that result in the bowel's inability to absorb certain nutrients. Some have already been mentioned. There may be a selective inability to absorb certain nutrients such as protein, minerals, fats, and sugars. Any disease that destroys the absorptive surface of the small intestine may result in the gut's inability to absorb any nutrient adequately.

Causes of malabsorption are:

- Gluten intolerance
- Bowel infections, including parasites
- Antibiotics

252 Medical Symptoms and Complications

- Crohn's disease
- Chronic pancreatitis
- Lactose intolerance
- Pernicious anemia
- Any disorder that prevents the bowel from absorbing nutrients, including tropical diseases

Questions

- Do you find that even when you eat adequately you still lose weight?
- Do you notice that your stools are greasy or oily and have a bad smell?
- Do you notice blood in your stool?
- Are you gluten or lactose intolerant?
- Do you require vitamin B_{12} injections?
- Have you traveled anywhere you could have acquired a gut infection, including parasites?

Irritable Bowel Syndrome

Irritable bowel syndrome (IBS) is a gastrointestinal condition that presents with abdominal pain or cramping, bloating, constipation or diarrhea, excessive flatulence, and possibly mucus in the stool. Symptoms are usually minor but may cause chronic problems. It is sometimes necessary to rule out more serious sources of symptoms before an accurate diagnosis of IBS is made.

Questions

- If you feel you have IBS, what symptoms do you have?
- What makes your symptoms better or worse?
- Does changing your diet or taking medications help?
- Have you been diagnosed with IBS by a physician?
- Have you been investigated for another gut illness that causes similar symptoms?

Gallbladder Disease

Gallbladder disease is the result of inflammation of the gallbladder, or cholecystitis, which may be associated with gallstones, or cholelithiasis. Symptoms of gallbladder disease include:

- Vague to severe pain of the upper abdomen, especially on the right, that may radiate to the right shoulder or back
- Nausea

Medical Symptoms and Complications   253

- Vomiting
- Intolerance of certain foods
- Fever
- Jaundice

Vague symptoms of nausea, food intolerances, and abdominal pain may linger for years undetected. An acute event of severe abdominal pain is what may lead someone to go to the emergency room, where a diagnosis is made using radiographic images or ultrasonography.

For those with an eating disorder, symptoms can make it difficult for someone to be expected to eat. Because symptoms are often insidious, symptoms of bloating and abdominal pain may be attributed to eating disorder behaviors such as vomiting, bingeing, and laxative abuse. Symptoms may also be attributed to intestinal motility disorder, gluten intolerance, or an acidic stomach. Irritable bowel syndrome and inflammatory bowel disease can cause these same symptoms, as well.

Questions

- Have you had these symptoms investigated by your doctor?
- Have you been told you may have gallbladder disease, including having gallstones?
- Have your skin and eyeballs ever turned yellow?
- Have you been taken to the emergency room for these symptoms?
- Do these symptoms affect eating disorder behaviors?
- How have you been managing these symptoms?
- Is there a history of gallbladder disease in your family?

Gastritis

Gastritis is inflammation of the lining of the stomach due to any number of causes. The most common symptoms are:

- Upper abdominal pain described as gnawing or burning
- Nausea
- Vomiting
- Pain may get worse or better with eating, depending on the kind of food.

The causes of gastritis may be due to the lining of the stomach being sensitive to stomach acid, helicobacter pylori (H. pylori) infection, alcohol excess, medications including non-steroidal anti-inflammatories, and autoimmune diseases such as Hashimoto's disease and vitamin B_{12} deficiency. Crohn's disease should also be considered.

254 Medical Symptoms and Complications

Questions

- Do you drink alcohol to excess?
- Do you think your abdominal pain increases with increased consumption of alcohol?
- Does eating make your symptoms worse or better?
- Do you take painkillers such as aspirin or ibuprofen on a regular basis?
- Have you been tested for H. pylori infection or parasites?
- Do you have thyroid disease or a problem absorbing vitamin B_{12} (pernicious anemia)?
- Could you have Crohn's disease?
- Does vomiting make symptoms worse?
- Does pain or nausea have an effect on the eating disorder?

Gastric (Peptic) and Duodenal Ulcers

Ulcers of the stomach or duodenum can present with upper abdominal pain. Pain may be similar to gastritis. The majority of individuals with these do not have any symptoms. Ulcers have the capacity to bleed. Seeing fresh blood or black coffee ground like matter in vomit or seeing dark red blood or black stools after a bowel movement may be signs of a bleeding ulcer. The causes of GI ulcers are very similar to those that cause gastritis and require similar investigations.

Questions

- Do you see blood when you vomit that looks red or like coffee grounds?
- Do you see dark red blood or have black stools with a bowel movement?
- Does stomach pain affect your ability to eat?
- Does the pain result in you needing to vomit to relieve pain?
- Does the pain make your eating disorder worse?
- Do you take anti-inflammatories?
- Have you been screened for H. pylori?
- Have you been investigated for inflammatory bowel disease?

Gastroesophageal Reflux Disorder (GERD)

Gastroesophageal reflux is caused by stomach contents entering the esophagus. The stomach contents will contain stomach acid, resulting in heartburn or burning sensation in the chest. Stomach contents may regurgitate and be tasted in the mouth as a sour liquid. Symptoms are often worse after eating, and especially while lying down. This backwash of stomach contents is usually blocked by the lower esophageal sphincter constricting and a pinching action where the stomach joins the esophagus. Symptoms

Medical Symptoms and Complications   255

are made worse by smoking and alcohol consumption. A condition called a *hiatal hernia* allows the upper part of the stomach to enter the chest, which in turn results in acid reflux.

For those who vomit as part of their eating disorder, reflux may be more common. Repeated reflux or vomiting can result in reflux esophagitis or inflammation of the esophagus caused by stomach acid. Chronic inflammation, ulcers and even scarring of the esophagus may result. Difficulty swallowing as well as food becoming trapped in the esophagus may arise. Nighttime reflux may trigger chronic coughing or laryngitis. Regurgitation or vomiting while sleeping may result in waking up choking.

Questions

- Do you notice a burning sensation in your chest, especially after eating?
- Do you notice food or an acidic fluid in your mouth possibly due to regurgitation?
- Are symptoms made worse by lying down?
- Do these symptoms become worse with an increased frequency of vomiting?
- Do you wake up choking in the night?
- Do you have difficulty swallowing or experience food getting caught in your esophagus?
- Does alcohol or smoking make your symptoms worse?

Pancreatitis

Pancreatitis is inflammation of the pancreas. It may be caused as a result of blockage of the bile duct by a gallstone, alcohol use, illicit drug use, cigarette smoking, high calcium levels, high-cholesterol, some medications, infections, cystic fibrosis, or cancer. There is a familial link as well. Symptoms may be acute or chronic.

Symptoms of pancreatitis include:

- Upper abdominal pain that may radiate to the back
- Fever
- Nausea
- Pain increasing with eating
- Weight loss
- Oily, smelly stools

As with many other gut disorders, symptoms of pancreatitis may affect one's ability to maintain adequate nutrition or increase the drive to vomit for symptom relief.

256 Medical Symptoms and Complications

Caution is required for those taking calcium supplements either for calcium replacement or to manage heartburn or gastric reflux symptoms. Calcium is taken by pregnant women for calcium replacement as well as to diminish heartburn due to acid reflux. Pregnant women should not increase recommended doses. Escalating abdominal discomfort, especially in those who are pregnant, may be symptoms of pancreatitis caused by calcium supplements. Women who are dealing with bulimia and pregnancy may have abdominal pains and heartburn symptoms incorrectly attributed to eating disorder behaviors, thus resulting in pancreatitis not being diagnosed. Pancreatitis can be fatal in hours; therefore, increasing abdominal discomfort in an individual taking calcium supplements should lead to an immediate investigation of pancreatitis. An intensive care admission may be necessary. It is common for those who are malnourished to take calcium supplements, as they will not be receiving calcium as they would otherwise through healthy eating.

Questions

- Along with your abdominal pain, do you have fever, and is your abdomen painful to touch?
- Could your pain be associated with alcohol excess or street drug use?
- Is there a family history of pancreatic disease in your family, including pancreatic cancer?
- Are you pregnant?
- Are you taking antacids for the pain?
- Do you take calcium supplements to prevent bone loss due to not having your periods or as replacement because of restricting eating patterns?
- Has the pain been increasing as you increase calcium supplement intake?
- Do you have a history of gallstones?
- Have you been losing weight since the pain has been progressing?
- What effect have these symptoms had on your eating disorder?

Lactose Intolerance

Lactose intolerance may present with symptoms of diarrhea, nausea, abdominal cramps, flatulence, and bloating. This is the result of an inability to digest the sugar lactose adequately. This is a sugar found in milk products. There is a deficiency of the enzyme, lactase, that breaks down lactose. Lactase is produced in the small intestines. As with all other conditions that result in abdominal pain and other GI symptoms, it can make it difficult for someone with an eating disorder to eat. Typically, foods containing milk products are avoided to manage uncomfortable feelings.

Medical Symptoms and Complications 257

Questions

- Are you intolerant of milk products?
- Does lactose intolerance affect how you eat?
- Does it have an effect on your eating disorder?
- Are you on a lactose-free diet?

Musculoskeletal System

Sore Joints

For those with eating disorders, joint pain may be due to over-exercising. Dehydration may result in decreased joint fluid, also resulting in sore joints. Restricting fluids or using diuretics and laxatives can contribute to these symptoms. As well, arthritis of the joints due to trauma or of genetic origin, such as rheumatoid arthritis, generates pain. Autoimmune diseases can cause joint pains and swelling, with Sjogren's syndrome and systemic lupus erythematosus being a couple.

Questions

- Do you experience joint pains? When and why?
- Could joint pains be the result of over-exercising, joint injury, dehydration from vomiting or restricting fluids, or because of laxative or diuretic use?
- Is there a history of rheumatoid arthritis in you or your family?
- Do you have an autoimmune disorder?
- Do you do any repetitive movements such as playing a musical instrument or keyboarding on a computer?
- Does joint pain affect the eating disorder, and in what way?

Sore Back

A sore back may result from over-exercising, especially where the back muscles are involved. Walking, running, dancing, and lifting are a few examples. Sitting for long periods of time, poor posture such as slouching, or bending excessively also create back strain. Pounding motions such as with running or horseback riding are worth enquiring about. Osteoporosis can lead to collapsing of vertebrae; collapsing of spinal discs also may develop due to repetitive back use or injury, causing chronic and sometimes severe back pain.

Questions

- Could your back pain be attributed to exercise, injury, or frequent bending?

258 Medical Symptoms and Complications

- Have you had a serious back injury from playing a sport such as soccer, rugby, tennis, or skating?
- Do you use your back for heavy work such as lifting or moving heavy objects at work or home?
- Do you garden?
- Do you do sit-ups or jumping jacks or run on hard surfaces for extended periods of time?
- Do you sit for prolonged periods of time, ride a horse, or do yoga?
- Do you have arthritis anywhere in your body?
- Do you have osteoporosis?
- Are you using Depo-Provera injections that may contribute to osteoporosis?
- Does back pain affect your eating disorder, such as limiting you from exercising?
- If you can't exercise due to back pain, what other eating disorder behaviors might you be using to compensate?
- Have you been investigated for cancer?

Sore Legs, Knees, Ankles, and Feet

Leg pains may result from overuse injuries due to over-exercising. Strain of the joints, muscles, and bones may result. *Shin splints* are a result of inflammation of muscle and the periosteum of the tibia due to overuse. Hairline bone fractures as well as full fractures, including in bones of the feet, may result from exercise and athletics. Osteoporosis will contribute to the risk of bone fractures. Playing a simple game of soccer or stepping off of a curb may cause ankle fractures for those with low bone mass. Knee pain may be the result of patellofemoral syndrome.

Sore Muscles, Muscle Cramps

Sore muscles, as with sore joints, can be a product of overuse. For those with exercise compulsion, this is a risk. Sore muscles can be a result of metabolic abnormalities including low potassium, calcium, and magnesium levels. Low electrolyte and mineral levels may result from starvation, diuretic, or laxative use.

Questions

- Do you have a history of metabolic abnormalities?
- Do you vomit or take laxatives or diuretics as part of the eating disorder?
- Could sore muscles be due to over-exercising, competitive athletics, or both?

Vertebral Spinous Process Pain

Because of wasting subcutaneous tissue, the spinous processes of the vertebrae are more likely to hurt with leaning against a chair or lying on the floor. Exercising while lying on the back, including yoga exercises, contributes to this pain.

Muscle Wasting

Due to starvation, muscles can waste. They become smaller in volume and mass. During starvation, the body compensates for the lack of protein consumed by breaking down muscle protein to meet metabolic needs. Physical weakness and tendon rupture become risks. It is a stealing from Peter to pay Paul scenario. Muscle wasting of the heart results in weakness of cardiac contractions, heart valve dysfunction, and heartbeat irregularities.

Questions

- Are you aware that wasting of muscles due to starvation also causes the heart to shrink and can lead to serious cardiac risks?

Muscle Weakness

Physical weakness may develop due to muscle wasting. Several other causes are mentioned in the section on the "Neurological System." Starvation, substance abuse, depression, and muscle toxicity from ipecac are to be considered.

Questions

- Do you use ipecac?
- Have you had electrolyte and mineral levels evaluated recently?

Sore Neck

Anything that can cause neck strain will cause neck pain. Sitting at a computer or reading for extended periods of time as well as neck injury from exercising are a few examples. Frequent vomiting over a toilet bowl may cause neck strain.

Endocrinological System

Symptoms of endocrinological origin have been covered extensively elsewhere, including hyperthyroidism, hypothyroidism, and insulin-dependent

260 Medical Symptoms and Complications

diabetes mellitus. See the sections on the "Gynecological System" and "Cardiovascular System".

An example of a disorder of endocrine origin is Addison's disease or primary adrenal insufficiency. It is caused by an inadequate amount of cortisol and possibly aldosterone being produced. Some symptoms are low blood pressure, weight loss, nausea, vomiting, diarrhea, and possible changes in mood and personality. These are virtually identical events seen in many with anorexia nervosa.

A 12-year-old girl was admitted to a hospital with many of the symptoms mentioned. It was assumed she had anorexia nervosa, and she was treated for this. Non-eating disorder medical causes for her symptoms were not investigated. She died. At autopsy they discovered she had Addison's disease. Regardless of any eating disorder suspicions, a thorough medical assessment needs to be in place to rule out other causes of troubling symptoms.

Respiratory System

Shortness of Breath

See "Chest Region" and "Cardiovascular System."

Wheezing

Wheezing may be associated with those who have a respiratory infection, asthma, or environmental sensitivities or who smoke. Smoke from tobacco, pot, hash, or other drugs all can inflame bronchial airways, resulting in wheezing. Smoking cigarettes is a common practice, but for those with eating disorders it may also be used as a method to curb appetite or increase metabolism.

Wheezing may be the result of food or vomit having been inhaled during a bingeing and vomiting episode that could partially block airways. This can lead to a lung infection.

Questions
*   Do you smoke anything?
*   Do you have environmental sensitivities?
*   Do you have a cold or flu?
*   Could you have inhaled food or vomit during a binge and vomit session?

Cough

Coughing will be commonly associated with the same triggers that result in wheezing. Coughing can be the result of gastroesophageal reflux.

Medical Symptoms and Complications 261

Inhaled food or vomit during binge and vomiting sessions would trigger coughing.

Tachypnea

Tachypnea or breathing fast will be associated with anything that deprives an individual of taking in an adequate amount of air. Any condition that constricts airways may result in tachypnea, as mentioned earlier.

With regard to those with eating disorders, fast breathing may result from abnormal metabolic states, with metabolic alkalosis being an example. Some cardiac arrhythmias can lead to oxygen deprivation resulting in quicker breathing. Tachypnea may be a symptom of a life-threatening metabolic or cardiac state. Tachypnea may also be associated with anxiety, including from panic attacks, hyperthyroidism, and stimulants.

Questions

- Do you ever find yourself breathing very quickly, and if you do, do you know why?
- Do you hyperventilate when anxious?
- Has this ever happened when you have been diagnosed with electrolyte disturbance?
- Do you notice your heart race or thump when you breathe fast?
- Are you anemic?
- Do you hyperventilate?

Irregular Respiration

Breathing can become irregular for the same reasons as those that cause tachypnea. An endocrine tumor that releases high levels of adrenaline from the adrenal glands, called a pheochromocytoma, may lead to a racing heart as well as fast and irregular breathing. An irregular heart that flips from one rhythm to another may affect respiratory rate. Electrolyte imbalances may affect respiratory function.

Colored Sputum

Purulent sputum is sputum infected with bacteria. This can be the result of bacterial-induced bronchitis or pneumonia. While viral-induced sputum will typically be clear, purulent sputum will be white or yellowish. Fever may be associated with lung infections.

Sputum that is green or gray will not likely be of bacterial origin. Green sputum is more likely to be caused by inspissated or thickened secretions in the lungs resulting from dehydration. A thick, mucousy grayish sputum may be found in those who smoke. Because smoke destroys the cilia in

262   Medical Symptoms and Complications

the airways that move debris out of the lungs, wads of dark, gray mucousy sputum may be coughed up to rid the lungs of unwanted matter in smokers. Inhaling food or vomit could result in lung infections.

Questions

- Do you ever cough up thick, creamy, yellow or dark sputum?
- If you are a smoker, do you wake up at night choking on thick, dark sputum?
- Could you be dehydrated?

Pain With Breathing

Pleurisy or inflammation of the lining around the lungs and inside the chest cavity can cause pain, especially with breathing. A rubbing sound may be heard with each breath due to friction of the lungs moving against the chest wall.

Pain with breathing may also be a result of fractured ribs. Those with eating disorders are prone to osteoporosis and are at higher risk of fractures, including of ribs. Exercise, athletic activities, hiking, and rock climbing may put someone with anorexia nervosa at increased risk of rib and other fractures. Sometimes rib fractures are spontaneous, not obviously caused by a particular physical activity. For those with advanced osteoporosis, a simple act of sneezing or coughing can fracture ribs.

Questions

- Did you have a cold or flu prior to chest pain?
- Have you been coughing a lot and hard?
- Were you doing any physical activity that could have fractured your ribs?

Dermatological System

Skin creates many symptoms and signs for those with eating disorders. Some will be of little consequence, while others, though subtle, may be an expression of an important concern.

Hair Loss

Hair loss may be a result of poor nutrition for those with eating disorders. It may also be the result of an illness or significant emotional event. Hair loss after illness or emotional stresses can take about three months to result in visible hair loss. Hair loss may be due to hormonal irregularities such as

Medical Symptoms and Complications   263

hypothyroidism and polycystic ovarian syndrome (PCOS). Deficiencies in vitamin D or iron are also triggers.

Hair loss can happen anywhere on the body. Where the hair loss occurs and the pattern of hair loss may help to determine the etiology or at least lead to appropriate investigations. Male pattern baldness in women may be the result of PCOS. General hair loss on the head may be due to nutritional deficiencies. Patchy hair loss could be due to medications such as lithium or due to trichotillomania.

Questions

- When did you first notice hair loss?
- Where is your hair loss?
- Have you gained weight or developed acne and oily skin, as well?
- Did hair loss occur after taking a medication, and what medication was this?
- Do you twirl and pull your hair out?
- Have you been receiving chemotherapy?
- Do you have a hormonal IUD?
- Could hair loss be due to stress or nutritional deficiencies?

Dry Skin

Dry skin may be a result of dehydration. It also may be due to a lack of nutrients such as zinc or over-washing or cleaning skin. Dry skin may be caused by excessively dry and cold environments such as on the prairies in winter, where temperatures are subzero. Eczema or psoriasis may give the appearance of dry skin and indeed be aggravated by dryness. Those who wash hands a lot in their work, such as those who work in a restaurant or in a health care facility, will develop dry and sometimes red or fissured fingers.

Questions

- Do you wash your skin obsessively?
- Do you have a germ phobia?
- Are you dehydrated?
- Do you have eczema or psoriasis?
- Do you work at a job that requires frequent hand washing?
- Have you had your thyroid checked?

Excessive Hair Growth

Excessive hair growth or hirsutism may be due to a familial trait to grow darker and more extensive hair than one hopes for. Hair is cosmetically

264 Medical Symptoms and Complications

very important. It also has variable cultural relevance depending on the community. Dark body and facial hair on women of Mediterranean heritage or southeast Asia will be more acceptable than in northern Europe or much of North America. Women will go to great lengths and expense to rid the body of unwanted hair. Make no mistake, unwanted hair can have the same negative body image influence that acne or being overweight has. Individuals may isolate in response. While polycystic ovarian syndrome can cause male pattern baldness in women, it can create excessive hair growth on the face and body. Attempts to have hair removed can be painful and expensive.

Questions

- Do you have any unwanted hair?
- Where is this hair?
- Why do you think you have this hair?
- Do you think that your hair distribution is a familial trait?
- Are you using any treatments to remove hair?
- Are you spending a lot of money for hair removal?
- Has anyone made a comment on your hair growth?
- Have you been medically assessed for polycystic ovarian syndrome?
- Are you taking hormones because you are transgender?

Acne

Acne is a common plight that may occur in puberty to later in life. It is ubiquitously loathed by those that experience it. Because acne primarily affects the face, it is nearly impossible to hide from it. For those with eating disorders, it may be a source of grief that triggers or ramps up existing depression. It affects body self-awareness, compounding already existing body dissatisfaction. Clinicians need to pay attention to individuals' concerns with having acne. It is not an exaggeration to say that acne can trigger suicidal thoughts.

Acne may be the result of naturally occurring hormones associated with adolescence. Acne may also develop due to secondary causes. The combined oral contraceptive pill typically prevents acne and is used to treat acne. When individuals discontinue the pill, acne may develop in response. Less often, the pill may exacerbate acne. Progesterone-only contraceptives have a propensity to trigger acne. Examples of these are the progesterone injection, progesterone-only pill, and intrauterine devices containing progesterone. Polycystic ovarian syndrome and hypothyroidism may also be causes.

Medical Symptoms and Complications 265

Questions

- Had you been prone to acne as a young teen?
- Did acne clear up then return, and when was this?
- Did acne begin after discontinuing a contraceptive containing estrogen and progesterone?
- Did acne begin or become worse with initiating a progesterone-based contraceptive?
- Do you have a hormonal IUD?
- How does acne affect your body image or eating disorder?

Lanugo

Lanugo is a fine, downy soft hair that grows on much of the body including the face in those with anorexia nervosa. It develops due to a chronic low weight state. It is believed to be a vestigial response to the body trying to warm itself.

Cracking in Corners of the Mouth

Cracks or fissures in the corners of the mouth, cheilosis, may result from frequent vomiting. Persistent fissuring may result from a fungus infecting the open sores, not allowing healing to take place. Antifungal creams may need to be applied to encourage healing. Vitamin deficiencies need to be considered. Fissures in the corners of the mouth are common in cold, dry climates.

Rashes

Rashes have many etiologies, a few of which are mentioned here. Rashes may be the result of nutritional deficiencies or obsessive washing. They may also be caused by self-harm due to cigarette burn, chemical irritation, or scratching. Rashes may develop due to infections caused by funguses, bacteria, or parasites. They may also evolve from scratching due to itching from any source including medications, food, or perfume sensitivites. Rashes may be of genetic origin such as eczema or psoriasis. Scurvy, a disorder resulting from lacking vitamin C, presents with a rash.

Questions

- Do you notice rashes, and where on your body do they occur?
- Do you have eczema or psoriasis?

266   Medical Symptoms and Complications

- Do you have rashes due to self-harm?
- What treatments do you use to deal with rashes?
- Do you experience rashes under stress?
- Do you have eczema or psoriasis?

Skin and Mucosal Ulcers

Ulcers of the skin or mucosal surfaces develop from several different etiologies. The location of ulcers may help to determine the cause. Ulcers of the genitals may be of sexually transmitted infection origin. Herpes simplex and syphilis are relatively common causes. Ulcers of the skin, as well as the genitals, can be caused by syphilis. Causes of mouth ulcers could be due to canker sores. They could also be from sexually transmitted infections.

Oral and/or genital ulcers may be symptoms of Crohn's disease and are likely to be incorrectly attributed to herpes simplex infections. A careful history inquiring as to abdominal pain, diarrhea, and blood in the stool may be helpful.

Questions

- When did these ulcers start?
- On what part of your body do you get ulcers?
- Do you get genital ulcers?
- Are you worried about having a herpes infection?
- Did you have increasing abdominal pain, diarrhea, or blood in your stool before the ulcers began?
- Is there a history of inflammatory bowel disease in you or your family?

Russell's Sign

Russell's sign are marks resulting from teeth rubbing on knuckles or fingers during the act of inducing vomiting. They are typically noticed involving the second and third metacarpophalangeal joint knuckles or fingers of either hand. Russell's sign over the fourth or fifth knuckles or finger may be due to individuals using their whole hand to trigger vomiting. The use of three or four fingers to induce vomiting will likely be due to the gag reflex diminishing in effect. Similar marks may be the result of having banged the hand or handling kittens and rabbits.

Questions

- What are those marks on your hands due to?
- Have they been caused by using your fingers to induce vomiting?

Medical Symptoms and Complications **267**

- Could those marks be caused by trauma, or do you have pets that scratch you?
- Do you require the use of more fingers as vomiting becomes harder to trigger?

Nail Damage

Nail irregularities may result from nutritional deficiencies. They may also be a product of stomach acid due to vomiting damaging the tissue around the nails. Caustic chemicals including acetylsalicylic acid solutions used deliberately to remove skin surrounding nails may be the cause as well. Another cause could be picking of the nails or cuticles. Some nail irregularities may be due to disease processes.

Questions

- Do you have any damage to your nails or skin surrounding them, and why?
- Do you pick at your nails or cuticles?
- Could the damage be caused by using your fingers to induce vomiting?
- Could the damage be due to the kind of physical work you do?
- Do you file your nails so they are pointed to give the appearance of longer, more slender fingers?

Bruising

Bruising is a concern to some. The most common cause would be due to trauma of one form or another. Many do not remember injuring themselves. Though bleeding disorders are feared to be the cause of "easy bruising," they are extremely rare.

Questions

- Could bruising be due to self-harm?

Petechiae

Petechiae are small flat red, purple, or black marks that can occur anywhere on the body. For those with eating disorders, petechiae may appear around the eyes due to pressure in the face from vomiting. They also may develop with exercise that creates pressure in the head such as push-ups or weight lifting. They also may occur from straining due to crying or giving birth. Some medications, including anti-inflammatories and some

268   Medical Symptoms and Complications

antibiotics, may be involved. Many of these risk factors are common in those with eating disorders. Petechiae are not dangerous by themselves but may be the result of important etiologies.

Questions

- Do you ever notice fine pinpoint marks on your skin, especially on your face?
- Do you think straining due to exercise and or vomiting could be the cause?
- Did these marks develop after you started a medication?
- Do you notice bleeding of your eyeballs with straining due to exercise or vomiting?

Urological System

Dysuria

Dysuria is pain with passing urine or urinating. Those with eating disorders may be at increased risk of urinary tract infections due to dehydration. Because of a decline in urinary frequency due to not drinking enough or eating foods with significant water content, bacterial overgrowth in the bladder escalates. Pain with urination may also be due to inflammation of the vagina and vulva as a result of a yeast or bacterial infection called bacterial vaginosis. Those with untreated diabetes may develop yeast vaginitis. A herpes simplex outbreak of the vulva may result in excruciating pain with voiding. Urinary tract infections (UTIs) will typically lead to an increase in urinary frequency and urgency. Vaginal or vulvar infections will more likely present with itching or burning but not urinary frequency and urgency. If vulvar itching or burning is associated with urinary frequency and urgency, then the individual may easily have vulvovaginitis *and* a urinary tract infection. Increasing frequency of both may result from intercourse. Friction due to intercourse may result in an inflamed meatus in a woman and lead to temporary symptoms of pain with voiding. In men, dysuria and a urethral discharge will usually be caused by a sexually transmitted infection. Vulvovaginitis associated with increased vaginal discharge and odor, itch or burning can be associated with vaginal intercourse.

Questions

- Does it ever hurt to pee?
- Have you ever had a bladder infection?
- Have you ever had a vaginal or vulvar infection that caused pain with urination?

Medical Symptoms and Complications 269

- Are your symptoms persistent, or do they come and go?
- Are you worried about having a sexually transmitted infection?
- Do you ride a bicycle?
- Have you had painful vulvar ulcers, possibly as a result of a herpes simplex outbreak?
- Does pain with urination or vaginal itch and burning happen after sex?
- Do you have a discharge from your penis?

Infrequent Urination

As mentioned earlier, dehydration will result in lower urinary output, possibly as a result of hyperaldosteronism or low blood volume. Some forms of renal disease prevent the kidneys from ridding the body of water and metabolites. Chronic low potassium levels from restricting, vomiting, and laxative and diuretic abuse may result in renal damage. Some renal disease may lead to toxicity and require dialysis. Declining urinary flow may be due to obstructions resulting from renal or ureteric calculi. Those with anorexia nervosa have an increased rate of calculi. Urinary obstruction is likely to cause flank or pelvic pains.

Questions

- Do you think that you do not urinate enough?
- Do you think this is due to not drinking enough fluids?
- Do you think you are losing fluid because of vomiting or laxative or diuretic use?
- Do you think you lose water due to sweating and breathing hard and fast with exercise?
- Have you been investigated for kidney disease?

Frequent Urination

Frequent urination may be related to a urinary tract infection. It also may be due to large fluid intake or diuretic use. Caffeine and alcohol are powerful diuretics. Untreated diabetes will increase blood glucose concentration, therefore resulting in massive urinary fluid loss. Some kinds of kidney disease allow for excessive urinary flow. Bladder cancer may present with urinary frequency and pain with voiding. Unresolved symptoms of urinary tract infections that are not associated with positive bacterial cultures may lead some to rely on alternative treatments. Anyone with unresolved UTI symptoms including those resorting to alternative treatments such as herbs should be investigated for cystitis and bladder cancer.

270 Medical Symptoms and Complications

Questions

- Do you get urinary tract infections, and do you think you may have one now?
- Do you pee more when you are anxious?
- Are you taking diuretics deliberately?
- Do you drink a lot of coffee or tea with caffeine or take caffeine pills?
- Is frequent urination due to alcohol consumption?
- Have you been losing weight since you have been peeing more, and if so, have you been tested for diabetes?
- Are you enjoying this weight loss?
- Is there a history of diabetes in your family?
- Have you been investigated for kidney disease or diabetes?
- If you have insulin dependent diabetes, are you withholding insulin to deliberately lose weight?

Flank Pain

Flank pain may have its origin in the kidneys. The pain may be caused from a kidney infection or renal pelvis obstruction. Obstruction may result from renal tumors or achalasia of the ureter, a neurogenic dysfunction of the ureter that inhibits urinary flow. Endometriosis infiltration of the ureter can also inhibit flow. Certainly injuries from contact sports may cause similar pain. Those with anorexia nervosa have an increased risk of kidney stone formation and urinary tract infections, largely as a result of dehydration. Rarely, flank pain may be due to a tumor of the kidney. Persisting or escalating flank pain must be investigated immediately

Questions

- How long have you had flank pain?
- Is it becoming worse, and do you have a fever as well?
- Do you have a history of renal stones, gallstones, or stones in the salivary gland ducts?
- Is there a history of stone formation in your family?

Pelvic Pain of Urological Origin

Pelvic pain of renal origin, as mentioned earlier, could result from a urinary tract infection, renal calculi in a ureter, and any cause of urinary tract obstruction. Look under the sections on the "Gastrointestinal System" and "Gynecological System" for causes of pelvic pain.

Gynecological System

Abdominal and Pelvic Pain of Gynecological Origin

There are several gynecological sources of abdominal pain including pelvic pain. A few are mentioned here. Gynecological anatomy includes the ovaries, fallopian tubes, uterus, supporting ligaments, vagina, and vulva. Other abdominal structures include those from several other systems. Abdominal and pelvic health issues of gynecological origin are mentioned here.

Endometriosis

Endometriosis is a condition where the lining of the uterus, the endometrium, grows outside the uterus. Normally during menstruation, the lining of the uterus, which naturally sloughs off during menstruation, drains out of the uterus into the vagina and then out of the vagina. Endometriosis is believed to be the result of retrograde bleeding through the fallopian tubes in which the blood, with tissue from the lining of the uterus, spilling onto any number of pelvic structures. Instead of the uterine lining tissue being degraded and removed by physiological processes, it implants. It can implant onto the ovaries, fallopian tubes, ligaments, uterus, bowel, bladder, ureters, and lining of the abdomen as well as blood vessels and nerves. This implanted tissue outside of the uterus will respond the same way the endometrium does during menstruation. The implanted tissue will cause pain and bleeding in these other structure. Therefore, pelvic pain during periods may increase, plus pain between periods may result in chronic pelvic pain that is intermittent or constant. The pelvic pain is often insidious and initially subtle, leading to endometriosis not being diagnosed for years or decades. Symptoms often start in the teen years and are attributed to being just normally painful periods.

Endometriosis is a serious condition that can result in years of severe menstrual pain, chronic pelvic pain, and pain with intercourse and is a major cause if infertility. It may cause adhesions of various pelvic organs, requiring surgery to release the adhesions. Endometrial deposits may invade bowel tissue, resulting in pain with bowel movements and rectal bleeding. Very rarely, it can travel to the chest, causing blood to appear in sputum.

Endometriosis causes significant physical and emotional carnage in those who experience it. Very painful periods as well as chronic pelvic pains between periods can have a strong effect on one's eating disorder. It may be difficult for someone in recovery who wants to increase nutrition to be motivated to eat during episodes of pain. It may also be an excuse to

272 Medical Symptoms and Complications

not eat or restrict further for the purpose of losing weight. Chronic pain from any source, including endometriosis, is demoralizing and can lead to exacerbation of depression and anxiety. The risk of infertility can plague some counting on having children. Those wishing to become pregnant in the future may worry for years they may not be fertile. For those where infertility has been concluded to be a certainty, individuals may carry much regret. Endometriosis has a familial or genetic link. The clinician should enquire as to whether other women in the individual's family have a history of this condition. Pelvic pain needs to be accurately diagnosed as soon as possible and successfully treated. Endometriosis can become an important impediment to recovery efforts.

An issue with abdominal and pelvic pains is that they are often dismissed as being eating disorder behavior induced. They may be wrongly attributed to pain caused from vomiting, laxative abuse, intestinal motility disorder, or constipation. It is possible to have eating disorder sources of abdominal symptoms compounded on top of those caused by endometriosis

Initial treatment for endometriosis usually involves prescribing a hormonal birth control method. The combined contraceptive pill containing a synthetic estrogen and progesterone, the progesterone-only pill, Depo-Provera injection, NuvaRing, contraceptive patch, and hormonal intrauterine systems may help with diminishing pelvic pain as well as arresting the progression of the disease.

Questions

- Do you have troublesome pelvic pains?
- Are they related to your periods or occur between periods, or both?
- When did they first start?
- Are the pains increasing?
- Do you experience pain with intercourse?
- Is there a history of endometriosis in your family?
- How do you deal with the pain?
- Do you use painkillers or hormonal methods to deal with pain?
- Have you seen a gynecologist?
- Have you had a laparoscopic procedure to diagnose and treat endometriosis?
- Have you had fallopian tube contrast dye injections to determine if you are likely fertile?

Pelvic Infections

Pelvic infections of gynecological origin may cause pelvic pains, but they also may not. Pelvic infections will often be the result of a sexually

Medical Symptoms and Complications 273

transmitted infection. There may or may not be pains with intercourse. Pelvic infections may also be of gut origin in the form of abscesses.

Questions

- Did your pelvic pain begin after a sexual encounter?
- Have you had STI testing?
- Have you had pelvic or abdominal surgery?
- Could you have inflammatory bowel disease?

Cervicitis

Cervicitis is inflammation of the cervix. Symptoms may include a change in vaginal discharge, possibly presenting with a bad odor and blood. It may be the result of a sexually transmitted infection including chlamydia, gonorrhea, genital herpes, or trichomoniasis. A non-sexually transmitted infection such as bacterial vaginosis may cause cervicitis. There may be spotting between periods or bleeding during or after intercourse. The cervix may be inflamed without an infection. Rarely, bleeding from an inflamed-looking cervix may be the result of cancer of the cervix.

Questions

- Have you been screened for STIs?
- Do you have a different discharge with a foul odor?
- Have you had a pap test or a screening for cancer of the cervix?

Ovarian Cysts

Ovarian cysts are usually of natural, physiological origin. Most are associated with normal functioning of the ovaries, which influences ovulation and menstrual activities. Some, however, may grow larger and create symptoms. Larger cysts usually rupture spontaneously, possibly resulting in brief pelvic pain on one side. Some cysts may not rupture and may keep growing, resulting in pelvic pressure, pain, or difficulty voiding. Torsion or twisting of the ovary may cause acute, severe pelvic pain.

For those with eating disorders, ovarian cysts may present with pelvic pains that have wrongly been attributed to eating disorder symptoms. Ovarian cysts can add to already existing other causes of pelvic pain such as endometriosis, urinary tract infections or obstructions, sexually transmitted infections, intestinal motility disorder, irritable bowel syndrome, and inflammatory bowel disease. Right-sided pelvic pain may be due to appendicitis. Endometriosis may create blood-filled ovarian cysts called endometriomas.

274 Medical Symptoms and Complications

Questions

- Is this pelvic pain different from your other pelvic pain?
- What diagnoses of pelvic pains have been made already?
- How is this pain different?
- Is this pain on one side of the pelvis or the other?
- Have you ever had an ovarian cyst?
- Is there a history of ovarian cysts in the family?
- Have you had your appendix removed?
- Do you have endometriosis?

Menstrual and Other Bleeding Irregularities

Menstrual irregularities may be usual for individuals or may be a result of various other causes. Some causes may be important, while others may not be.

Amenorrhea is the menstrual irregularity most often associated with anorexia nervosa. Amenorrhea is defined as not experiencing three or more periods in a row that would otherwise be expected. With regard to anorexia nervosa, it will be a product of alterations in endogenous hormone status derived from stress and weight loss. It may also occur in women who are athletic. A combination of weight loss and increased physical activity may contribute to developing amenorrhea. Before amenorrhea occurs, periods may become irregular as well as shorter and lighter. Period cramps also diminish. Other reasons for amenorrhea are pregnancy, menopause, and hormonal contraception, including hormonal IUDs. Surgical causes include hysterectomy or oophorectomy.

Excessive bleeding from the vagina may be due to a number of causes. Important reasons for unusual bleeding include pregnancy and pelvic infections. An ectopic pregnancy, sometimes associated with the copper IUD, may be fatal. Other causes that can be expected are the use of progesterone-only contraceptives such as the progesterone-only pill, progesterone injections, and hormonal intrauterine devices and are not harmful unless bleeding is excessive or associated with pregnancy. Bleeding during or after intercourse may result from inflammation of the cervix. Excessive thickening of the lining of the uterus, growths such as uterine polyps, and uterine fibroids may cause bleeding. Hormonal abnormalities due to hyperthyroidism, hypothyroidism, polycystic ovarian syndrome, or a pituitary tumor called a prolactinoma are also causes of irregular uterine bleeding.

For those with eating disorders, any of these causes of bleeding are possible. Of course, weight loss, emotional stress, and high-level athleticism may lead to irregular bleeding. Because ectopic pregnancy is the leading cause of death in pregnant women, pregnancy must be ruled out immediately. Spotting in someone with anorexia nervosa who has not had periods for months or years may be due to bleeding in pregnancy. Physical and emotional stresses may alter periods as well. Those who travel where there is much walking may have irregular or absent periods. Even though amenorrhea may be associated with anovulation, it cannot be assumed that someone who does not have her periods is not fertile. Someone with anorexia nervosa who usually experiences amenorrhea may develop intermittent bleeding when she develops amorous feelings for a new partner. Spotting or the return of period-like bleeding may be the result of weight gain and be an indication of improved nutrition.

Questions

- Could you be pregnant?
- Do you use a copper IUD?
- Could spotting be due to improving nutrition or weight?
- Could you be spotting or have an unexpected period because you have missed taking birth control pills, or could your hormonal intrauterine device have been expelled?
- Do you fear bleeding after having not had your period for some time is due to weight gain?
- Since you have noticed bleeding, has this had an effect on your eating disorder behaviors?
- Have you been very physically active, including while traveling?
- How does bleeding make you feel?
- Are you worried about having a sexually transmitted infection?
- Do you feel weak or faint due to blood loss?

Unusual Vaginal Discharge and Vulvar Irritation or Pain (Vulvovaginitis)

Most vaginal discharges are physiological, while some are problematic. Discharges that are unchanging and without symptoms are likely of no concern. Some discharges are associated with vaginal and vulvar itching or burning or have a bad odor. These symptoms may or may not be associated with a change in discharge volume. Symptoms may be due to fungal or bacterial overgrowths or are the result of STIs such as chlamydia, gonorrhea, trichomonas, or genital herpes. The risk of vulvovaginitis is increased with IUD use. Retained foreign bodies such as tampons, condoms, or tissue contribute to malodorous discharges. Retained tampons can result in toxic shock syndrome, which is very serious and even life threatening.

For those with eating disorders who experience recurring vulvovaginitis, symptoms may have a profound effect on mood and anxiety. Chronic unresolved symptoms can aggravate depression and anxiety and negatively

276   Medical Symptoms and Complications

affect esteem. Chronic vulvovaginitis can be very difficult to cure, as symptoms frequently return following treatment.

Questions

- Do you experience an unusual vaginal discharge?
- Is the discharge associated with vaginal itching or burning, or does it have a bad odor?
- Does it hurt to have intercourse since you first noticed these symptoms?
- Is there any chance that there is a retained tampon or condom?
- Are you worried that you may have a sexually transmitted infection?
- Do you notice painful, open sores in the vulva?
- Do you have an IUD?
- Have you noticed pelvic pains since developing these symptoms?
- Have these symptoms had an effect on your eating disorder?
- Are they causing anxiety or depression because of resistant treatment?

Pelvic and Abdominal Pain of Unknown Origin

Although abdominal and pelvic pains will always have a cause, sometimes with meticulous histories as well as thorough laboratory and radiological investigations, a definitive etiology cannot be identified. In this situation it becomes a waiting game. Hopefully, pain will resolve on its own. Sometimes pains persist or even increase, at which time we need to revisit the concerns. Many origins of abdominal and pelvic pains are insidious and occult and will only be able to be diagnosed when more salient symptoms develop. Endometriosis, inflammatory bowel disease, and some cancers are slow to present with identifiable features. A high index of suspicion for all serious pathologies is required. Close monitoring of symptoms, even if vague, is recommended.

Questions

- Have you had thorough investigations for all causes of your pain?
- How are you managing pain symptoms?
- How are you able to cope with pain not knowing what is causing it?
- Are you optimistic the pain will resolve on its own?
- Do you fear the pain will never go away?
- Do you worry that the pain could be the result of a serious illness?
- How is this affecting your moods and eating disorder behaviors?

General Constitutional Symptoms

Vague constitutional symptoms that are sometimes expressed as "I don't feel well," "I'm tired," "I have no energy," or "I'm exhausted" are the bane

Medical Symptoms and Complications 277

of many clinicians. It becomes a "Where do I start?" scenario. It is very easy to want to pay little attention to such concerns. Often the reasons for these symptoms are not particularly serious or have been stated several times over long periods of time without any resolution, leading to us becoming complacent. We may dismiss these concerns as crying wolf one more time.

I remember a patient I met for the first time while working in a clinic. When I asked why she was here to see me, the first words out of her mouth were "I'm tired." I was already an hour and a half behind seeing patients, and all my examining rooms were full. I did pay attention enough to ask her why she thought she could be tired. She said that she had visited a dentist who prescribed her a medication I had never heard of before. It was to manage dental pain. Within minutes she was in a coma, totally unresponsive. Being too late to wait for an ambulance to arrive, I had to think on my feet. I had never heard of the drug before, so I looked it up in a pharmaceutical book and discovered that it was a synthetic narcotic (I'm flipping through a book while she is nearing respiratory arrest). Fortunately, there was a pharmacy next door that carried Narcan, an antidote used to reverse a narcotic overdose. After she was given the medication intramuscularly, within a minute she woke up fully alert. If I hadn't taken the initial very brief history when I did, she would have most certainly died. It turns out she had extensive dental damage as a result of severe vomiting behavior associated with anorexia nervosa. She did not deliberately overdose, nor did she take more than the recommended dose. Her emaciated state likely contributed to low tolerance for the narcotic. She was the first patient I had ever seen with anorexia nervosa in private practice.

References

Mårild, K., Størdal, K., Bulik, C. M., Rewers, M., Ekbom, A., Liu, E., & Ludvigsson, J. F. (2017). Celiac disease and anorexia nervosa: A nationwide study. *Pediatrics*, 139(5). pii: e20164367. doi: 10.1542/peds.2016–4367. Epub 2017 Apr 3.

Mascolo, M., Dee, E., Townsend, R., Brinton, J. T., & Mehler, P. S. (2015). Severe gastric dilatation due to superior mesenteric artery syndrome in anorexia nervosa. *Int Journal Eat Disord*, 48(5): 532–534. doi: 10.1002/eat.22385. Epub 2015 Jan 30.

Mustelin, L., Raevuori, A., Kaprio, J., & Keski-Rahkonen, A. (2014). Association between eating disorders and migraine may be explained by major depression. *Int Journal Eat Disord*, 47(8): 884–887. doi: 10.1002/eat.22311. Epub 2014 May 30.

Sachs, K. V., Harnke, B., Mehler, P. S., & Krantz, M. J. (2016). Cardiovascular complications of anorexia nervosa: A systematic review. *Int Journal Eat Disord*, 49(3): 238–248. doi: 10.1002/eat.22481. Epub 2015 Dec 29.

Sundararaghavan, S., Pitts, T. Y., Suarez, W. A., & Johnstone, C. (2005). Chest pain among adolescents with anorexia nervosa. *Pediatr Emerg Care*, 21(9): 603–605.

Wotton, C. J., James, A., & Goldacre, M. J. (2016). Coexistence of eating disorders and autoimmune diseases: Record linkage cohort study, UK. *Int Journal Eat Disord*, 49(7): 663–672. doi: 10.1002/eat.22544. Epub 2016 Jun 23.

Index

abdomen 29; cramps in 189–190; pain in 271, 276
abnormal bleeding 231
absent or on hold eating disorder behaviors 212
abuse and neglect, coping with 20
abuse history 91–94
accomplishments and skills 96
acne 264–265; control of 19–20
acting as if efforts are being made to eat 177
active listening techniques 48
addresses 65–66; email 66
advocates 45
affirmations 158
age or developmental related history 54–55
allergies and sensitivities 22, 102–103
allowing situations-ducks in a row 217–219
alone, avoidance of eating 171
alternate plans 185
alternative eating disorder behaviors 215
amenorrhea 112, 177–178, 274–275
American Psychiatric Association 2
ana apps 3
animation 9
ankles, sore 258
anorexic look 26
anosmia 239
anxiety 196–197
apps 3
arms 29
artificial increasing of weight 178
artistic activities 89–91
art of give and take 47–48
assumptions, avoiding 60
athletic activities 91
athletic body 27

attention seeking motivation 18–19
aversion behaviors 160–161
avoiding behaviors 161–169

back, sore 257–258
backsliding 52
balance, poor 235–236
Balanchine, George 10
beautiful look 26
bedroom, eating in the 171
being busy 158
binge eating and related behaviors 141–147
birth dates, client 64
bleeding: abnormal 231; excessive menstrual 274–275; with vomiting 195–196
blemishes 30
body areas, focused 27–31
body calipers 141
body gauging behaviors 137–141; clothing 140–141; mirrors 139–140; scales 137–138
body images 22–23; dance and 10; desired 26–27; distorted 31–32; family history and 78; focused body areas and 27–31; focuses of 22–32; not desired 23–26
body mass index (BMI) 24
body regions 225–226
bones, prominent 28
Botox 198
braces, excuses with 180
breastfeeding 127
breast size and shape 29–30
breathing, pain with 262
brief eating disorder history 44
browsing history, deletion of computer 180
bruising 267

buddies, eating disorder 159
buff, athletic, toned, healthy look 27
bulimia nervosa 2
bulk-forming laxatives 123
busyness 158
buttocks 29
buying food (false information) 178

cachectic look 26; metabolism boosters 136
caffeine 136
calorie burning and metabolism altering behaviors: exercise as 130–135; heating blankets 135–136; nonchemical methods 136–137
calorie burning foods 149
calorie counting 155–156
car, eating in the 171
carbohydrate reducing diets 150–151
cardiovascular system: abnormal bleeding 231; feeling generally cold or having cold and blue extremities 230–231; palpitations 194–195, 226–227; shortness of breath 195, 229–230; syncope 194–195, 227–229
caregiver information 68–69
catch-up 58–59
celebrities 10–11
celiac disease 250–251
certification driven histories 56–57
cervicitis 273
change: motivation for 51; stages of 52
changing in kind, eating disorder behaviors 213
Charcot-Marie-Tooth syndrome 31
checking fridge when others are around, then removing food as if one has eating it 178
chest pain or pressure 195, 231–233
chewing and spitting 169
chewing food several times 162
children of those with eating disorders 78–79
child-sized portions 167
chopsticks 166
cigarettes 157
citing doctor or nutritionists' recommendations (false information) 179–180
cleaning something disgusting 160
cleanses 148
clients, demographic and contact information for 62–69
clockwise eating 174

clothing 140–141
cold, feeling 230–231
colored sputum 261–262
competition motivation 11
compounding risk 70
computer browsing history, deletion of 180
condiments, strong 168
confidentiality, client 55–56
consequences of eating disorder behaviors 216–217
contact information 62–64; reliability and 64–65
contact person 66
contraception 103–104, 112; avoidance of 165
control motivation 12–13
CoolSculpting 200
coordination concerns 234–235
cotton ball diet 153
cough 260–261
counterclockwise eating 174
counting: calorie 155–156; serving 156
cracking in corners of mouth 265
cramps: abdominal 189–190; muscle 258
Crohn's disease 68, 109–110, 249–250
cryolipolysis 200
current health status 99
cutlery 174
cutting of food 174
cyberbullying 5–6
cysts, ovarian 273–274

daily planning 182
damaged hands 191
dance 10
dark plates 166
dead anorexics and bulimics, photos of 8
death: efforts to prevent 197; in family history 82–83; sudden cardiac 228
deformities, physical 30–31
dehydration 163–164
delaying 161–163
dementia 241–242
demographics and contact information 62–69
dermatological system: acne 19–20, 264–265; bruising 267; cracking in corners of mouth 265; dry skin 263; excessive hair growth 263–264; hair loss 262–263; nail damage 162; petechiae 267–268; rashes 265–266; Russell's sign 266–267; skin and mucosal ulcers 266
dessert, avoiding 167

280 Index

detoxifying 148
developmental history 73–74
diabetes mellitus 127–129
diagnostic criteria for eating disorders 2–3
dialogue, negative 14–15
diarrhea 190–191
DiClemente, C. C. 52
diet pills, over-the-counter 136
diets 147–148; carbohydrate reducing 150–151; cotton ball 153; fat calorie reducing 149–150; genetically modified food restricted 180; protein reducing 151; vegetarian 152
direct questions 49–50
disabilities, physical 31
disability insurance motivation 16–17
discharge, unusual vaginal 275–276
distorted body image 31–32
diuretics 126–127
dizziness 194–195
documenting 183
dog walking 133
drinking water every hour 170
drooping eyelids 242
drugs and alcohol: enquiring about history of use of 89; in family history 82; self-medication using 100; use and addictions to 70, 201–203
dry skin 263
dumpster diving 146–147
duodenal ulcers 254
dysgeusia 238–239
dysuria 268–269

eating: of food with strong odors that can be smelled on one's breath 178; in front of a mirror 159; only when people notice 180; with others, not eating before 180; portion of food in a restaurant, then having the rest packed up to go 179
eating disorder behaviors 116–117; absent or on hold 212; allowing situations-ducks in a row 217–219; alternative 215; binge eating and related 141–147; body gauging behaviors 137–141; calorie burning and metabolism altering 130–137; changing in kind 213; consequences of 216–217; eating disorder and non-eating disorder use for each suspected 205–206; false information 175–181; hiding behaviors

217; *how* questions about 207–208; increasing, decreasing, staying the same 211–212; intent of 221–222; linked 213; mutually exclusive 213–214; non-triggers 214–215; organizing behaviors 181–186; past, recent, present, and future uses of 207; patterns 215–216; preventing situations 219; purging 117–130; quantifying of 219–221; restricting 147–169; rules aiding restricting of food 169–175; substance use 201–203; surgery and other cosmetic altering methods 197–201; symptom management 186–197; triggers 214; *what* questions about 208; *when* questions about 209–210; *where* questions about 210; *who* questions about 211; *why* questions about 209; why stop? 222–223
eating disorder buddies 159
eating disorder history: complexities of assessing eating disorders and 1; fundamentals of taking (*see* interviews); general (*see* general eating disorder history); reasons for taking a detailed 42–43; what gets in the way of a good 53–54; when to take a brief 44
eating disorders 1; body image in 22–32; children of those with 78–79; diagnostic criteria for 2–3; family history of 76–77; financial costs of 37–38; food sources and 37; money sources for 39–40; motivations for engaging in (*see* motivations for engaging in an eating disorder); personality triad in 32–37; terminology of 48–49; transportation and 37
eating disorder voice 14
eating out: avoidance of 170; eating a portion of food in a restaurant, then having the rest packed up to go 179
emaciated look 26
Email 46
Email addresses 66
emetics 120
emotional abuse 93
emotional risks 70
endocrinological system 259–260
endometriosis 271–272
enemas 125–126
engaging 44–45; failures with 45–46; helping someone feel at ease and 46–47

Index   281

ethnicity 113–114
excessive hair growth 263–264
excessive menstrual bleeding 274–275
excessive spices on food 160–161
excuse to fail motivation 13
exercise 130–135, 206
extremities, cold and blue 230–231
eyelids, drooping 242

face 27–28; surgery procedures on 198
facial swelling 243–244
failure, fear of 97–98
fainting 194–195, 227–229
falling 194–195
false information 175–176; acting as
    if efforts are being made to eat 177;
    buying food 178; checking fridge when
    others are around, then removing food
    as if one has eaten it 178; citing doctor
    or nutritionists' recommendations
    179–180; deleting browsing history
    on the computer 180; eating a portion
    of food in a restaurant, then having
    the rest packed up to go 179; eating
    food with strong odors that can be
    smelled on one's breath 178; excuses
    with wearing braces 180; genetically
    modified food restricted diet 180; if one
    can't avoid eating with others, don't eat
    before 180; increasing weight artificially
    178; only eat when people notice 180;
    playing music or running water in the
    bathroom to hide vomiting sounds 179;
    purchasing tampons to hide not having
    periods 177–178; recalibrating scales
    178–179; red eyes 179; talking as if
    individuals do not have weight control
    issues 180–181; telling others they are
    sick so they have an excuse to not eat
    176; ways to look healthier 178
family history 74–75; basic food dynamics
    in the family in 77–78; children of
    those with eating disorders and 78–79;
    deaths in 82–83; family and eating
    disorder history in 76; family body
    image and weight issues in 78; family
    lineage and eating disorders in 77;
    illnesses in 80–81; interviewing family
    members about 75–76; living situation
    in 85; losses in 84; mental health and
    drug or alcohol use in 82; moves in
    84–85; pets in 79–80; regrets and 84

fasting 148
fat 23
fat calorie reducing diets 149–150
fear foods 151–152
fear of failure 97–98
fear of losing partner if weight gained 18
feet, sore 258
fiber 169
fidgeting 132
fielding new concerns during therapy 59
financial costs of eating disorders 37–38
financial motivations for engaging in
    eating disorders 17–18
first interview, who should be at 55–56
fit in, conform, belong, motivations to 12
flabby 25
flank pain 270
fluid loading 164–165
fluid restriction 163–164
focused time in therapy 59
food allergies 22, 102–103
food associations 161
food containers, avoidance of eating
    out of 171
food sources 37
foods with different flavors, eating various
    166
forgetfulness 241
frequent urination 269–270
friends and other peers 86

gallbladder disease 252–253
gastric (peptic) ulcers 254
gastritis 253–254
gastroesophageal reflux disorder (GERD)
    254–255
gastrointestinal system 246; celiac disease
    250–251; Crohn's disease 249–250;
    gallbladder disease 252–253; gastric
    (peptic) and duodenal ulcers 254;
    gastritis 253–254; gastroesophageal
    reflux disorder (GERD) 254–255;
    intestinal motility disorder 247–249;
    irritable bowel syndrome (IBS)
    252; lactose intolerance 256–257;
    malabsorption syndrome 251–252;
    pancreatitis 255–256; superior
    mesenteric artery syndrome
    (SMAS) 247
gender dysphoria 13–14
gender fluid persons 14
gender identity and breasts 30

282 Index

gender orientation 89
general constitutional symptoms 276–277
general eating disorder history: abuse history in 91–94; accomplishments and skills in 96; artistic activities in 89–91; athletic activities in 91; dating in 88; demographics and contact information 62–69; developmental history in 73–74; drugs and alcohol in 89; failures in 97–98; family history in 74–85; gender orientation in 89; general medical history and 98–113; history of chief complaint in 70; life goals in 96–97; previous and ongoing eating disorder treatment history in 70–72; previous psychiatric diagnoses in 72; psychological history in 72; risk assessment in 69–70; self-harm in 95–96; sexual experiences in 89; social history in 86–88; surgery in 109–110; writing and 91
general medical history: allergies and sensitivities in 22, 102–103; contraception in 103–104; current health status in 99; ethnicity and 113–114; height and weight history in 98–99; hormone treatment in 105; immunizations in 101–102; infectious diseases in 110–111; medications in 100–101; menstrual history in 111–113; past medical history in 100; postpartum period 108–109; pregnancy in 105–108; religion in 114
genetically modified food restricted diet 180
genetically related health concerns 73–74
grabbing of thighs, arms, abdomen, buttocks, or hips 141
grazing 143
gross 23–24
gum chewing 157–158; sugar-free 168
gyms 133–134
gynecological system 271–276; abdominal and pelvic pain 271; cervicitis 273; endometriosis 271–272; menstrual irregularities 112, 178, 274–275; ovarian cysts 273–274; pelvic infections 272–273; unusual vaginal discharge and vulvar irritation or pain 275–276

hair growth, excessive 263–264
hair loss 262–263

hands, damaged 191
headaches including migraine 237–238
head region 243–246; facial swelling 243–244; hearing loss 245; sore or sensitive teeth 244–245; tinnitus 245–246
health concerns during childhood 73
healthier looking individuals 178
healthy body look 27
hearing loss 245
heating blankets 135–136
height and weight history 98–99
hiding behaviors 217
hirsutism 263–264
history of chief complaint 70
hoarding 144–145
hormone treatment 105
horseback riding 132
horseradish 168
hospitalization motivation 15–16
hot spices 120
house cleaning 132–133
how questions 207–208
humongous 24–25
hunger relief 186–187
hypersensitivity 36–37

idols and other people 10–11
illness, feigning 176
illnesses in family history 80–81
immunizations 101–102
inability to smell (anosmia) 239
increasing, decreasing, staying the same, eating disorder behaviors 211–212
increasing weight artificially 178
indigestion 188–189
infections, pelvic 272–273
infectious diseases 110–111
infrequent urination 269
injuries, sports 133
insulin-dependent diabetes mellitus (IDDM) 127–129
intake assessment 44
intent of eating disorder behaviors 221–222
internet, the 3–6
interviews: age or developmental related history and 54–55; art of give and take in 47–48; breakdown of weekly 58–59; certification driven histories and 56–57; clients who need 43–44; engaging with 44–46; of family members 75–76; how

Index   283

to ask questions in 48–50; how to have someone feel at ease in 46–47; key points for 60–61; language used in 48; letting the clients speak in 50; personal writing as source of information and 56; reconnecting 56; recovery history and 52–53; sensitive questions in 50; taking notes in 57–58; who should be at first 55–56
intestinal motility disorder 119, 247–249
invisible goal 27
involuntary movements 239
ipecac 120
irregular respiration 261
irritable bowel syndrome (IBS) 252

joints, sore 257
journaling 56, 183
junk foods 142–143; sugar-free 168

keeping the family together motivation 18
knees: appearance of 30; sore 258

labels, food 155
labiaplasty 198–199
labor delivery 73
lactose intolerance 256–257
lacto-vegetarian diets 152
language used in interviews 48
large or big 24
laxatives 122–125, 205–206
legs, sore 258
licking chopsticks or forks 166
life goals 96–97
lifeline 20
linked eating disorder behaviors 213
lip injections 198
liposuction 198
lists 184
living arrangements 66–68
living situation 85
looking hot 27
losses and family history 84
low self-esteem 11
low weight 26
lunch-sized portions 167

maintaining medical instability 14
makeup 200
malabsorption syndrome 251–252
manipulative behaviors 176
mantras 158

markers 119
meal and snack reduction 148
measuring food 154
measuring tapes 141
media 20–21; *see also* social media
medical instability, maintaining 14
medical risks 69–70
medical symptoms and complicating health concerns 224–226; cardiovascular 226–231; chest region 195, 231–233; dermatological system 262–268; endocrinological system 259–260; gastrointestinal system 246–257; general constitutional symptoms 276–277; gynecological system 271–276; head region 243–246; musculoskeletal system 257–259; neurological system 233–242; pelvic and abdominal pain of unknown origin 276; respiratory system 260–262; urological system 268–270
medications 100–101; avoidance of 165–166; hormone treatment 105
memory loss 240–241
menstrual history 111–113
menstrual irregularities 112, 178, 274–275
mental health and family history 82
metabolism boosters 136; sleeping as 159; weight gain secondary to metabolic stress and 196
migraine 237–238
milestones, developmental 73
minute to minute plan 182
mirrors 139–140; eating in front of 159
mixed foods, avoidance of 175
modeling 21–22
money sources for eating disorders 39–40
motivating behaviors 158–160
motivational forces 51
motivation for change 51
motivations for engaging in an eating disorder 3; acne control 19–20; animation 9; apps 3; attention seeking 18–19; competition 11; control 12–13; coping with abuse and neglect 20; cyberbullying 5–6; dance 10; excuse to fail 13; fear of losing partner if weight gained 18; fit in, conform, belong 12; food allergies 22; gender dysphoria 13–14; idols and other people 10–11; the internet and 3–5; keeping the

family together 18; lifeline 20; low self-esteem 11; maintain medical instability 14; media 20–21; modeling 21–22; negative dialogue 14–15; photographic images 6–9; punish others 13; slow suicide 13; social media 4–5; stay in hospital 15–16; stay on disability insurance 16–17; student loans 17–18; superiority to others 12
mouth: cracking in corners of 265; injury to throat or 192–193
moves in family history 84–85
muscles: cramping of 258; sore 258; spasms of 240; wasting of 259; weakness in 259
musculoskeletal system 257–259
mustard 168
mutually exclusive eating disorder behaviors 213–214
Myers, Mike 114

nails: damage to 267; painting of 162
names of clients 64
neck, sore 259
negative calorie foods 149
negative dialogue 14–15
negative motivating forces 3
neurofibromatosis 31
neurological system: coordination concerns 234–235; dementia 241–242; drooping eyelids 242; forgetfulness 241; headaches including migraine 237–238; inability to smell (anosmia) 239; involuntary movements 239; memory loss 240–241; muscle spasm 240; numbness, tingling, and sensory loss 233–234; pain 242–243; poor balance 235–236; poor taste (dysgeusia) 238–239; visual disturbances 242; weakness 236–237
nicotine 136
nonchemical methods of altering metabolism 136–137
nonhuman photographic images 9
non-triggers, eating disorder behaviors 214–215
not desired body images 23–26
note-taking 57–58
numbness, tingling, and sensory loss 233–234

obese 24
obsessive-compulsive disorder (OCD) 34
offering food to others 167

old photos 8
open-ended questions 49–50
opposite hand, eating with 162
order, eating in specific 174
organizing behaviors 181–186; alternate plans 185; documenting 183; eating disorder action tools or packages 184; lists 184; for recover 185–186; specific plans 182–183
out of shape 25–26
ovarian cysts 273–274
over-the-counter diet pills 136
ovo-vegetarian diets 152

pain 242–243; abdominal 271, 276; with breathing 262; flank 270; musculoskeletal system 257–259; pelvic 270, 271, 276; vertebral spinous process 259; vulvar 275–276
painting of nails 162
palpitations 194–195, 226–227
pancreatitis 255–256
PANDAS syndrome 111
parotid gland swelling 244
past, recent, present, and future uses of eating disorder behaviors 207
past medical history 100
patterns: eating disorder behaviors 215–216; not eating in 168
peer pressure 12
pelvic infections 272–273
pelvic pain: of gynecological origin 271; of unknown origin 276; of urological origin 270
people pleasing trait 32–34
peppermint 166
percentage of food, reducing the 149
perfectionism 34–36
personality triad 32–37
personal writing 56
petechiae 267–268
pets 79–80
phlebotomy 129
phone numbers 65
photographic images 6–9
physical abuse 93–94
physical deformities 30–31
physical disabilities 31
picking apart food 168–169
plateaus 52
plates and bowls, eating from specific 174
playing music or running water in the bathroom to hide vomiting sounds 179

Index   285

pleurisy 262
poor balance 235–236
poor taste (dysgeusia) 238–239
popcorn 151–152
portions, small 167
postpartum period 108–109
powerful look 27
pregnancy 73, 105–108; postpartum period 108–109
pretty look 26
preventing situations 219
pro-ana kits 184
pro-ana scrapbooks 183
pro-ana websites 4
Prochaska, J. O. 52
procrastination 35–36
pro-mia websites 4
prominent bones 28
prostitution 39–40
protein reducing diets 151
psychiatric diagnoses, previous 72
psychological history 72
punishment of others motivation 13
purchasing tampons to hide not having periods 177–178
purging behaviors: breastfeeding 127; diuretics 126–127; enemas 125–126; laxatives 122–125; phlebotomy 129; rumination 129–130; suppositories 125; vomiting 117–122; withholding insulin 127–129

quantifying of eating disorder behaviors 219–221
questions: *how* 207–208; how to ask 48–50; key points for 60–61; to leave out 50–51; sensitive 50; types of 49–50; *what* 208; *when* 209–210; *where* 210; *who* 211; *why* 209

rashes 265–266
reasons for stopping eating disorder behaviors 222–223
recalibrating of scales 178–179
reconnecting 56
recovery, organizing for 185–186
recovery history 52–53
rectal bleeding 195–196
red eyes 179
reducing the available volume of food 149; in single day only 169
reduction, meal and snack 148
refeeding syndrome 185

regrets and family history 84
religion 114
religious meaning in patterns of eating 174
respiratory system 260–262; *See also* shortness of breath
restricting eating behaviors: asking for lunch or child-sized portions 167; aversion behaviors 160–161; avoiding 161–169; being busy 158; calorie burning foods 149; calorie counting 155–156; carbohydrate reducing diets 150–151; cigarettes 157; cotton ball diet 153; counting servings 156; definitions and meanings 147–148; dehydration 163–164; delaying 161–163; false information and 175–181; fat calorie reducing diets 149–150; fear foods 151–152; fluid loading 164–165; gum chewing 157–158; meal and snack reduction 148; measuring food 154; medication avoidance 165; motivating behaviors 158–160; protein reducing diets 151; reading labels on food containers 155; reducing the available volume of food 149; reducing the percentage of food 149; reducing the weight of food 149; rituals 174–175; rules aiding 169–175; safe food choices 151; selective eating 152–153; skipping meals and snacks 148; throwing food away 164; time rules 171–174; vegetarian diets 152; weighing food 154
risk assessment 69–70, 205
rituals 174–175
rubber bands, wearing 159
rules aiding restricting of food 169–175
rumination 129–130
Russell's sign 266–267

safe food choices 151
safety screening 59
salt 120
sayings 158
scales 137–138; recalibrating of 178–179
school 87–88
secret eating 171
selective eating 152–153
self-esteem, low 11
self harm 95–96
selfies 7
self-phlebotomy 129
sensitive questions 50

servings, counting 156
setting utensils down between bites 162
sex trade 39–40
sexual abuse 94
sexual attractiveness 27
sexual experiences 89
shin splints 258
shorthand abbreviations 57
shortness of breath 195, 229–230
short-term plans 182
single day reductions in food 169
sitting straight 132
size, clothing 140
skin: bruising 267; dry 263; and mucosal
    ulcers 266; petechiae 267–268; rashes
    265–266
skipping meals and snacks 148
sleeping over 6 hours per night 159
slow suicide 13
smart waters 194
smoking 157
snack foods 142–143, 151; sugar-food 168
social history 86–88
social media 4–5; communicating through
    66; cyberbullying on 5–6
So I Married an Axe Murderer 114
soreness 257–259
sore or sensitive teeth 244–245
sore throat from other causes 192–193
special status 19
specific plans 182–183
spitting and chewing 169
spoiling food 160–161
sports participation 132–133
sputum, colored 261–262
stacking magazines and removing them
    with weight loss 159
stages of change 52
Stages of Change model 52
stealing food 145–146
Stevia 167–168
stimulant laxatives 123
stomach 29
stopping of eating disorder behaviors
    222–223
student loans motivation 17–18
subjective binges 142
substance use 201–203
sudden cardiac death 228
sugar substitutes 167–168
suicide: contact information in cases of
    potential 62–63; slow 13

superiority to others 12
superior mesenteric artery syndrome
    (SMAS) 247
superstition 174
suppositories 125
surgery: for blemishes 30; breast reduction
    29–30; facial procedures 198; gender
    dysphoria and 14; in general medical
    history 109–110; labiaplasty 198–199;
    liposuction 198; tummy tuck 29
swelling, facial 243–244
swimming 132
symptom management behaviors
    186–197; abdominal cramps 189–190;
    anxiety 196–197; blood with vomiting
    and rectal bleeding 195–196; damaged
    hands 191; death prevention 197;
    diarrhea 190–191; dizziness, falling,
    fainting, and palpitations 194–195;
    indigestion 188–189; mouth or throat
    injury 192; relieving hunger 186–187;
    shortness of breath and chest pains 195;
    sore throat from other causes 192–193;
    teeth and gum damage 191–192;
    water retention 193–194; weight gain
    secondary to metabolic stress 196
syncope 194–195, 227–229

tachypnea 261
talking as if individuals do not have weight
    control issues 180–181
teeth: damage to gums and 191–192; sore
    or sensitive 244–245
terminology of eating disorders 48–49
text messaging 46
thighs 28
thin, trim and slight 26
thinspirational pictures 4, 7–8
throat injury 192–193
throwing food away 164
time rules 171–174
tinnitus 245–246
toned body 27
tools, eating disorder 184
torsades de pointes 240
touching of food, avoidance of 174
transportation 37
trap lines 143–144, 216
treatment history, previous and ongoing
    eating disorder 70–72
triggers, eating disorder behaviors 214
tummy tucks 29

ulcers: gastric and duodenal 254; skin and mucosal 266
underdressing 140
underweight 26
unsafe foods 151
updated histories 58
urination: frequent 269–270; infrequent 269

vaginal discharge, unusual 275–276
vague l constitutional symptoms 276–277
vegan diets 152
vegetarian diets 152
venting 50, 59
vertebral spinous process pain 259
visual disturbances 242
volume of food, reducing the available 149
vomiting 117–122, 206
vulvar irritation 275–276

walking the dog 133
wasting, muscle 259
water every hour 170

water retention 193–194
weakness 236–237; muscle 259
weekly interviews 58–59
weekly planning 182
weighing, daily 170
weighing food 154
weight gain secondary to metabolic stress 196
weight of food, reducing the 149
weight phobia disorder 137
what questions 208
wheezing 260
when questions 209–210
where questions 210
white foods, avoidance of 170
whitening of teeth 162
who questions 211
why questions 209
withholding of insulin 127–129
work experiences 86
World Health Organization 2
writing 56, 91
writing weight on one hand and goal weight on the other 158

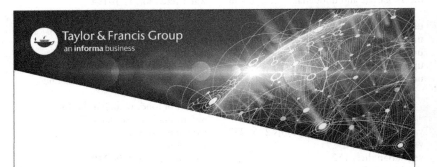